WHAT JESUS DEMANDS FROM THE WORLD

What JESUS DEMANDS *from the* WORLD

JOHN PIPER

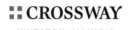
CROSSWAY

WHEATON, ILLINOIS

ISBN-13: 978-1-4335-2057-0
ISBN-10: 1-4335-2057-5
ePub ISBN: 978-1-4335-2070-9
PDF ISBN: 978-1-4335-2058-7
Mobipocket ISBN: 978-1-4335-2069-3

Library of Congress Cataloging-in-Publication Data
Piper, John, 1946-
    What Jesus demands from the world / John Piper.
      p.   cm.
    Includes index.
    ISBN 13: 978-1-58134-845-3 (hc : alk. paper)
    ISBN 10: 1-58134-845-2
    1. Jesus Christ—Teachings. 2. Bible. N.T. Gospels—Criticism, interpretation, etc. I. Title.
BS2415.P49   2006
241.5—dc22   2006021810

Crossway is a publishing ministry of Good News Publishers.

LB		20	19	18	17	16	15	14	13	12	11
13	12	11	10	9	8	7	6	5	4	3	2	1

To
Benjamin and Melissa
living the love of Jesus

Contents

All authority in heaven and on earth

has been given to me.

JESUS

ACKNOWLEDGMENTS

This book was possible because generosity has flowed to me from more streams than I can mention here, indeed more streams than I know. But I gladly mention several. The elders and congregation of Bethlehem Baptist Church gave me a five-month leave from preaching. This was part of their kindness on the twenty-fifth anniversary of our ministry together at the church. Without this extended time away, this book would not have been written.

The happy combination of solitude and fellowship at Tyndale House in Cambridge, England, with its abundant resources, provided the ideal setting for this kind of research and writing. Bruce Winter, whose long and faithful tenure as Warden was coming to an end while I was there, was gracious and stimulating in his welcome and friendship. The staff and readers of Tyndale House made our stay a glad and fruitful season. God knows the anonymous hands that opened to make this stay possible.

David Mathis, Justin Taylor, and Ted Griffin read the manuscript with care and helped me make hundreds of improvements. Carol Steinbach again gathered her team and prepared the Scripture and Person Indexes, which will help readers find their way around more easily. Lane Dennis and his team at Crossway Books encouraged and supported this project from conception to reality. My wife Noël set up house in a new place, set me free to write, and read every word with the eyes that only a gifted wife can bring. Everything I do hangs on her support.

When someone asks, "How long did it take you to write this book?" I often answer, "Sixty years." I know it's not a satisfactory answer. But it does tell the truth that the streams of generosity that have come together to create this book have been flowing into my life from the start. I do not doubt that experiences I had from Summit Drive Grade School in Greenville, South Carolina, in the 1950s to the University of Munich in the early 1970s and the ministry of the Word for twenty-five years at Bethlehem shaped what is in this book. There is no separating life and the labor of writing.

For all the countless streams of generosity—known and unknown—that have flowed into my life, I thank Jesus, who created me and called me and governs all my days, as he does the governments of the world and the galaxies of the universe. I pray that he will use this book to make himself known and treasured and obeyed as the only Savior from our sin and the only Sovereign over the world.

SUGGESTIONS FOR
HOW TO READ THIS BOOK

Long books seem daunting because we think we should start at the front and read to the back and not skip anything. I don't expect most people to read this book that way. I hope some will. I did structure the book so that matters at the front may help the reader understand matters further on. And there is a kind of foundation, progression, and climax. But the chapters have enough independence that most of them can be read without the others. It will be obvious when one chapter depends on another.

Therefore, I invite you to step in anywhere. You don't have to read the Introduction first. I hope that the way Jesus' commands are interwoven will draw you further in, from one issue to another.

I have tried to keep the chapters relatively short so that in general they can be read at one sitting for those who only have limited time from day to day. This is why some of the chapters deal with the same command from different angles. I thought it better to handle the matter in several chapters rather than in one long one.

Since the focus is on the commands of Jesus in this book, much about his life and death is not here. If you want to see how I have tried to portray these more fully, you can look at two other (shorter!) books where I deal with Jesus and his death: *Seeing and Savoring Jesus Christ* (Crossway Books, 2004) and *Fifty Reasons Why Jesus Came to Die* (Crossway Books, 2006). And, of course, there are important books by others that I will be referring to along the way.

Most of all I hope you will pray as you read. Even if you are not accustomed to praying, ask God to protect you from any mistakes I may have made and to confirm to you what is true. In the end, what matters is the effect that God produces in our lives through his written word by his Spirit. That's what makes prayer so crucial. In prayer we ask God to transform us in that way.

Finally, may the living Jesus fulfill the purpose of his word as you read: "These things I have spoken to you, that my joy may be in you, and that your joy may be full" (John 15:11).

Introduction:
The Aim of the Book

The aim of this book is God-glorifying obedience to Jesus. To that end I am seeking to obey Jesus' last command: "Make disciples of all nations . . . *teaching them to observe all that I have commanded you*" (Matt. 28:19-20). Jesus' final command was to teach all his commandments.

The Impossible Final Command

Actually, the final command was more precise than that. He did *not* say, "Teach them all my commandments." He said, "Teach them *to observe* all my commandments." You can teach a parrot all of Jesus' commandments. But you cannot teach a parrot to *observe* them. Parrots will not repent, and worship Jesus, and lay up treasures in heaven, and love their enemies, and go out like sheep in the midst of wolves to herald the kingdom of God.

Teaching people to parrot all that Jesus commanded is easy. Teaching them to *observe* all that Jesus commanded is *impossible*. Jesus used that word. When a rich man could not bring himself to let go of his riches and follow him, Jesus said, "It is easier for a camel to go through the eye of a needle than for a rich person to enter the kingdom of God. . . . With man it is *impossible*, but not with God. For all things are possible with God" (Mark 10:25-27).

Therefore, the person who sets himself to obey Jesus' final commission—for example, to teach a rich man to *observe* the command to "renounce all that he has" (Luke 14:33)—attempts the impossible. But Jesus said it was *not* impossible. "All things are possible with God." So the greatest challenge in writing this book has been to discern God's way of making impossible obedience possible.

Jesus said that this impossible goal happens through *teaching*. "Make disciples . . . *teaching* them to observe all that I have commanded you." There is, of course, more to it than that—like the atoning death of Jesus (Mark 10:45) and the work of the Holy Spirit (John 14:26) and prayer (Matt. 6:13). But in the end Jesus focused on teaching. I take this to mean that God has chosen to do the impossible through the teaching of all that Jesus commanded. That's what I pray this book will prove to be—a kind of teaching that God will use to bring about impossible obedience to Jesus. And all of that for the glory of God.

Teaching and Obedience That Glorify God

The reason I emphasize the glory of God is because Jesus did. He said, "Let your light shine before others, so that they may see your good works and *give glory to your Father who is in heaven*" (Matt. 5:16). The ultimate goal of Jesus' commandments is not that we observe them by doing good works. The *ultimate* goal is that God be glorified. The obedience of good works is penultimate. But what is ultimate is that in our obedient lives God be displayed as the most beautiful reality in the world. That is Jesus' ultimate goal[1] and mine.

This helps me answer the question: What kind of teaching of Jesus' commandments might God be willing to use to bring about such impossible obedience? If the aim of obedience is ultimately the glory of God, then it is probable that the teaching God will use is the kind that keeps his glory at the center. Therefore, my aim has been to keep the supremely valuable beauty of God in proper focus throughout the book.

---

[1] See especially *Demand #47*.

Keeping the Commandments Connected to Jesus and His Work

How then do we keep the beauty of God in proper focus in relation to Jesus' commandments? By treating the meaning and motivation of the commands in connection with the person and work of Jesus. The person and work of Jesus are the primary means by which God has glorified himself in the world. No revelation of God's glory is greater. Jesus said, "Whoever has seen me has seen the Father" (John 14:9). Therefore, his *person* is the manifestation of the glory of God. To see him as he really is means seeing the infinitely valuable beauty of God. Jesus also said, as he was praying, "I glorified you on earth, having accomplished the work that you gave me to do" (John 17:4). Therefore, his *work* is a manifestation of the glory of God. When we see what he achieved and how he did it, we see the majesty and greatness of God.

Therefore, my aim has been *to probe the meaning and the motivation of Jesus' commands in connection with his person and work.* What emerges again and again is that what he is commanding is a life that displays the worth of his person and the effect of his work. His intention is that we not disconnect what he commands from who he is and what he has done.

We should not be surprised, then, that Jesus' final, climactic command is that we teach all nations to observe all that he commanded. This leads to his ultimate purpose. When obedience to his commands happens, what the world sees is the fruit of Jesus' glorious work and the worth of his glorious person. In other words, they see the glory of God. This is why Jesus came and why his mission remains until he comes.

A Sketch of the Person and Work of Jesus

Anticipating what we will see later in the book, the briefest sketch of Jesus' person and work should be given here, so that from the start the commands rest on their proper foundation. Jesus came into the world, sent by God, as the long-awaited Jewish Messiah. When

Jesus asked his disciples who they thought he was, Peter answered, "You are the Christ [that is, Messiah], the Son of the living God." To this Jesus responded, "Blessed are you, Simon Bar-Jonah! For flesh and blood has not revealed this to you, but my Father who is in heaven" (Matt. 16:16-17).

When Jesus was on trial for his life, the charge was blasphemy, and eventually treason against Caesar, because of his apparent claims to be the Messiah, the King of Israel, the Son of God. The Jewish high priest asked him, "Are you the Christ, the Son of the Blessed?" And Jesus said, "I am, and you will see the Son of Man seated at the right hand of Power, and coming with the clouds of heaven" (Mark 14:61-62).

WHY JESUS FAVORED THE TITLE SON OF MAN

Even though Jesus acknowledged that he was the Messiah, the Son of God, his favorite designation for himself was "Son of Man." At one level this title carries the obvious meaning that Jesus was truly human. But because of its use by the prophet Daniel, it probably is a very exalted claim of universal authority.

> Behold, with the clouds of heaven there came one like a son of man, and he came to the Ancient of Days and was presented before him. And to him was given dominion and glory and a kingdom, that all peoples, nations, and languages should serve him; his dominion is an everlasting dominion, which shall not pass away, and his kingdom one that shall not be destroyed. (Dan. 7:13-14)

The reason Jesus favored the title *Son of Man* for himself was that the terms *Messiah* and *Son of God* were loaded with popular political pretensions. They would give the wrong impression about the nature of his messiahship. They could easily imply that he fit in with the conceptions of the day that the Messiah would conquer Rome and liberate Israel and set up his earthly kingdom. But Jesus had to navigate these political waters by presenting himself as truly the Messiah, even the divine Son of God with universal authority, but also reject the popular notion that the Messiah would not suffer but immediately rule.

The term *Son of Man* proved most useful in this regard because though it did carry exalted claims for those who had ears to hear, on the face of it he was not making explicit claims to political power. Under this favorite title (while not rejecting the others), Jesus was able to make his claims that the long-awaited messianic kingdom of God had come in his ministry.[2]

THE KINGDOM OF GOD HAD COME INTO HISTORY

The Jewish people longed for the day when the Messiah would come and bring the kingdom of God. The kingdom would mean that the enemies of Israel are defeated, sins are wiped away, diseases are healed, the dead are raised, and righteousness, joy, and peace hold sway on the earth with the Messiah on the throne. Jesus arrived and said, "The time is fulfilled, and the kingdom of God is at hand; repent and believe in the gospel" (Mark 1:15). What he meant was that in his own ministry the liberating, saving reign of God had arrived. "If it is by the finger of God that I cast out demons, then *the kingdom of God has come upon you* . . . the kingdom of God is *in the midst of you*" (Luke 11:20; 17:21).

But there was a mystery. Jesus called it "the secret of the kingdom of God" (Mark 4:11). The mystery was that the kingdom of God had come in history *before* its final, triumphant manifestation. Fulfillment was here, but consummation was not here.[3] The kingdom would arrive in two stages. In the first stage the Messiah would come and suffer, and in the second stage the Messiah would come in glory (Luke 24:46; Mark 14:62).

---

[2] For a helpful overview of the titles of Jesus in the Gospels in the space of twelve pages see Craig L. Blomberg, *Jesus and the Gospels* (Nashville: Broadman & Holman, 1997), 401-412.

[3] For an excellent book-length treatment of the kingdom of God in the ministry of Jesus see George Ladd, *The Presence of the Future* (Grand Rapids, Mich.: Eerdmans, 1974).

He Came to Serve and Die for Sins and Rise Again

Therefore, the primary work of Jesus on the earth during his first coming was to suffer and die for the forgiveness of sins. He said, "Even the Son of Man came not to be served but to serve, and to give his life as a ransom for many" (Mark 10:45). And at the Last Supper with his disciples, he took the cup and said, "This is my blood of the covenant, which is poured out for many for the forgiveness of sins" (Matt. 26:28).

Dying was not his only mission. But it was central. In shedding his blood he purchased the new-covenant promises. The new covenant was God's promise that all who enter the coming kingdom will have their sins forgiven, will have the law written on their hearts, and will know God personally (Jer. 31:31-34). The blessings of this covenant are crucial in enabling us to obey Jesus' commandments. Which makes Jesus' death of supreme importance in bringing about the impossible obedience that he demands.

But there was more to his mission. When John the Baptist was perplexed about whether Jesus was really the Messiah, he sent word to him from prison: "Are you the one who is to come, or shall we look for another?" Jesus answered, "Go and tell John what you hear and see: the blind receive their sight and the lame walk, lepers are cleansed and the deaf hear, and the dead are raised up, and the poor have good news preached to them. And blessed is the one who is not offended by me" (Matt. 11:3-6). In other words, "All my healing and preaching are a demonstration of my messiahship, but don't take offense that I am not fulfilling the political expectation of earthly rule. I *am* the one who is to come, but my central mission (in this first coming) is suffering—to give my life as a ransom for many."

When his mission was accomplished, after three days in the grave, Jesus rose from the dead. This was God's plan. It was an act of supreme authority over death. "No one takes [my life] from me, but I lay it down of my own accord. I have authority to lay it down, and I have authority to take it up again. This charge I have received from my Father" (John 10:18). When he was raised, he appeared to his disciples on many occasions and gave them proof that he

THE ROOTS OF DISILLUSIONMENT

The upshot of those days in Germany was a growing disillusionment with the historical effort to reconstruct a Jesus of history behind the unified portrayal of Jesus in the New Testament Gospels. I detected a good bit of what seemed to be scholarly disingenuousness. Scholarly articles would begin with a healthy dose of "perhaps," "probably," "possibly," and other nuanced qualifiers, but by the end of the article there had emerged (out of nowhere it seemed to me) a confidence that something reliable and useful had been found. For my part I saw massive minds assembling, with great scholarly touch, a house of cards.

It helps to be sixty years old. I have watched the cards collapse over and over. For example, who of us today can give any serious account of the reconstructions of the historical Jesus by Milan Machoveč (*Jesus für Atheisten*, 1972), Herbert Braun (*Jesus*, 1969), or Kurt Niederwimmer (*Jesus*, 1968)? But these were the cutting-edge reconstructions that, by the standards of the guild, I had to come to terms with. The first two argued with Bultmann that the kingdom of God in Jesus' ministry was a mythological construct that could be dispensed with today as we find the political (Machoveč was a Marxist) and existential "meaning" of Jesus for us. Niederwimmer exploited, as the book jacket said, "the assured results of depth psychology" to find in the kingdom of God "the objectification of a collective process of consciousness." I was not impressed with the fruit of the Second Quest. I had seen glorious things in the Jesus of the Gospels, and the Quest was offering me husks and ashes.

I found myself at home in these amazing words of Adolf Schlatter as he defined what he believed scholarship (*die Wissenschaft*) should be.

> I keep myself as free as possible from conjectures and avoid therefore the effort to overturn them. This does not seem like a fruitful business to me. For conjectures are not overturned by producing more of the same. They sink away when one sees that observation

is more fruitful than conjecture. . . . I call *Wissenschaft* [scholar-
ship] the observation of what exists (*des Vorhandenen*), not the
attempt to imagine what is not visible. Perhaps one will object that
the guesswork of conjecture excites and entertains while observation is a hard and difficult work. That's true; play is easier than
work. But the Gospel is misunderstood when one makes a play-
thing out of it.[4]

The conviction was growing in me that life is too short and the
church is too precious for a minister of the Word to spend his life
trying to recreate a conjectured Jesus. There was work to be done—
very hard work—to see what is really there in the God-given portrayal of Jesus in the New Testament Gospels.

WHAT HOPE FOR THE THIRD QUEST?

The Third Quest for the Historical Jesus "began in the early 1980s,
fueled by some new archaeological and manuscript data, some
new methodological refinements, and some new enthusiasm that
historical research did not need to lead to a dead end."[5] It is still
in process, and there are surveys available of what is happening.[6]
Ben Witherington observes, "The desire to say something new and
fresh characterizes almost all of the [Third Quest] works exam-
ined in this study, sometimes to the extreme of preferring the new
over the probable."[7] My own assessment of what is happening is
this: To the degree that the present reconstructions of the historical
Jesus depart from the portrayal found in the Gospels of the New
Testament, they will be forgotten the same way Machoveč, Braun,
and Niederwimmer are forgotten.

There are reasons why this is so.

---

[4] Adolf Schlatter, *Der Evangelist Matthäus*, 6th ed. (Stuttgart: Calver Verlag, 1963), xi. My
translation.
[5] Witherington, *The Jesus Quest,* 12-13.
[6] Besides Witherington's overview cited in the previous footnote, see Larry Hurtado, "A
Taxonomy of Recent Historical-Jesus Work," in *Whose Historical Jesus?* ed. William E. Arnal
and Michel Desjardins (Waterloo, Ontario: Wilfrid Laurier University Press, 1997), 272-295;
Jonathan Knight, *Jesus: An Historical and Theological Investigation* (London: T&T Clark
International, 2004), 15-56; *The Historical Jesus in Recent Research*, ed. Dunn and McKnight.
[7] Witherington, *The Jesus Quest,* 247.

First, no reliable or lasting portrait of Jesus has ever been reconstructed from going behind what the four Gospels portray. There is no reason to think this will change. The reason is at hand: When you abandon *das Vorhandenen* (what exists at hand) for conjectures, you turn scholarship into an academic game. What is needed to give the game life is toys. And everybody knows the market and the academy demand new toys every generation. They cannot last. The tragedy is how much damage they do to people who do not have roots in the Gospels—and do not have the benefit of being sixty years old.

THE GOSPELS HAVE NOT BEEN OVERTHROWN

Second, the portrayal of Jesus in the four Gospels has not been overthrown by scholarship. The appearance of overthrow arises from the unwarranted creation of criteria of authenticity that by definition will rule out aspects of the New Testament portrayal. Thankfully, God has raised up several generations of careful, rigorous, and faithful scholars who are not cowed by the radical critics and who patiently go about their work establishing the historical credibility of the four Gospels. I thank God for them. I don't mean that they provide proof of the Gospels. I mean they show that the attacks on the historical validity of the portrayal of Jesus in the Gospels are not compelling.[8]

FRAGMENTS LEAD TO ARBITRARY RECONSTRUCTIONS

Third, the attempt to reconstruct a reliable, compelling portrait of Jesus behind the Gospels is an illusion because by definition the

---

[8] In this connection, the following books offer counterarguments to the Third Quest and the Quest in general: Craig L. Blomberg, *The Historical Reliability of the Gospels* (Downers Grove, Ill.: InterVarsity Press, 1987); Craig L. Blomberg, *Jesus and the Gospels* (Nashville: Broadman & Holman, 1997); Craig L. Blomberg, *The Historical Reliability of John's Gospel* (Downers Grove, Ill.: InterVarsity Press, 1998); D. A. Carson, *The Gospel According to John* (Grand Rapids, Mich.: Eerdmans, 1991), 40-68; *Jesus Under Fire*, ed. Michael J. Wilkins and J. P. Moreland (Grand Rapids, Mich.: Zondervan, 1995); Paul Barnett, *The Truth About Jesus: The Challenge of the Evidence* (Sydney: Aquila Press, 1994); Luke Timothy Johnson, *The Real Jesus: The Misguided Quest for the Historical Jesus and the Truth of the Traditional Gospels* (San Francisco: HarperSanFrancisco, 1996); Gregory Boyd, *Cynic, Sage or Son of God? Recovering the Real Jesus in an Age of Revisionist Replies* (Grand Rapids, Mich.: Baker, 1995); Gary Habermas, *The Historical Jesus: Ancient Evidence for the Life of Christ* (Joplin, Mo.: College Press, 1996); Lee Strobel, *The Case for Christ: A Journalist's Personal Investigation of the Evidence for Jesus* (Grand Rapids, Mich.: Zondervan, 1998).

method adopted only offers fragments without immediate context. Floating sayings and events can only be connected arbitrarily. That means the mind of the scholar, not the reality of Jesus, is governing the reconstruction. Luke Timothy Johnson has made this point effectively:

> When the compositions are fragmented, chopped into small pieces, and arranged in arbitrary sequences, they do not work at all. The literary compositions of the New Testament are analyzed best when their literary integrity is respected and appreciated. Approached in this fashion, they can be appreciated as witnesses and interpretations of religious experience and convictions.[9]

ONLY THE GOSPELS REMAIN

Fourth, the portrayal of Jesus in the Gospels of the New Testament is the only portrayal that has any chance of shaping the church and the world over the long haul. This is because it is the only one that people have access to. Whatever the Questers may construct, it will usually be read by only a handful of people. And even if they turn it into a blockbuster movie, seen by millions, that will pass without so much as a memory in ten years, while the Gospels will still be in the hands of the masses. I will wager my life that this was God's idea and that it will be worth all my remaining breath to try to understand what is actually there and teach it faithfully.

MY APPROACH IN THIS BOOK

In addition to what I said about method under the subheading, "A Word About Method" in the Introduction, it may be helpful to point out here that the process of selecting which commands to discuss was complex. I gathered and recorded all the commands by reading the Gospels. This included implied commands (for example, "Blessed are the merciful" implies "Be merciful"). This list was over five hundred, counting the multiple restatements among the Gospels.

---

[9] Johnson, *The Real Jesus*, 167.

The next step was to distinguish commands that would have abiding significance for faith and life. That is, I excluded commands like "Pick up your bed, and go home" (Mark 2:11). Finally there was a process of grouping and categorizing. After several passes, I was able to include all the commands in about thirty categories. These groupings formed the initial structure of the chapters. Some expanded, and the chapters were divided into two or more. Hence the round number of fifty chapters. I do not claim to have commented on every command. My hope is that enough categories and enough specific commands are handled to give help even for those I may have passed over.

THE JESUS OF THE GOSPELS IS THE MOST RADICAL

The fifth and final reason why reconstructions of Jesus that attempt to go behind the Gospels will not last and will fail to shape the church long-term is that the most radical Jesus is the one portrayed in the Gospels. So many of the reconstructions of Jesus behind the Gospels are motivated by the desire to liberate Jesus from the domesticated traditions of the church that fit Jesus into this world in predictable and compromising ways. That is a good desire. But their approach accomplishes the very opposite of what is hoped for. To the degree that the church is trained to distrust the Jesus of the Gospels and to look for ever new human creations of Christ, the real Jesus is blurred, and his power to break free from the unbiblical traditions that bind him is blunted.

This is the point that Luke Timothy Johnson makes so well: The critical need in the church and the world is the "real Jesus" of the Gospels. Johnson's words are a fitting conclusion to this Word to Biblical Scholars and a launching pad for *What Jesus Demands from the World*.

> Does the church act triumphalistically, or treat its people arrogantly? Is it an agent for the suppression of human needs and aspirations? Does it foster intolerance and small-mindedness? Does the church proclaim a gospel of success and offer Jesus as a better

business partner? Does it encourage an ethos of prosperity to the neglect of the earth's good, or an individualistic spirituality to the neglect of the world's needy? Are its leaders corrupt and coercive? Such distortions of Christianity can find no harsher critic, no more radical rejecter, than the Jesus found *only* in the pages of the New Testament, the Jesus who was himself emptied out for others and called his followers to do the same.

The Jesus to whom Saint Francis of Assisi appealed in his call for a poor and giving rather than a powerful and grasping church was not the Historical Jesus but the Jesus of the Gospels. One must only wonder why this Jesus is not also the "real Jesus" for those who declare a desire for religious truth, and theological integrity, and honest history.[10]

---

[10] Ibid., 177.

Demand #1

You Must Be Born Again

Jesus answered . . . "Do not marvel that I said to you, 'You must be born again.'"—John 3:5, 7

Jesus answered him, "Truly, truly, I say to you, unless one is born again, he cannot see the kingdom of God."—John 3:3

I n the third chapter of John's Gospel, Jesus is speaking to "a man of the Pharisees named Nicodemus, a ruler of the Jews" (John 3:1). Pharisees were the experts in the Jewish Scriptures. This is why Jesus was astonished that Nicodemus was baffled about what Jesus meant by "You must be born again." Nicodemus asks, "How can a man be born when he is old? Can he enter a second time into his mother's womb and be born?" (John 3:4). Jesus responds, "Are you the teacher of Israel and yet you do not understand these things?" (John 3:10).

A New Spirit I Will Put Within You

In other words, an expert in the Jewish Scriptures should not be baffled by Jesus' demand, "You must be born again." Why not? Because there are so many clues in the Jewish Scriptures that Jesus and Nicodemus had in common. God had promised a day when he would cause his people to be born again. One of God's clearest promises is in the book of Ezekiel. Jesus echoed Ezekiel's words when he said, "Unless one is born of water and the Spirit, he cannot enter the kingdom of God" (John 3:5). Being "born again" is described as a birth from water and Spirit. Those two terms, "water" and "Spirit," are linked in Ezekiel 36:25-27. God says:

> I will sprinkle clean water on you, and you shall be clean from all
> your uncleannesses, and from all your idols I will cleanse you. And
> I will give you a new heart, and a new spirit I will put within you.
> And I will remove the heart of stone from your flesh and give you
> a heart of flesh. And I will put my Spirit within you, and cause you
> to walk in my statutes and be careful to obey my rules.

God promises cleansing from sin and the gift of a new human spirit by the presence of his own divine Spirit. Jesus thinks Nicodemus should make the connection between his demand to be born again and Ezekiel's promise of a new spirit and the gift of God's Spirit. But he doesn't. So Jesus explains further by describing the role of God's Spirit in bringing about this new spirit: "That which is born of the flesh is flesh, and that which is born of the Spirit is spirit" (John 3:6).

THE DEAD CANNOT SEE

Flesh is what we are by nature. It refers to ordinary humanity. By our first birth we are only flesh. This natural human condition, as we experience it, is spiritually lifeless. We are not born spiritually alive with a heart that loves God. We are born spiritually dead.

That's what Jesus implied when he said to a would-be disciple who wanted to go home to a funeral, "Leave the *dead* to bury their own dead" (Luke 9:60). In other words, some are physically dead and need burying. Some are spiritually dead and can bury them. He implied it again when, in his parable of the prodigal son, the father says, "This my son was *dead*, and is alive again" (Luke 15:24). That's why "unless one is born again he cannot see the kingdom of God" (John 3:3). The dead can't see. That is, they can't see God's kingdom as supremely desirable. It looks foolish or mythical or boring. So they "cannot enter the kingdom of God" (John 3:5). They cannot because it is foolishness to them.

Jesus sees all of humanity divided into two parts: those who are merely born once—"born of the flesh," "the (spiritually) dead"— and those who are "born again" by the Spirit of God—those who are alive to God and see his kingdom as true and supremely desirable.

THE WIND BLOWS WHERE IT WILL

Nicodemus is not entirely wrong to be baffled. There is a mystery. Jesus says so in John 3:8, "The wind blows where it wishes, and you hear its sound, but you do not know where it comes from or where it goes. So it is with everyone who is born of the Spirit." In other words, "Nicodemus, you need new spiritual life—a second birth."

And what Jesus demands from Nicodemus, he demands from all. He is speaking to everyone in the world. No one is excluded. No ethnic group has a greater bent toward life. Dead is dead—whatever our color, ethnicity, culture, or class. We need spiritual eyes. Our first birth will not get us into the kingdom of God. But we do not cause ourselves to be born again. The Spirit does that. And the Spirit is free and blows in ways we do not comprehend. We must be born again. But this is a gift of God.

Look away from yourself. Seek from God what he alone can do for you. Moral improvement of the old you is not what you need. New life is what the whole world needs. It is radical and supernatural. It is outside our control. The dead do not give themselves new life. We must be born again—"not . . . of the will of the flesh nor of the will of man, but of God" (John 1:13). That is what Jesus demands from the world.

Demand #2

REPENT

From that time Jesus began to preach, saying, "Repent, for the kingdom of heaven is at hand." —MATT. 4:17

I have not come to call the righteous but sinners to repentance. —LUKE 5:32

The men of Nineveh will rise up at the judgment with this generation and condemn it, for they repented at the preaching of Jonah, and behold, something greater than Jonah is here. —MATT. 12:41

Unless you repent, you will all likewise perish. —LUKE 13:3, 5

The first demand of Jesus' public ministry was, "Repent." He spoke this command indiscriminately to all who would listen. It was a call for radical inward change toward God and man.

WHAT IS REPENTANCE?

Two things show us that repentance is an internal change of mind and heart rather than mere sorrow for sin or mere improvement of behavior. First, the meaning of the Greek word behind the English "repent" (μετανοέω, *metanoeō*) points in this direction. It has two parts: *meta* and *noeō*. The second part (*noeō*) refers to the mind and its thoughts and perceptions and dispositions and purposes. The first part (*meta*) is a prefix that regularly means movement or change. In view of the way this prefix regularly functions,[1] we may infer that the basic meaning of *repent* is to experience a change of the mind's perceptions and dispositions and purposes.

The other factor that points to this meaning of *repent* is the way Luke 3:8 describes the relationship between repentance and new behavior. It says, "Bear fruits *in keeping with* repentance." Then it gives examples of the fruits: "Whoever has two tunics is to share with him who has none, and whoever has food is to do likewise" (Luke 3:11). This means that repenting is what happens inside of us. Then this change leads to the fruits of new behavior. Repentance is not the new deeds, but the inward change that bears the fruit of new deeds. Jesus is demanding that we experience this inward change.

SIN: AN ASSAULT ON GOD

Why? His answer is that we are sinners. "I have not come to call the righteous but *sinners* to repentance" (Luke 5:32). What was Jesus' view of sin? In the parable of the prodigal son, Jesus describes the son's sin like this: "He squandered his property in reckless living . . . [and] devoured [it] with prostitutes" (Luke 15:13, 30). But when the prodigal repents he says, "Father, I have sinned *against heaven* and before you. I am no longer worthy to be called your son" (Luke 15:21). Therefore, throwing your life away on reckless living and prostitutes is not just humanly hurtful; it is an offense against heaven—that is, against God. That's the essential nature of sin. It's an assault on God.

We see this again in the way Jesus taught his disciples to pray. He said that they should pray, "Forgive us our *sins*, for we ourselves forgive everyone who is *indebted* to us" (Luke 11:4). In other words, sins that God forgives are compared to the ones people commit against us, and those are called *debts*. Therefore, Jesus' view of sin is that it dishonors God and puts us in *debt* to restore the divine

[1] For example, *meta* is used as a prefix in the words *metabainō* (transfer or change from one place to another), *metaballō* (change one's way of thinking), *metagō* (lead or move from one place to another), *metatithēmi* (convey from one place to another, put in another place, transfer), *metamorphoō* (change in a manner visible to others, be transfigured), *metastrephō* (cause a change in state or condition, change, alter), and *metaschēmatizō* (change the form of something, transform, change), etc.

honor we had defamed by our God-belittling behavior or attitudes. Later we will see how that debt gets paid by Jesus himself (Mark 10:45). But for us to enjoy that gift he says we must repent.

Repenting means experiencing a change of mind so that we can see God as true and beautiful and worthy of all our praise and all our obedience. This change of mind also embraces Jesus in the same way. We know this because Jesus said, "If God were your Father, you would love *me*, for I came from God" (John 8:42). Seeing God with a new mind includes seeing Jesus with a new mind.

THE UNIVERSAL NEED FOR REPENTANCE

No one is excluded from Jesus' demand to repent. He made this clear when a group of people came to him with news of two calamities. Innocent people had been killed by Pilate's massacre and by the fall of the tower of Siloam (Luke 13:1-4). Jesus took the occasion to warn even the bearers of the news: "Unless you repent, you will all likewise perish" (Luke 13:5). In other words, don't think calamities mean that some people are sinners in need of repentance and others aren't. *All* need repentance. Just as all need to be born again (John 3:7), so all must repent because all are sinners.

When Jesus said, "I have not come to call the righteous but sinners to repentance" (Luke 5:32), he did not mean that some persons are good enough not to need repentance. He meant some *think* they are (Luke 18:9), and others have already repented and have been set right with God. For example, the rich young ruler desired "to justify himself" (Luke 10:29), while "the tax collector . . . beat his breast, saying, 'God, be merciful to me, a sinner!' [and he] went down to his house justified [by God!]" (Luke 18:13-14). (For more on Luke 18:9-15, see *Demand #20*.)

THERE IS AN URGENCY TO THIS DEMAND BECAUSE JUDGMENT IS COMING

Therefore, none is excluded. All need repentance. And the need is urgent. Jesus said, "Unless you repent, you will all likewise *perish*."

What did he mean by *perish*? He meant that the final judgment of God will fall on those who don't repent. "The men of Nineveh will rise up at the judgment with this generation and condemn it, for they repented at the preaching of Jonah, and behold, something greater than Jonah is here" (Matt. 12:41). Jesus, the Son of God, is warning people of the judgment to come and is offering escape if we will repent. If we will not repent, Jesus has one message for us: "Woe to you" (Matt. 11:21).

This is why his demand for repentance is part of his central message concerning the kingdom of God. He preached that the long-awaited kingdom of God is present in his ministry. "The time is fulfilled, and the kingdom of God is at hand; repent and believe in the gospel" (Mark 1:15). The gospel—the good news—is that the rule of God has arrived in Jesus to save sinners before the kingdom arrives at his second coming in judgment. So the demand to repent is based on the gracious *offer* that is present to forgive and on the gracious *warning* that someday those who refuse the offer will perish in God's judgment.

To All Nations Beginning from Jerusalem

After he had risen from the dead, Jesus made sure that his apostles would continue the call for repentance throughout the world. He said, "Thus it is written, that the Christ should suffer and on the third day rise from the dead, and that *repentance* and forgiveness of sins should be proclaimed in his name to all nations, beginning from Jerusalem" (Luke 24:46-47). So the demand of Jesus to repent goes to all the nations. It comes to us, whoever we are and wherever we are, and lays claim on us. This is the demand of Jesus to every soul: Repent. Be changed deep within. Replace all God-dishonoring, Christ-belittling perceptions and dispositions and purposes with God-treasuring, Christ-exalting ones.

COME TO ME

Come to me, all who labor and are heavy laden, and I will give you rest. —MATT. 11:28

Jesus stood up and cried out, "If anyone thirsts, let him come to me and drink." —JOHN 7:37

Jesus said to them, "I am the bread of life; whoever comes to me shall not hunger." —JOHN 6:35

You refuse to come to me that you may have life. —JOHN 5:40

When he had said these things, he cried out with a loud voice, "Lazarus, come out." The man who had died came out. —JOHN 11:43-44

When a person is born anew and experiences repentance, his attitude about Jesus changes. Jesus himself becomes the central focus and supreme value of life. Before the new birth happens and repentance occurs, a hundred other things seem more important and more attractive: health, family, job, friends, sports, music, food, sex, hobbies, retirement. But when God gives the radical change of new birth and repentance, Jesus himself becomes our supreme treasure.

HIS YOKE IS EASY, AND HIS BURDEN IS LIGHT

Therefore, his demand that we come to him is not burdensome. It means coming to the one who has become everything to us. Jesus did not come into the world mainly to bring a new religion or a new law. He came to offer himself for our eternal enjoyment and to do whatever he had to do—including death—to remove every obstacle to this everlasting joy in him. "These things I have spoken to you, that my joy may be in you, and that your joy may be full" (John 15:11). When Jesus demands that we do things—like "Come to me"—the essence of these demands is that we experience the life that most fully savors and spreads his supreme worth.

As Jesus looks out over the religions of the world—including the Judaism of his day—he sees people who are laboring under heavy loads to earn the favor of whatever deity they believe in. He did not come to replace that God-appeasing load with another one. He came to carry that load and call us to himself for rest. "Come to me, all who labor and are heavy laden, and I will give you rest. Take my yoke upon you, and learn from me, for I am gentle and lowly in heart, and you will find rest for your souls. For my yoke is easy, and my burden is light" (Matt. 11:28-30). Make no mistake, there *is* a yoke and a burden when we come to Jesus (there would be no demands if this were not true), but the yoke is easy, and the burden is light.

There Is a Burden, But It's Not Jesus

But perhaps it's not easy and light the way we think it is. Jesus also said, "The gate is narrow and the way is *hard* that leads to life" (Matt. 7:14). The reason it is hard is not because Jesus is a hard taskmaster. It's hard because the world is a hard place to enjoy Jesus above all. Our own suicidal tendency to enjoy other things more must be crushed (Matt. 5:29-30). And besides our own sin, many people are angered that we do not love what they love. So Jesus warned, "Some of you they will put to death. You will be hated by all for my name's sake" (Luke 21:16-17).

But Jesus is not the burden. When we come to him, he is the burden-lifter, the soul-satisfier, and the life-giver. "Jesus stood up and cried out, 'If anyone thirsts, let him come to me and drink'" (John 7:37). Coming to Jesus means coming to drink. And the water we drink in fellowship with Jesus gives everlasting life. "Whoever drinks of the water that I will give him will never be thirsty forever.

The water that I will give him will become in him a spring of water welling up to eternal life" (John 4:14). The demand that we come to Jesus is the demand to come to the fountain of life and drink.

Jesus is not satisfied to lure us into obedience with images of life-giving water. He will also draw us with promises of life-sustaining bread. "I am the bread of life; he who comes to me shall not hunger" (John 6:35). Jesus himself is the bread of heaven—the source and essence of everlasting life. He will draw us with promises of deliverance from perishing (John 3:16). The demand that we come to him is therefore like the demand of a father to his child in a burning window, "Jump to me!" Or like the demand of a rich, strong, tender, handsome husband to an unfaithful wife, "Come home!" Or like the demand of a rescue squad that finds you on the point of death, dehydrated after days in the desert, "Drink this!"

"You Refuse to Come to Me That You May Have Life"

But the personal tragedy of sin and spiritual blindness is that people do not come. Jesus grieved over his people. "O Jerusalem, Jerusalem, the city that kills the prophets and stones those who are sent to it! How often would I have gathered your children together as a hen gathers her brood under her wings, and you would not!" (Matt. 23:37). "You search the Scriptures because you think that in them you have eternal life; and it is they that bear witness about me, yet you refuse to come to me that you may have life" (John 5:39-40).

Why don't people come to Jesus? At one level the answer is because they "*refuse* to come." In other words, people do not *want* to come. Some call this the choice of free will. Jesus would probably say it is the choice of a will enslaved to sin. "Truly, truly, I say to you, everyone who commits sin is a *slave* to sin" (John 8:34). Jesus would say that people do not come to him because they are enslaved to their supreme preference for other things. "The light has come into the world, and people loved the darkness rather than the light . . . everyone who does wicked things hates the light and does not come to the light" (John 3:19-20).

How then has anyone ever come, since we are all enslaved to sin and spiritually dead (see *Demand #1*)? Jesus' answer was that God, in his great mercy, overcomes our resistance and draws us: "No one can come to me unless the Father who sent me draws him" (John 6:44). "No one can come to me unless it is granted him by the Father" (John 6:65). God grants the gift of new birth and repentance, which opens the eyes of the spiritually blind to the truth and beauty of Jesus. When this happens, all suicidal objections fall. We are finally free. And, finally free from slavery, we come.

"LAZARUS, COME OUT!"

Jesus came into the world to gather his flock from all the world (John 11:52). He lays down his life for them and demands that they come to him. Though he weeps over those who do not come, he will not be frustrated in his design. He will succeed in gathering a people for himself. He speaks with absolute sovereignty when he says, "I have other sheep that are not of this fold. I must bring them also, and they will listen to my voice. So there will be one flock, one shepherd" (John 10:16). He *must* bring them. They *will* heed his voice. They *will* come.

When you hear the voice of Jesus saying, "Come to me," pray that God would give you eyes to see Jesus as irresistibly true and beautiful. Pray that you would hear this command the way Lazarus did when he was dead. "[Jesus] cried out with a loud voice, 'Lazarus, come out.' The man who had died came [out of his grave]" (John 11:43-44). When you come to Jesus like this, you will never cease to praise and thank him for his sovereign grace.

Demand #4

BELIEVE IN ME

Let not your hearts be troubled. Believe in God; believe also in me. —JOHN 14:1

Believe me that I am in the Father and the Father is in me, or else believe on account of the works themselves. —JOHN 14:11

While you have the light, believe in the light, that you may become sons of light. —JOHN 12:36

[Jesus] said to Thomas, "Put your finger here, and see my hands; and put out your hand, and place it in my side. Do not disbelieve, but believe." —JOHN 20:27

Why does Jesus demand that we believe in him? And what does believing in him really mean? The reason Jesus demands that we believe in him is that all human beings are in a desperate situation, and only Jesus can rescue us. He demands belief in himself because we cannot rescue ourselves but must look entirely to him for help. Jesus is the only one who can save us from this danger. For our own sake he demands that we trust him. It is as though a fireman finds you almost unconscious in a burning building that is about to collapse, throws his insulated tarp over you, picks you up, and says, "Hold still as I carry you. Don't move. Don't try to help me. I will get you out. You must let me do it. Trust me."

THE DESPERATE SITUATION WE ARE IN

Of course, most people don't feel the need for a divine fireman to rescue them. So what is this desperate situation that only Jesus can rescue us from? Jesus put it like this. Notice the words "perish," "condemned," and "wrath of God."

> For God so loved the world, that he gave his only Son, that whoever believes in him should not perish but have eternal life. For God did not send the Son into the world to condemn the world, but in order that the world might be saved through him. Whoever believes in him is not condemned; but whoever does not believe is condemned already, because he has not believed in the name of the only Son of God. . . . Whoever believes in the Son has eternal life; whoever does not obey the Son shall not see life, but the wrath of God remains on him. (John 3:16-18, 36)

The desperate situation we are in, Jesus says, is that we are under the wrath of God. This is owing to our sin (see *Demand #2*). God is just, and his anger is rightly kindled against human attitudes and behaviors that belittle his worth and treat him as insignificant. All of us have done this. In fact, we do it every day.

God Sent Jesus to Die in Our Place

But the amazing truth is that God has sent his Son Jesus into the world not to add to this condemnation, but to rescue us from it. And the way Jesus rescues us is by taking the condemnation on himself, dying in our place, and then demanding not heroic acts of penance but that we trust him. Jesus said, "I am the good shepherd. The good shepherd lays down his life for the sheep" (John 10:11). In other words, Jesus' death was purposeful. He intentionally laid it down in our place.

Jesus saw himself as the fulfillment of the astonishing prophesy of Isaiah 53 (cf. Luke 22:37; Isa. 53:12). Isaiah prophesied seven hundred years before Jesus came that a Servant of the Lord would come to die for his people.

> We esteemed him stricken, smitten by God, and afflicted. But he was wounded for our transgressions; he was crushed for our iniquities; upon him was the chastisement that brought us peace, and with his stripes we are healed. All we like sheep have gone

astray; we have turned every one to his own way; and the LORD has laid on him the iniquity of us all. (Isa. 53:4-6)

The reason Jesus demands that we believe on him is that there is nothing we can add to this rescue from the wrath of God. Jesus became our substitute. The sins that should have brought condemnation on us, God laid on Jesus. God's love planned an amazing exchange: Jesus endured what we deserved so that we might enjoy what he deserved—eternal life. And the way we come to enjoy this life is by believing in Jesus. That's what he said: "Truly, truly, I say to you, whoever *believes* has eternal life" (John 6:47; cf. Luke 8:12).

WHAT DOES BELIEVING IN JESUS MEAN?

Therefore, not many questions are more important than this: What does believing in him really mean? First, it means first believing certain historical facts to be true. When Jesus' disciple Thomas doubted that Jesus was raised physically from the dead, Jesus came to him and said, "Put your finger here, and see my hands; and put out your hand, and place it in my side. Do not disbelieve, but believe" (John 20:27). Belief is not a leap in the dark. It has foundations and content. It is based on what really happened in history.

But believing in Jesus means more than knowing true things about Jesus. It means trusting him as a living person for who he really is. This is why Jesus spoke of simply believing *in him*. "Believe in God; believe also *in me*" (John 14:1; cf. Matt. 18:6). Believing *in* Jesus is more than believing *about* Jesus. We trust *him*.

BEING SATISFIED WITH ALL THAT GOD IS FOR US IN JESUS

Notice that Jesus offers himself to us not merely as a rescuer to be trusted but as living water to be drunk—not to mention offering himself to us as Shepherd (Matt. 26:31), Bridegroom (Matt. 9:15), Treasure (Matt. 13:44), King (John 18:36), etc. What does it mean to "believe in" Jesus as life-giving water?

Jesus said, "If anyone thirsts, let him come to me and drink" (John 7:37). "Whoever drinks of the water that I will give him will never be thirsty forever. The water that I will give him will become in him a spring of water welling up to eternal life" (John 4:14). In another place, Jesus connected this drinking with believing in him and coming to him: "I am the bread of life; whoever *comes* to me shall not hunger, and whoever *believes* in me shall never thirst" (John 6:35). In other words, believing in Jesus and drinking the water that wells up to eternal life are the same.

Believing in Jesus when he offers himself to us as life-giving water does not mean merely believing *that* this water gives life. Water gives life when we drink it. Jesus gives life by being trusted. Trusting Jesus as water, therefore, means drinking the water. That is, it means "receiving" Jesus and all the life-giving grace of God that comes to us in him. "Whoever *receives* me receives him who sent me" (Matt. 10:40; cf. John 13:20). Believing in Jesus includes drinking Jesus as the soul-thirst-quenching water of life. That is, it means savoring and being satisfied with all that God is for us in Jesus.

The Fireman Illustration Was Inadequate

So the illustration I used above of trusting the fireman is insufficient. It's true as far as it goes. Jesus is a rescuer. We must hold still, not move, and let him carry us to safety out of the burning wrath of God. But it is possible to trust a fireman that you do not admire. He may be an adulterer and drunk in his time off. He doesn't ask you to believe in him for all that he is, or to receive him, or to savor his life. But Jesus does. He is so much more than a rescuer. Therefore, believing in him is more than trusting in his rescue skills.

Jesus came not only to rescue us from condemnation but also that we might enjoy everlasting life, which means that we might experience all that God is for us in him. "This is eternal life," he said, "that they know you the only true God, and Jesus Christ whom you have sent" (John 17:3). He knows what we need far better than we do. We need rescue from the wrath of God, and we need a soul-satisfying relationship with God. This is what Jesus came to give. It comes to us in one way alone—by believing in him. Therefore, he gives his demand to the world: "Believe in me."

Demand #5

LOVE ME

Whoever loves father or mother more than me is not worthy of me, and whoever loves son or daughter more than me is not worthy of me. —MATT. 10:37

Jesus said to them, "If God were your Father, you would love me, for I proceeded and came forth from God." —JOHN 8:42, RSV

JESUS COMMANDS THE EMOTIONS

I recall reading a book in college that argued: Love cannot be a feeling because it is commanded, and you can't command the feelings. In other words, love must simply be an act of the will or a deed of the body without involving the emotions or affections. But the problem with this argument is that the premise is false: Jesus *does* command the feelings. He demands that our emotions be one way and not another.[1]

He demands, for example, that we *rejoice* in certain circumstances (Matt. 5:12), and that we *fear* the right person (Luke 12:5), and that we not *feel shame* over him (Luke 9:26), and that we forgive *from the heart* (Matt. 18:35), and so on. If a feeling is proper

---

[1] The most thorough study on emotions in the New Testament is now Matthew Elliott's *Faithful Feelings: Emotion in the New Testament* (Leicester, England: Inter-Varsity Press, 2005). He writes, "Part of the essence of the Christian is how he or she feels. We must recover some of the insight of Jonathan Edwards, Calvin, Augustine and others as they rightly emphasize the role of emotion in the believer's life. With a little work we can come up with a clear idea of the emotional characteristics of the members of the kingdom of God. They love God and each other, they take joy in what Jesus has done in the past and what he will do in the future. They have secure hope that God will triumph. They become angry at sin and injustice and are jealous for God. They embrace the sorrow of the suffering as their own and grieve over sin. But this emotional life is rarely glimpsed in our theologies where emotion is not emphasized as a sign of true faith. Not only do Christians live the ethics of the kingdom, they also feel the attitudes and emotions of the kingdom. This is part of the picture that is very clear in the New Testament. These feelings are a result of good theology and are a necessary component of faith" (263-264).

to have, Jesus can demand it. The fact that I may be too corrupt to experience the emotions that I ought to have does not change my duty to have them. If Jesus commands it, I should have it. My moral inability to produce it does not remove my guilt; it reveals my corruption. It makes me desperate for a new heart—which Jesus came to give (see *Demand #1*).

LOVE FOR JESUS IS NOT LESS THAN DEEP AFFECTION

Jesus' demand that we love him may involve *more* than deep feelings of admiration for his attributes and enjoyment of his fellowship and attraction to his presence and affection for his kinship, but it does not involve *less*. At least two things that he said show this. He said, for example, that our love for him must exceed the love we have for mother and father and son and daughter. "Whoever loves father or mother more than me is not worthy of me, and whoever loves son or daughter more than me is not worthy of me" (Matt. 10:37). The love that binds us to these relationships is not mere willpower. It is deep with affection. Jesus says that the love we must have for him is not less than that, but more.

The other evidence that Jesus requires our love to be more than good deeds is in John 14:15. Jesus said, "If you love me, you will keep my commandments." Sometimes people use these words to say: Loving Jesus *is* keeping his commandments. That's not what it says. It says that keeping Jesus' commandments comes *from* our love for him. It does not *separate* deeds from love, but it does *distinguish* them. First we love him. Then because of this—overflowing from this—we do what he says. Love is not synonymous with commandment-keeping; it is the root of it. So the love that Jesus demands is something very deep and strong—like the closest family bonds of affection that we have, but greater than that and more than that.

LOVE FOR JESUS SPRINGS FROM A NEW NATURE

Jesus' demand to be loved like this implies that we must have a new nature—a new heart. How else can we love someone we have never seen more affectionately than we love our dear children? Loving like this is not in our fallen human nature. Jesus made this plain when he said to those who did not love him, "If God were your Father, you would love me" (John 8:42). In other words, "The reason you do not love me is that you are not in the family of God. You don't have the family nature—the family spirit, the family heart, preferences, tendencies, inclinations. God is not your Father."

Jesus came as God's unique, divine Son (Matt. 11:27) so that fallen sinners like us could become non-divine sons of God with hearts and ways like his. "To all who did receive him, who believed in his name, [Jesus] gave the right to become children of God" (John 1:12). That's why Jesus could say, "Love your enemies . . . and you will be sons of the Most High" (Luke 6:35). Through the new birth (*Demand #1*) and faith (*Demand #4*), Jesus gives us the rights and the inclinations of the children of God. At the center of those inclinations is love for Jesus, God's Son.

He Who Is Forgiven Little, Loves Little

How God enables us to love Jesus more than we love our closest friends and relatives is not a total mystery. The gift of the new birth and repentance—the new nature of a child of God—is brought about through seeing the glory of Jesus' love *for us*. Jesus taught this provocatively at a dinner party. A strict Pharisee, who had little love for Jesus, invited Jesus to dinner. While they were reclining at the low Middle-Eastern table, a prostitute entered and poured ointment—mingled with her tears—on Jesus' bare feet and wiped his feet with her hair. The Pharisee was indignant that Jesus would allow this.

So Jesus asked a question of the Pharisee: If a moneylender forgave two debtors, one who owed him five thousand dollars and the other fifty, which would love him more? He answered, "The one, I suppose, for whom he cancelled the larger debt." Jesus agreed, then said, "Do you see this woman? I entered your house; you gave me no water for my feet, but she has wet my feet with her tears and wiped them with her hair. You gave me no kiss, but from the time I came in she has not ceased to kiss my feet. You did not anoint my head with oil, but she has anointed my feet with ointment." Then Jesus concluded: "She loved much. But he who is forgiven little, loves little" (Luke 7:36-48).

This is a story about the way great love for Jesus comes into being. It comes into being when we are given eyes to see the beauty of Jesus in the way he loved us first. We did not love him first. He loved us first (John 15:16). Our love for Jesus is awakened when our hearts are broken because of our sin (unlike the judgmental Pharisee) and when we taste the sweetness of Jesus' forgiving love preceding and awakening our love for him.

THE DEMAND THAT WE LOVE HIM IS AN ACT OF LOVE

There is no doubt that this love will produce the fruit of obedience to Jesus' other commandments (John 14:15), and that it will incline us to fulfill the ministry he gives us to do (John 21:15-22), and that it will produce a longing that Jesus be honored and blessed (John 14:28; 5:23). But beneath all this fruit is the fundamental reality of heartfelt love for Jesus—strong feelings of admiration for his attributes, abiding enjoyment of his fellowship, undying attraction to his presence, warm affection for his kinship, and strong gratitude for loving us before we loved him.

These emotions and this fruit are what Jesus meant when he referred to our being "worthy" of him: "Whoever loves father or mother more than me is not *worthy* of me' (Matt. 10:37). Loving Jesus with these affections and with this fruit makes us "worthy" of Jesus. This does not mean that we deserve Jesus, as in the phrase "the laborer is *worthy* of his wages" (Luke 10:7, literal translation). It means that Jesus deserves this kind of love. Our worthiness means that he has produced in us affections and behaviors that are suitable and fit for his worth. They correspond properly to his value. (Compare the use of the word "worthy" in the phrase, "Bear fruits worthy of [that is, suitable to] repentance," Luke 3:8, literal translation.)

Jesus demands that he be loved by the world because he is infinitely worthy to be loved. And since our love for him is the enjoyment of his glory and presence and care, therefore Jesus' demand that we love him is one more way that his love overflows on us.

Demand #6

LISTEN TO ME

He called the people to him again and said to them, "Hear me, all of you, and understand."—MARK 7:14

As he said these things, he called out, "He who has ears to hear, let him hear."—LUKE 8:8

Take care then how you hear.—LUKE 8:18

And a woman named Martha welcomed him into her house. And she had a sister called Mary, who sat at the Lord's feet and listened to his teaching. But Martha was distracted with much serving. And she went up to him and said, "Lord, do you not care that my sister has left me to serve alone? Tell her then to help me." But the Lord answered her, "Martha, Martha, you are anxious and troubled about many things, but one thing is necessary. Mary has chosen the good portion, which will not be taken away from her."—LUKE 10:38-42

The entire life and work of Jesus is one great argument why we should listen to his word. Page after page of the New Testament Gospels pile up reasons to turn off the television and listen to Jesus. Here are some of those reasons—and why so many don't listen.

NO ONE EVER SPOKE LIKE THIS MAN

Jesus' ministry was so astonishing and so threatening that his adversaries wanted him out of the way. So the Pharisees "sent officers to arrest him" (John 7:32). But to their dismay the officers came back empty-handed, not because Jesus had good bodyguards, but because his teaching was so stunning. "The officers . . . came to the chief priests and Pharisees, who said to them, 'Why did you not bring him?' The officers answered, 'No one ever spoke like this man!'" (John 7:45-46). When they listened to Jesus, they could not follow through with their mission to arrest him.

JESUS SPEAKS THE VERY WORDS OF GOD

When Jesus finished his famous Sermon on the Mount, "the crowds were astonished at his teaching, for he was teaching them as one who had authority, and not as their scribes" (Matt. 7:28-29). This authority was not because of a personality trait or a pedagogical technique. The reason is much deeper. His words have authority and power, Jesus says, because they are the words of God. "I have not spoken on my own authority, but the Father who sent me has himself given me a commandment—what to say and what to speak" (John 12:49). "What I say, therefore, I say as the Father has told me" (John 12:50; cf. 8:28). "The word that you hear is not mine but the Father's who sent me" (John 14:24). Jesus' words have authority because when he speaks, God speaks. Jesus speaks *from* God the Father and *as* God the Son.

JESUS' WORDS SILENCE SUPERNATURAL POWERS

But the authority of Jesus' words is not only the compelling power of God-revealed truth. There is another dimension. It also carries the force to defeat supernatural powers. Once when Jesus met a demon-possessed man he rebuked him and said, "Be silent, and come out of him!" (Mark 1:25). When the demon convulsed the man and came out, the crowd was amazed and said, "What is this? A new teaching with authority! He commands even the unclean spirits, and they obey him" (Mark 1:27). This same power of Jesus' word healed leprosy (Matt. 8:3), deafness (Mark 7:34-35), and blindness (Matt. 9:28-30). And most remarkable of all, with a simple word three times Jesus raised the dead. "Little girl, I say to you, arise"

(Mark 5:41-42). "Young man, I say to you, arise" (Luke 7:14-15). "Lazarus, come out" (John 11:43-44).

JESUS HAS THE WORDS OF ETERNAL LIFE

Therefore, Jesus' words were *life* in more ways than one. They could sustain physical life and restore physical life. But more important than that they were the indispensable way to *eternal* life. It is a wonderful thing to be raised from the dead—but not if you are simply going to perish later in hell. The most precious thing about the words of Jesus, and the most important reason to listen to him, is that his words lead to eternal life.

Once when Jesus had finished teaching some hard things, "Many of his disciples turned back and no longer walked with him." So Jesus said to the twelve apostles whom he had chosen, "Do you want to go away as well?" To which Peter responded, "Lord, to whom shall we go? You have the words of eternal life" (John 6:66-68). This was not mere enthusiasm for a charismatic teacher. Jesus confirmed Peter's judgment: "It is the Spirit who gives life; the flesh is of no avail. The words that I have spoken to you are spirit and life" (John 6:63). Jesus agrees. He speaks the words of eternal life. Everyone who wants eternal life should listen to the words of Jesus.

How do Jesus' words give eternal life? We have already seen that eternal life comes through believing in Jesus: "This is the will of my Father, that everyone who looks on the Son and believes in him should have eternal life" (John 6:40; see *Demand #4*). The reason the words of Jesus lead to eternal life is that they awaken this faith. Belief in Jesus does not come by the waving of a magic wand. It comes by hearing the word of God through Jesus.

JESUS' WORDS AWAKEN FAITH

One of Jesus' most important parables was about sowing seed on four kinds of soil. The seed represents the word. One kind of soil is the trampled path where the seed falls and the birds snatch it away. Jesus explains it like this: "The ones along the path are those who have heard. Then the devil comes and takes away the word from their hearts, so that they may *not believe and be saved*" (Luke 8:12). What this shows is that Jesus sees his word as the key to believing and being saved. If the word is taken away, there will be no faith in Jesus. And if there is no faith in Jesus, there will be no salvation— no eternal life. First comes hearing the word of Jesus, then comes belief in Jesus, then comes eternal life. "Whoever *hears* my word and *believes* him who sent me has eternal *life*" (John 5:24).

The reason Jesus' words awaken faith in him is that they reveal who he really is and what he does to obtain eternal life for us. We see the glory of Jesus and the all-sufficiency of his work through his word. But not everybody does. Some hear his words, but do not hear them as true and compelling. They see what he is talking about, but do not see it as beautiful and convincing. So Jesus said, "This is why I speak to them in parables, because seeing they do not see, and hearing they do not hear, nor do they understand" (Matt. 13:13).

WHY DO THEY NOT HEAR AND BELIEVE?

Why do so many people not hear what Jesus is saying? Jesus said to his most bitter adversaries, "You seek to kill me because my word finds no place in you" (John 8:37). That is a striking phrase: "My word finds no place in you." Their minds and hearts are shaped (or stuffed) in such a way that when he speaks, what he says won't fit in their hearts. This seems to imply that there is a certain readiness for Jesus' word that goes before his word and enables us to hear him. That is in fact what Jesus teaches.

When Jesus was on trial at the end of his life, Pilate pressed him to confess that he claimed to be the king of the Jews. Jesus responded by saying, "For this purpose I was born and for this purpose I have come into the world—to bear witness to the truth" (John 18:37). Jesus came to speak the truth. His words are truth. Pilate responded cynically, "What is truth?" In other words, there was "no place" in Pilate for Jesus' words. But that did not take Jesus off guard. Nor did it mean that Pilate had hindered God's plan. Jesus had the final and decisive word about Pilate: "Everyone who is *of the truth* listens to my voice" (John 18:37).

So now we have another striking phrase—not only, "My word finds no place in you," but also the even more remarkable phrase, "Everyone who is *of the truth* listens to my voice." On the one hand, there are people whose hearts and minds have *no room* for the voice of Jesus. And on the other hand, there are people who are "*of the truth.*" They listen to Jesus. They do have room for his word. There is, you might say, a truth-shaped readiness to hear the voice of Jesus.

WHOEVER IS OF GOD HEARS THE WORDS OF GOD

Jesus describes these two kinds of listeners with two other phrases: If they do not hear they are not "of God," and if they hear they are his "sheep." The non-listeners he describes like this: "Whoever is *of God* hears the words of God. The reason why you do not hear them is that you are not *of God*" (John 8:47). Now we have three descriptions of the non-listeners: they have "no place" for Jesus' word, they are not "of the truth," and they are not "of God." This is a sobering revelation. It means that our condition as fallen sinners unfits us for hearing the truth—especially as it comes from Jesus.

We are not neutral like a metronome wand poised straight up between truth and error—waiting dispassionately to be inclined to one side or the other. No, we are heavily tilted toward selfishness and all the errors that support it. When Jesus speaks, unless God acts to give us ears to hear and eyes to see, there will be no place in us for the words of Jesus.

This explains why Jesus said:

> I thank you, Father, Lord of heaven and earth, that you have hidden these things from the wise and understanding and revealed them to little children; yes, Father, for such was your gracious will. All things have been handed over to me by my Father, and no one knows who the Son is except the Father, or who the Father is except the Son and anyone to whom the Son chooses to reveal him. (Luke 10:21-22)

When he had said this, he turned to his disciples and said, "Blessed are the eyes that see what you see!" (Luke 10:23). Blessed indeed! Blessed *by God*. This seeing is the work of God. Only God can give us eyes to see and ears to hear. That's why Jesus says that those who do not listen to his words are not "of God" (John 8:47). This is the *blessing* we desperately need—the blessing that God would make in our hearts a place for the truth.

"My Sheep Hear My Voice"

Finally, Jesus calls those who do have a place for truth his *sheep*: "My sheep hear my voice, and I know them, and they follow me" (John 10:27). Therefore, we can know we are his sheep if we listen to his voice. We know we are his sheep if there is a truth-shaped place for his word in our hearts, and we welcome what he says.

Therefore, I urge you on behalf of Jesus, listen to his word. Be like Mary and sit at his feet (Luke 10:39, 42). Don't turn away from the command of his Father given on the Mount of Transfiguration: "This is my beloved Son, with whom I am well pleased; *listen to him*" (Matt. 17:5). Don't miss the merciful attraction in the words, "Heaven and earth will pass away, but my words will not pass away" (Mark 13:31). Don't hate yourself by rejecting the one who said, "These things I have spoken to you . . . that your joy may be full" (John 15:11; cf. 17:13). Listen to Jesus.

Demand #7

ABIDE IN ME

Abide in me, and I in you. As the branch cannot bear fruit by itself, unless it abides in the vine, neither can you, unless you abide in me. —JOHN 15:4

As the Father has loved me, so have I loved you. Abide in my love. —JOHN 15:9

If you abide in my word, you are truly my disciples, and you will know the truth, and the truth will set you free. —JOHN 8:31-32

J esus' demands are for a lifetime. He does not demand a single decision to repent or come or believe or love or listen. All these continue. The transformation of repentance continues. Coming to Jesus again and again continues. Believing in him hour by hour continues. Listening to his word as the daily source of spiritual life continues. Jesus demands the engagement of our minds and hearts every day of our lives.

A transaction with Jesus in the past that has no ongoing expression in our lives was a false transaction. When Jesus said, "If you abide in my word, you are truly my disciples" (John 8:31), he meant that if we *don't* abide, we are *not* truly his disciples. And the opposite of *true* disciples is *false* disciples. That's what we are if we count on past experiences without ongoing devotion to Jesus.

A LIFELONG EXTENSION OF ENCOUNTERING JESUS

One way that Jesus taught the necessity of an ongoing devotion was to demand, "Abide in me." There is nothing uniquely religious about the word *abide*. In the language of the New Testament, it is the ordinary word for "stay" or "continue" or sometimes "dwell." Jesus meant: "Stay in me. Continue in me. Keep me for your dwelling." It is the lifelong extension of encountering Jesus.

The context of this demand is the analogy of a vine and its branches. Jesus compares himself to the vine, and us to branches:

> Abide in me, and I in you. As the branch cannot bear fruit by itself, unless it abides in the vine, neither can you, unless you abide in me. I am the vine; you are the branches. Whoever abides in me and I in him, he it is that bears much fruit, for apart from me you can do nothing. (John 15:4-5)

This picture helps us understand what Jesus meant by abiding in him. The main point of the analogy is that power to bear fruit—that is, power to live a fruitful life of Christ-like love (John 15:12)—flows from Jesus if we stay vitally connected to him. Then we are like a branch connected to the vine so that all the life-sustaining, fruit-producing sap can flow into it. Jesus is explicit in claiming to be the power that we need to live fruitful lives. He says, "Apart from me you can do nothing." Abiding in Jesus means staying vitally connected to the life-giving, power-giving, fruit-producing branch, namely, Jesus.

The Moment-by-Moment Cause of Every Good Thing

In other words, Jesus demands that he be the moment-by-moment cause of every good thing in our lives. "Apart from me you can do *nothing*." Nothing! Really? Well, we could sin and stop bearing fruit and perish without him. But that's not what he promises to produce. He means: "Without me you can do nothing truly good, truly God-honoring and Christ-exalting and self-abasing and eternally helpful for others." Abiding in Jesus means staying vitally connected, hour by hour, to the one who alone produces in our lives everything he demands.

IF YOU ABIDE, YOU BEAR FRUIT

But practically, what does this mean in our experience? What is this "staying vitally connected"? How do we do this? One important part of the answer is to make clear that abiding in Jesus is *not* the same as bearing fruit or keeping his commandments. Fruit-bearing and commandment-keeping is the *result* of abiding. *If* we abide, we bear fruit.

Jesus does not contradict this when he says, "If you keep my commandments, you will abide in my love" (John 15:10). This does not mean: Keeping his commandments *is* abiding in his love. That would be like saying: Fruit *is* being connected to the vine. No. Fruit is the *result* of our being connected to the vine. They are not the same thing. What Jesus means is that if you don't keep the commandments, that is, if you don't bear the fruit of love (for love is the sum of his commandments, John 15:12), you have ceased to abide in him. For the truth stands: "Whoever abides in me . . . bears much fruit" (John 15:5).

So the answer to our question, "How do we abide in Jesus?" is *not* "by bearing fruit" or "by keeping the commandments." That misses the whole point. The point is to discover *how* to bear fruit. The answer is, by abiding in Jesus. And so the question becomes: How do we abide in Jesus? What does it mean in actual experience?

PRACTICALLY, HOW DO WE ABIDE IN JESUS?

Jesus uses two other similar phrases that point to the answer. He refers to abiding in his *love*. And he refers to abiding in his *word*. Both of these point toward abiding as continual *trust* in the truth of Jesus' words and in the certainty of his love.

ABIDING MEANS TRUSTING IN JESUS' LOVE

Not to abide in Jesus' love would mean that we stop believing that we are loved by Jesus. We look at our circumstances—perhaps persecution or disease or abandonment—and we conclude that we are not loved by Jesus anymore. That's the opposite of abiding in the love of Jesus. So abiding in his love means continuing to believe, moment by moment, that we are loved.

Everything that comes into our lives under Jesus' sovereign authority (Matt. 8:8) is part of his love for us. If it is pleasant, he says, "That's how my Father cares for the birds of the air and the lilies of the field; how much more you!" (cf. Matt. 6:26-30). And if it is painful, he says, "Fear not, the worst that can happen is death, and I have overcome death. I will be with you to the end. And you will be repaid at the resurrection of the just" (cf. Matt. 10:28; 28:20; John 11:25-26; Luke 14:14). Abiding in Jesus means trusting that this is true—and true *for you*. That is, it means living on this truth moment by moment. It flows to us like sap flows to a branch. We receive it and get our life from it every day.

ABIDING MEANS TRUSTING IN JESUS' WORD

Similarly, this is true with the phrase, "Abide in my *word*" (John 8:31). This cannot mean merely, "Keep my commandments." Rather it means, "Keep on trusting my word. Keep on trusting what I have revealed to you about myself and my Father and my work." The context of John 8:31-32 confirms this: "Jesus said to the Jews who had believed in him, 'If you abide in my word, you are truly my disciples, and you will know the truth, and the truth will set you free.'" The result of abiding in Jesus' word is being set free. From what? From sin. That's the slavery Jesus has in mind, as John 8:34 shows: "Everyone who commits sin is a *slave to sin*." So freedom from sin is the fruit of abiding in the word. "If you abide in my word . . . the truth will set you free." Not sinning is the *fruit*, not the *definition*, of abiding in the word. So keeping the commandments of Jesus, which is another way of describing liberation from sin, is not the meaning of abiding in his word, but the fruit of it.

So we conclude that abiding in Jesus—in his love and in his word—is trusting that he really is loving us at every moment and that everything he has revealed about himself and his work for us and our future with him is true. We are taken back to what we saw in the chapter on believing in Jesus (*Demand* #4). Believing in Jesus as our living water means *drinking* the water—savoring it and being satisfied with it. So it is with the sap that flows from the vine to the branch. We receive it, drink it, savor it, and satisfy our souls with it. This daily ever-renewed satisfaction in Jesus is the key to bearing fruit.[1] This is what it means to abide in Jesus.

JESUS KEEPS US ABIDING

As easy as it seems to abide, to stay implanted, to drink, to rest in Jesus, the truth is that we are often tempted to find our life-giving sap from another plant. And besides our own sinful tendencies, the devil himself wants to snatch us out of the vine, and we must pray daily, Jesus said, that God would "deliver us from evil" (Matt. 6:13). Therefore, we need to remind ourselves that Jesus does not leave us to ourselves. Even though he commands us to abide in him—and we are responsible to abide there, and guilty if we don't abide—nevertheless he himself keeps us there. And we would not abide there without his crucial keeping.

Jesus showed us this in at least three ways. He said that no one can snatch his own sheep (that is, his own true branches) out of his hand.

> My sheep hear my voice, and I know them, and they follow me. I give them eternal life, and they will never perish, and no one will snatch them out of my hand. My Father, who has given them to me, is greater than all, and no one is able to snatch them out of the Father's hand. (John 10:27-29)

Then he prayed to his Father that God would cause us to keep on abiding in his name (that is, in Jesus). "Holy Father, keep them in your name, which you have given me. . . . While I was with them, I kept them in your name . . . and not one of them has been lost except the son of destruction, that the Scripture might be fulfilled"

---

[1] I have tried to explain this and give many practical examples of how this works in real life in the book *The Purifying Power of Living by Faith in FUTURE GRACE* (Sisters, Ore.: Multnomah, 1995).

(John 17:11-12). So it is *God* who does the decisive work in keeping us in the vine.

Then Jesus himself illustrated how he prays for his own disciples and preserves them from falling away. He predicted Simon Peter's three denials on the night before his death. But then he spoke with sovereign authority to Simon in words that should encourage all of us. "Simon, Simon, behold, Satan demanded to have you, that he might sift you like wheat, but I have prayed for you that your faith may not fail. And when you have turned again, strengthen your brothers" (Luke 22:31-32). Jesus prayed for Simon's keeping and knew it would happen. He said, "*when* you have turned," not "*if* you turn." God's answer to Jesus' prayer was sovereignly decisive. Yes, Simon's faith faltered, and he sinned by denying Jesus. But his faith did not fail utterly. He was not cut off from the vine. Jesus prayed for him. And there is no reason to think Jesus has ceased praying for us this way today.[2]

We are not idle in the battle to abide in Jesus. But in the end the battle is assured because it does not depend finally on us. Jesus wins. No one can snatch us out of his hand. He and his Father are greater than all. Therefore, his demand that we abide in him is that we keep trusting the one who keeps us trusting.

---

[2] Some commentators on the Bible disagree that Jesus keeps his own by making sure that they keep abiding in him. They point, understandably, to John 15:1-2, 6: "I am the true vine, and my Father is the vinedresser. Every branch of mine that does not bear fruit he takes away, and every branch that does bear fruit he prunes, that it may bear more fruit. . . . If anyone does not abide in me he is thrown away like a branch and withers; and the branches are gathered, thrown into the fire, and burned." Does this mean that we can be truly attached to the life-giving vine and then later be "taken away" and "thrown into the fire"? I don't think that is what Jesus is saying, mainly because of the three reasons given above. Rather, I think Jesus means that there are those who appear to be truly in the vine, but are not. They have a kind of attachment, but it is not real and life-giving. Judas is the clearest example in Jesus' ministry. He was "attached" to Jesus for three years: there was a kind of influence flowing into him, and he received many blessings from Jesus. But he was not truly attached in a life-giving way. So eventually he was "taken away"—not away from true life, but away from the artificial attachment that looked real for a season but was not.

Demand #8

TAKE UP YOUR CROSS
AND FOLLOW ME

If anyone would come after me, let him deny himself and take up his cross and follow me. For whoever would save his life will lose it, but whoever loses his life for my sake will find it. —MATT. 16:24-25

Follow me, and I will make you become fishers of men. —MARK 1:17

I am the light of the world; he who follows me will not walk in darkness, but will have the light of life. —JOHN 8:12

Follow me, and leave the dead to bury their own dead. —MATT. 8:22

If you would be perfect, go, sell what you possess and give to the poor, and you will have treasure in heaven; and come, follow me. —MATT. 19:21

Jesus was fully human and fully God (John 1:1, 14). He was not God with a human veneer—like a costume. He was a real, flesh-and-blood man, a carpenter's son (Mark 6:3). So when he said to fishermen or tax collectors, "Follow me," their obedience was a concrete, physical act of putting their feet on the ground and walking behind Jesus and being part of his traveling team.

FOLLOWING JESUS WHEN HE IS NOT HERE

But Jesus knew that he would not always be on earth to have followers in this physical sense. "I am going to him who sent me. . . . I tell you the truth: it is to your advantage that I go away, for if I do not go away, the Helper will not come to you. But if I go, I will send him to you" (John 16:5, 7). Jesus was fully aware that the movement he began would continue after he had gone back to his Father in heaven. This was his plan (see *Demand #45*).

Therefore, the demand that we follow him was relevant not only for his physical days on earth but for all time. He made this clear at the end of his earthly ministry. He had risen from the dead and was about to ascend to the Father. He told Peter that he would suffer martyrdom someday after Jesus was gone. Peter wondered if he was the only one and asked Jesus what would happen to his fellow apostle, John. Jesus answered, "If it is my will that he remain until I come, what is that to you? You follow me!" (John 21:22).

What this implies about "following Jesus" is that it happens after he is gone. Until Jesus comes again, he expects his disciples on earth to "follow" him. So following Jesus is not limited to physically walking around Palestine behind him. Jesus demands it of every person in every country in every age.

FOLLOWING JESUS MEANS JOINING HIM IN WHAT HE WAS SENT TO DO

When Jesus said to Peter and Andrew, who were fishermen by trade, "Follow me, and *I will make you become fishers of men*" (Mark 1:17), he was using imagery relevant to them for something that applies to everyone who follows Jesus. The demand to follow Jesus means that everyone should join him in what he came to do. And he tells us repeatedly what that was. "The Son of Man came . . . to give his life as a ransom for many" (Mark 10:45). "The Son of Man came to seek and to save the lost" (Luke 19:10). "I have not come to call the righteous but sinners to repentance" (Luke 5:32). "I came that they may have life and have it abundantly" (John 10:10). "What shall I say? 'Father, save me from this hour'? But for this purpose I have come to this hour. Father, glorify your name" (John 12:27-28).

In summary, then, he came to "die for the nation [of Israel], and not for the nation only, but also to gather into one the children of

God who are scattered abroad" (John 11:51-52). He came to *gather* a people—specifically, to gather a people in allegiance to himself for the glory of his Father—by dying to save them from their sins and to give them eternal life and a new ethic of love like his (John 13:34-35). Therefore, when he demands that we follow him, he means that we join him in that task of gathering: "Whoever does not *gather* with me scatters" (Luke 11:23). There are no neutral followers; we either scatter or gather. Following Jesus means continuing the work he came to do—gathering a people in allegiance to him for the glory of his Father.

FOLLOWING JESUS INTO SUFFERING

Continuing the work he came to do even includes the suffering he came to do. Following Jesus means that we share in his suffering. When Jesus calls us to follow him, this is where he puts the emphasis. He knows he is heading to the cross, and he demands that we do the same. He designs his entire life and ministry to go to Jerusalem and be killed. "I must go on my way today and tomorrow and the day following, for it cannot be that a prophet should perish away from Jerusalem" (Luke 13:33).

So he "set his face to go to Jerusalem" (Luke 9:51). And he knew exactly what would happen there. It was all planned by his Father when he sent him into the world. "See, we are going up to Jerusalem, and the Son of Man will be delivered over to the chief priests and the scribes, and they will condemn him to death and deliver him over to the Gentiles. And they will mock him and spit on him, and flog him and kill him. And after three days he will rise" (Mark 10:33-34). That's the plan—down to the details of being spit on.

That was the design of his life. And he knew that his own pain would also fall on those who followed him. "If they persecuted me, they will also persecute you" (John 15:20). So the unflinching focus of his demand was that we follow him in suffering. "If anyone would come after me, let him deny himself and take up his cross and follow me" (Matt. 16:24). Jesus put the emphasis on self-denial and cross-bearing.

Suffering for Jesus with Joy Shows His Supreme Value

He did not die to make this life easy for us or prosperous. He died to remove every obstacle to our everlasting joy in making much of him. And he calls us to follow him in his sufferings because this life of joyful suffering for Jesus' sake (Matt. 5:12) shows that he is more valuable than all the earthly rewards that the world lives for (Matt. 13:44; 6:19-20). If you follow Jesus only because he makes life easy now, it will look to the world as though you really love what they love, and Jesus just happens to provide it for you. But if you suffer with Jesus in the pathway of love because he is your supreme treasure, then it will be apparent to the world that your heart is set on a different fortune than theirs. This is why Jesus demands that we deny ourselves and take up our cross and follow him.

Suffering for Jesus Is Temporary; Pleasure in Jesus Is Eternal

Of course, the pain is temporary. He does not call us to eternal suffering. That's what he rescues us from. "Whoever loves his life loses it, and whoever hates his life *in this world* will keep it for *eternal life*" (John 12:25). "Whoever loses his life for my sake and the gospel's will *save* it" (Mark 8:35). Suffering for Jesus is temporary. Pleasure in Jesus is eternal. When Peter said (perhaps with a tinge of self-pity), "See, we have left everything and followed you," Jesus responded, without coddling Peter's self-pity, "Everyone who has left houses or brothers or sisters or father or mother or children or lands, for my name's sake, will receive a hundredfold and will inherit eternal life" (Matt. 19:27, 29). In other words, there is no ultimate sacrifice in following Jesus. "You will be repaid at the resurrection of the just" (Luke 14:14). "Your reward is great in heaven" (Matt. 5:12).

Even before heaven, joy abounds along the hard road that leads through death to resurrection. Nothing can compare with the joy of walking in the light with Jesus as opposed to walking in the darkness without him. Jesus said, "I am the light of the world. Whoever follows me will not walk in darkness, but will have the light of life" (John 8:12). Following Jesus does indeed lead through suffering and death. But the path is luminous with life and truth. Jesus promised, "I am with you always, to the end of the age" (Matt. 28:20). And where Jesus is present there is joy—joy in sorrow for now, but joy nevertheless. "These things I have spoken to you, that my joy may be in you, and that your joy may be full" (John 15:11).

Ruptures in Relationships with People

This is why the ruptures caused by following Jesus are not devastating. There are ruptures in relationships with people, relationships with possessions, and relationships with our vocation. Jesus has jolting ways of describing the cost of following him in relation to people. "Follow me, and leave the dead to bury their own dead" (Matt. 8:22). "If anyone comes to me and does not hate his own father and mother and wife and children and brothers and sisters, yes, and even his own life, he cannot be my disciple" (Luke 14:26). In other words, following Jesus is so supremely important that it calls for behaviors that are sometimes going to look like *hate* to the world. I have seen this lived out in agonizing choices that missionaries make to take their little children to risky places and leave aging parents behind, well cared for, but perhaps never to be seen on earth again. Some call it loveless. But Jesus has his eyes on the nations and what love demands in their case.

Ruptures in Relationships with Possessions

Following Jesus also ruptures our relationship with possessions. There once was a rich young man who loved his possessions too much. So Jesus cut to the heart of his idolatry with the demand, "If you would be perfect, go, sell what you possess and give to the poor, and you will have treasure in heaven; and come, follow me" (Matt. 19:21, see *Demand #20*). If something gets in the way of following Jesus, we must get rid of it.

And this is not unique to that rich man but applies to all of us:

"*Any one* of you who does not renounce all that he has cannot be my disciple" (Luke 14:33). Renouncing what you have may not always mean selling it all. Jesus commended Zacchaeus for giving *half* of his goods to the poor (Luke 19:8-9). But renouncing *all* does mean that everything we have is totally at Jesus' disposal for purposes that please him and that it must never get in the way of radical obedience to his command of love.

RUPTURES IN RELATIONSHIPS WITH VOCATION

Then there is the rupture that following Jesus brings to our vocation. When Jesus called the twelve to follow him, none of them was a professional Jesus-follower. They were fishermen and tax collectors and the like. They had jobs. Incredibly, it went something like this: "As [Jesus] passed by, he saw Levi the son of Alphaeus sitting at the tax booth, and he said to him, 'Follow me.' And he rose and followed him" (Mark 2:14). Just like that! (As far as we know.) For most of us it was not that simple. But it does happen.

And it may happen to you. Not everyone should leave his vocation to follow Jesus. When one man wanted to leave his homeland and follow Jesus, Jesus said, "Go home to your friends and tell them how much the Lord has done for you, and how he has had mercy on you" (Mark 5:19). Most of us should stay where we are and follow Jesus in all the radical ways of love demanded by our present position and relationships.[1] But not everyone. For some— perhaps you (even as you read this)—following Jesus will mean a risky rupture in your vocation. Do not be afraid to follow him away from the familiar.

FOLLOWING JESUS IS COSTLY AND WORTH IT

Jesus has no desire to trick you into following him with a kind of bait and switch. He is utterly up front about the cost. In fact, he urges you to count the cost. "For which of you, desiring to build a

---

[1] For more on what obedience to Jesus looks like in the secular workplace, see the chapter "Making Much of Christ from 8 to 5" in John Piper, *Don't Waste Your Life* (Wheaton, Ill.: Crossway Books, 2003), 131-154.

tower, does not first sit down and count the cost, whether he has enough to complete it? . . . Or what king, going out to encounter another king in war, will not sit down first and deliberate whether he is able with ten thousand to meet him who comes against him with twenty thousand?" (Luke 14:28, 31). Let the call to follow Jesus be clear and honest. "In the world you will have tribulation. But take heart; I have overcome the world" (John 16:33). It is costly, and it is worth it.

LOVE GOD WITH ALL YOUR HEART, SOUL, MIND, AND STRENGTH

Jesus answered, "The most important [commandment] is, 'Hear, O Israel: The Lord our God, the Lord is one. And you shall love the Lord your God with all your heart and with all your soul and with all your mind and with all your strength.'"—MARK 12:29-30

Woe to you Pharisees! For you tithe mint and rue and every herb, and neglect justice and the love of God. These you ought to have done, without neglecting the others.—LUKE 11:42

But I know that you do not have the love of God within you. I have come in my Father's name, and you do not receive me. If another comes in his own name, you will receive him.—JOHN 5:42-43

Jesus came to restore human beings to the kind of relationship with God and each other that we were created for. The most important thing he has to say about that restored relationship with God is that we were meant to love God with all our heart and soul and mind and strength. Jesus assumes that loving God means loving him for who he really is, and so his vision of who God is permeates all that he says.

KNOW GOD, AND LOVE HIM FOR ALL THAT HE IS

God is the Creator. He created human beings (Matt. 19:4) and all the universe (Mark 13:19). He sustains all he made, governing its smallest details of birds and lilies. "Are not two sparrows sold for a penny? And not one of them will fall to the ground apart from your Father" (Matt. 10:29; cf. 6:30). He is a God of wisdom (Luke 11:49) and righteousness (Matt. 6:33) and power (Matt. 22:29) and wrath (John 3:36) and compassion (Luke 15:20) and love (John 3:16). He is a person, not a mere force, and can be known as a Father who loves us as his children (John 1:12; 16:27). Jesus demands of us, "Love this God. Love him with all that you are for all that he is."

To love God we must know him. God would not be honored by groundless love. In fact, there is no such thing. If we do not know anything about God, there is nothing in our mind to awaken love. If love does not come from knowing God, there is no point in calling it love *for God*. There may be some vague attraction in our heart or some unfocused gratitude in our souls, but if they do not arise from knowing God, they are not love for God.

JESUS: REVELATION OF GOD, LITMUS TEST OF OUR LOVE FOR GOD

Therefore, Jesus came into the world to make God known, that he might be truly loved. Jesus said to his disciples:

> "If you had known me, you would have known my Father also. From now on you do know him and have seen him." Philip said to him, "Lord, show us the Father, and it is enough for us." Jesus said to him, "Have I been with you so long, and you still do not know me, Philip? Whoever has seen me has seen the Father. How can you say, 'Show us the Father'?" (John 14:7-9)

Jesus so deeply reveals God that receiving Jesus becomes the test of loving God and having him as our Father. "If God were your Father, you would love me" (John 8:42). If we won't have Jesus, we don't have God. He made himself the measure of our knowing and loving God. "I know that you do not have the love of God within you. I have come in my Father's name, and you do not receive me. If another comes in his own name, you will receive him. How can you believe, when you receive glory from one another and do not seek the glory that comes from the only God?" (John 5:42-44).

In other words, Jesus is so fully God-reflecting and God-exalting that denying him means denying God. Jesus knows that his adversaries "do not have the love of God within [them]" because they do not receive him. "The one who rejects me rejects him who sent me" (Luke 10:16). If they loved God, they would love him. He makes God known more clearly and more fully than any other revelation. Therefore, it cannot be that one has love for God but rejects Jesus.

"I Made Known to Them Your Name"

Therefore, if we are to love God, we must know him as he is revealed in Jesus. Before Jesus came, God awakened love by the revelation of himself in his word—which always pointed toward Jesus. "You search the Scriptures," Jesus said, "because you think that in them you have eternal life; and it is they that bear witness about me" (John 5:39). But now that Jesus has come, it is the revelation of Jesus himself that awakens love to God. "No one knows the Father except the Son and anyone to whom the Son chooses to reveal him" (Matt. 11:27).

This is what Jesus did for his disciples. He made God known. In Jesus' prayer in John 17, he says, "I made known to them your name, and I will continue to make it known" (v. 26). This is the long-awaited fulfillment of the prophecy in the Law of Moses: "The LORD your God will circumcise your heart and the heart of your offspring, so that you will love the LORD your God with all your heart and with all your soul, that you may live" (Deut. 30:6). Jesus is the fulfillment of that prophecy. Therefore, we cannot love God apart from the revelation of Jesus who changes our hearts to know God so that we see him as compellingly beautiful.

Seeing and Savoring God as Compellingly Beautiful

The reason I use the phrase "compellingly beautiful" is to stress two things. One is that loving God is not a mere decision. You cannot merely decide to love classical music or country western music, much less God. The music must become compelling. If you don't love it, something must change inside you. That change makes it possible for the mind to experience the music with a compelling sense of its attractiveness. So it is with God. You do not merely decide to love him. Something changes inside you, and as a result he becomes compellingly attractive. His glory—his beauty—compels your admiration and delight.

The other thing I am emphasizing in the phrase "compellingly beautiful" is that love for God is not essentially behavior but affection—not deeds but delight. God's glory becomes our supreme pleasure. We begin to prefer above all else to know him and see him and be with him and be like him. There are several important reasons for believing that love for God is most essentially an experience of the affections, not behavior.

LOVING GOD IS FIRST, LOVING OUR NEIGHBOR IS SECOND

First, Jesus distinguished the first and second commandment. He said, "You shall love the Lord your God with all your heart and with all your soul and with all your mind. This is the great and first commandment. And a second is like it: You shall love your neighbor as yourself" (Matt. 22:37-39). Therefore, loving God cannot be defined as loving our neighbor. They are different. Loving God is first. Loving our neighbor is second. The first is primary and depends on no greater obedience. The second is secondary and depends on loving God. They are not separated, for true love for God will always bring about love for people. But they are different. This means that the behaviors of love toward others are not the essential meaning of loving God. They are the overflow or fruit of loving God. Loving God is not the way we treat others. It is a compelling admiration and delight in God.

"THEIR HEART IS FAR FROM ME"

Second, Jesus said to the Pharisees when they criticized the freedom of his disciples, "Well did Isaiah prophesy of you hypocrites, as it is written, 'This people honors me with their lips, but their heart is far from me; in vain do they worship me'" (Mark 7:6-7). Jesus says that external actions—even religious ones directed toward him—are not the essence of worship. They are not the essence of love. What happens in the heart is essential. The external behaviors will be pleasing to God when they flow from a heart that freely admires and delights in God—that is, when they flow from love for God.

THE OPPOSITE OF LOVING GOD IS HATING AND DESPISING

Third, Jesus said, "No one can serve two masters, for either he will hate the one and love the other, or he will be devoted to the one and despise the other. You cannot serve God and money" (Matt. 6:24). The opposite of loving God is "hating" and "despising." These are strong emotional words. They imply that the positive counterpart is also a strong emotion. So loving God is a strong inward emotion, not a mere outward action. But someone might say that "serve" is the key word here and implies that love for God is serving God. But that is not what it says. It says that the reason you cannot serve two masters (God and money) is that behind the behaviors of serving are two diametrically opposed passions: hate versus love, devotion versus despising. Jesus does not equate loving God with serving God. He roots serving God in loving God.

AN ADULTEROUS GENERATION SEEKS FOR A SIGN

Fourth, when the Pharisees, who had no love for Jesus (or God, John 5:42), said to him, "Teacher, we wish to see a sign from you," Jesus replied in a way that shed light on the nature of loving God. He said, "An evil and adulterous generation seeks for a sign, but no sign will be given to it except the sign of the prophet Jonah" (Matt. 12:39). Why does he call them "adulterous" for seeking a sign? Because God was Israel's husband (Ezek. 16:8), and Jesus was God coming to reclaim his unfaithful wife. That's why he alludes to himself as the "bridegroom" (Matt. 25:1ff.).

Why would a wife (Israel represented by her leaders) stand before her husband (Jesus) and demand a sign that he was her husband? Jesus says it is not owing to innocent ignorance. It's owing to an *adulterous* heart. In other words, Israel does not love her husband. She loves other suitors—like the praise of men (Matt. 23:6) and money (Luke 16:14). What this teaches us about the love Jesus demands for God is that it is like a faithful wife's love for her husband—not mere external behavior but heartfelt affection and admiration and delight. It should be modeled not on the service of a slave, but on the Song of Songs. "We will exult and rejoice in you; we will extol your love more than wine; rightly do they love you" (Song 1:4).

With Heart, Soul, Mind, and Strength

When Jesus demands that we love God with all of our heart, soul, mind, and strength, he means that every faculty and every capacity of our being should express the fullness of our affection for God—the fullness of all the ways that we treasure him. These four faculties and capacities overlap in meaning:[1] heart, soul, mind, and strength. But they are not identical. "Heart" highlights the center of our volitional and emotional life without excluding thought (Luke 1:51). "Soul" highlights our life as a whole, though sometimes distinguished from the body (Matt. 10:28). "Mind" highlights our thinking capacity. And "strength" highlights the capacity to make vigorous efforts both bodily and mentally (Mark 5:4; Luke 21:36).

The function of these faculties and capacities in relation to loving God is to demonstrate that love.[2] It may be that "heart" is men-

---

[1] Concerning "heart" and "mind," consider that the one other place in the four Gospels where "mind" (διάνοια) occurs other than in the command to love God "with all your mind" (ἐν ὅλῃ τῇ διανοίᾳ σου) is Luke 1:51, where it is translated "thoughts" and happens in the "heart": "He has shown strength with his arm; he has scattered the proud in the *thoughts* [διανοίᾳ] of their hearts." So "mind" and "heart" are not always distinct. Concerning "heart" and "soul," consider that Jesus said, "Do not fear those who kill the body but cannot kill the *soul*. Rather fear him who can destroy both *soul* and body in hell" (Matt. 10:28). This implies that "soul" is the fullness of life or personhood apart from the body. Therefore, it would include the "heart," even though it is more.

[2] In the command to love God "*with* all your heart and *with* all your soul and *with* all your mind and *with* all your strength" the Greek prepositions behind the English translation "with" are not the same each time this command is used in the Gospels. All three gospels are quoting Deuteronomy 6:5 where the Hebrew preposition used is בְּ (בְּכָל־לְבָבְךָ וּבְכָל־נַפְשְׁךָ וּבְכָל־מְאֹדֶךָ). But

tioned first because it is seen most especially as the *source* of love that is expressed through the soul (life), mind (thought), and strength (effort). Luke especially seems to take it that way, because he uses a different Greek preposition in the phrase "*with* all your heart" than he does in translating the other three phrases (see note 2). In any case, the point is that every faculty and capacity that we have should display at every moment that God is our supreme treasure.

EVERY CAPACITY TREASURES GOD ABOVE ALL THINGS

Loving God is most essentially treasuring God. And loving him with *all* the heart and *all* the soul and *all* the mind and *all* the strength means that every faculty and every capacity treasures God above all things and in such a way that our treasuring of any other thing is also a treasuring of God. In other words, there may be other good things that we may rightly treasure in some measure. But we may not treasure them in the place of God. We may only treasure them as expressions of treasuring God. If one of our human capacities finds pleasure in anyone or anything in such a way that this pleasure is not also a delight in God, then we have not loved God with all that capacity.

This way of seeing love for God is confirmed by the way God was loved in the Psalms. Jesus saw himself as the goal and focus and fulfillment of the Old Testament Scriptures, including the Psalms (Matt. 5:17; Luke 24:27; John 5:39). We would expect him to demand a love that extends and fulfills what the psalmists expe-

---

Matthew 22:37 translates the preposition with ἐν every time (ἀγαπήσεις κύριον τὸν θεόν σου ἐν ὅλῃ τῇ καρδίᾳ σου καὶ ἐν ὅλῃ τῇ ψυχῇ σου καὶ ἐν ὅλῃ τῇ διανοίᾳ σου). Mark 12:30 translates it with ἐξ every time (ἀγαπήσεις κύριον τὸν θεόν σου ἐξ ὅλης τῆς καρδίας σου καὶ ἐξ ὅλης τῇ ψυχῇ σου καὶ ἐξ ὅλης τῆς διανοίας σου καὶ ἐξ ὅλης τῆς ἰσχύος σου). Because of this, I am inclined to see ἐν and ἐξ as two ways of expressing the same instrumental meaning of the Hebrew word ב. In other words, both mean more or less "by." The heart and soul and mind and strength are the instruments *by* which we demonstrate love for God. A slight variation to this interpretation is suggested by Luke's peculiar way of translating Deuteronomy 6:5. He uses the preposition ἐξ in relation to "heart" but ἐν in relation to "soul," "strength," and "mind" (ἀγαπήσει κύριον τὸν θεόν σου ἐξ ὅλης [τῆς] καρδίας σου καὶ ἐν ὅλῃ τῇ ψυχῇ σου καὶ ἐν ὅλῃ τῇ ἰσχύϊ σου καὶ ἐν ὅλῃ τῇ διανοίᾳ σου, καὶ τὸν πλησίον σου ὡς σεαυτόν, Luke 10:27). One wonders if Luke intended to say that the heart is the "source" (hence ἐξ), while the soul, mind, and strength are the spheres in which this love is demonstrated (hence ἐν). That would fit what I am stressing, namely, that love for God is a matter most essentially of the affections (of the heart) and secondarily demonstrated in the action of the life of mental and physical effort.

rienced. In the Psalms we read of love to God that is absolutely exclusive: "Whom have I in heaven but you? And there is nothing on earth that I desire besides you" (Ps. 73:25). "I say to the LORD, 'You are my Lord; I have no good apart from you'" (Ps. 16:2). What can this exclusivity possibly mean, since the psalmists also speak, for example, of loving other people (Ps. 16:3)?

We get a clue in Psalm 43:4 where the psalmist says, "Then I will go to the altar of God, to *God my exceeding joy.*" This last phrase ("my exceeding joy") is literally, "the gladness of my rejoicing" or "the joy of my exultation."[3] This points to God as the joy of all our joys. In all my rejoicing over all the good things that God has made, God himself is the heart of my joy, the gladness of my joy. In all my rejoicing in everything, there is a central rejoicing in God. Every joy that does not have God as the central gladness of the joy is a hollow joy and in the end will burst like a bubble. This is what led Augustine to pray, "He loves thee too little who loves anything together with Thee, which he loves not for thy sake."[4]

LET NOT YOUR LOVE GROW COLD

Therefore, I conclude that Jesus' demand to love God with all our heart and soul and mind and strength means that every impulse and every act of every faculty and every capacity should be an expression of treasuring God above all things. Jesus warned that this most important of all demands would be widely forsaken in the last days. "Because lawlessness is increased, most people's love will grow cold" (Matt. 24:12, NASB).

Beware lest your love for God grow cold in these days. Remember, we will love him to the degree that we know him. And remember that only Jesus can make him known in truth and fullness (Matt. 11:27). Therefore, look steadily at Jesus and pray that he would reveal God as compellingly beautiful. "Whoever has seen me has seen the Father" (John 14:9).

---

[3] The Hebrew phrase is two words for joy or rejoicing (שִׂמְחַת גִּילִי).
[4] Saint Augustine, *Confessions*, Book 10, Chapter XXIX.

Keeping my focus on God

Jan 8

Adonai   Merciful   Gracious   Redeemer
My God   My Protection   My Guide in truth

Keeping my focus on others

Demand #10

REJOICE AND LEAP FOR JOY

Blessed are you when people hate you and when they exclude you and revile you and spurn your name as evil, on account of the Son of Man! Rejoice in that day, and leap for joy, for behold, your reward is great in heaven; for so their fathers did to the prophets. —LUKE 6:22-23

Behold, I have given you authority to tread on serpents and scorpions, and over all the power of the enemy, and nothing shall hurt you. Nevertheless, do not rejoice in this, that the spirits are subject to you, but rejoice that your names are written in heaven. —LUKE 10:19-20

The kingdom of heaven is like treasure hidden in a field, which a man found and covered up. Then in his joy he goes and sells all that he has and buys that field. —MATT. 13:44

These things I have spoken to you, that my joy may be in you, and that your joy may be full. —JOHN 15:11

SURPRISED BY JOY

Jesus' demand that we "rejoice . . . and leap for joy" (Luke 6:23; cf. Matt. 5:12) is astonishing for so many reasons that it would take whole books to unfold all of its surprising implications.[1] Half a

---

[1] I wrote a little book to get people started on this path, *The Dangerous Duty of Delight* (Sisters, Ore.: Multnomah, 2001), and a bigger book to go deeper, *Desiring God: Meditations of a Christian Hedonist* (Sisters, Ore.: Multnomah, 2003).

century ago C. S. Lewis responded to this surprise by looking at the inescapable evidence in the Gospels. He wrote:

> If we consider the unblushing promises of reward and the stagger-ing nature of the rewards promised in the Gospels, it would seem that our Lord finds our desires not too strong, but too weak. We are half-hearted creatures, fooling about with drink and sex and ambition when infinite joy is offered us, like an ignorant child who wants to go on making mud pies in a slum because he cannot imagine what is meant by the offer of a holiday at the sea. We are far too easily pleased.[2]

In other words, the demand that we be happy is not marginal or super-fluous. It is a shocking wake-up call to people who are finding their happiness in all the wrong places. Jesus' solution to our love affair with sin is not merely that we tear out our sin-loving eyes (Matt. 5:29), but that we be mastered by joy in a new reality, namely, God.

IN HIS JOY HE GOES AND SELLS ALL THAT HE HAS

Central to his preaching was the announcement that the kingdom of heaven had come near. He meant that he was the King and that his work was the arrival of the saving rule of God (Luke 11:20; 17:20-21). So he told a very short parable to show how people come into the kingdom. He said, "The kingdom of heaven is like treasure hid-den in a field, which a man found and covered up. Then *in his joy* he goes and sells all that he has and buys that field" (Matt. 13:44).

The parable means that God's saving presence and sovereign reign are so valuable that when people see them for what they really are—treasure hidden in the field—they count everything as nothing compared to the vast fortune of being part of that reign. And Jesus leaves no doubt about the internal experience of that "conversion." It is joy-driven. He says, "*In his joy* he goes and sells all that he has and buys that field."

---

[2] C. S. Lewis, *The Weight of Glory, and Other Addresses* (Grand Rapids, Mich.: Eerdmans, 1965), 2.

It cannot be otherwise. Jesus came into the world with *good* news, not bad news. He does not call us to a willpower religion that feels only duty and no delight. He calls us to himself and to his Father. Therefore, he calls us to joy. Of course, it is not joy in things. Jesus is not preaching a health, wealth, and prosperity gospel—one of America's most lamentable exports to the world. It is joy in *God* and in his *Son*.

This is why the parable describes coming to the kingdom as "selling all." The demand for joy does not encourage us to retreat one millimeter from the radical demand of Luke 14:33, "Any one of you who does not renounce all that he has cannot be my disciple." We renounce all those joy-giving things because we have found the treasure hidden in the field and we have been given eyes to see that this treasure—this glorious God—is infinitely more valuable than everything we possess or could possess in this world. This is why we renounce it all with joy.

SELF-DENIAL AND THE QUEST FOR JOY

This is the meaning of self-denial. Renounce everything on earth in order that you might have Jesus. Sell all, so that you might have the kingdom. C. S. Lewis captures the spirit of Jesus' demand for self-denial when he says:

> The New Testament has lots to say about self-denial, but not about self-denial as an end in itself. We are told to deny ourselves and to take up our crosses in order that we may follow Christ; and nearly every description of what we shall ultimately find if we do so contains an appeal to desire.[3]

In other words, we deny ourselves because beyond self-denial is great reward. Jonathan Edwards goes even deeper in his analysis of how Jesus' demand for self-denial relates to his demand for joy.

---

[3] Ibid., 1.

Self-denial will also be reckoned amongst the troubles of the godly. . . . But whoever has tried self-denial can give in his testimony that they never experience greater pleasure and joys than after great acts of self-denial. Self-denial destroys the very root and foundation of sorrow, and is nothing else but the lancing of a grievous and painful sore that effects a cure and brings abundance of health as a recompense for the pain of the operation.[4]

If this is true, then Jesus' demand for self-denial is another way of calling us to radically pursue our deepest and most lasting joy. They are not competing commands. They are like the command to be cancer-free and the command to have surgery.

OUR JOY IS NOT MAINLY IN PROSPERITY BUT IN OBEDIENCE AND PAIN

What astonishes us most immediately when Jesus says, "Rejoice . . . and leap for joy" is that he is saying it precisely in the context of pain. "Blessed are you when people hate you and when they exclude you and revile you and spurn your name as evil, on account of the Son of Man! Rejoice in that day, and leap for joy" (Luke 6:22-23). When Jesus demands that we rejoice, he has not forgotten the kind of world we live in. It is filled with suffering. And he promises that some of that suffering will fall on us as his disciples. "They will lay their hands on you and persecute you, delivering you up to the synagogues and prisons . . . and some of you they will put to death. You will be hated by all for my name's sake" (Luke 21:12, 16-17). "If they have called the master of the house Beelzebul, how much more will they malign those of his household" (Matt. 10:25). "If they persecuted me, they will also persecute you" (John 15:20).

Jesus has not forgotten that. In fact, he demands that we follow

---

[4] Jonathan Edwards, "The Pleasantness of Religion," in *The Sermons of Jonathan Edwards: A Reader*, ed. Wilson H. Kimnach, Kenneth P. Minkema, and Douglas A. Sweeney (New Haven, Conn: Yale University Press, 1999), 23-24.

him in that painful path of love (see *Demand #8*). Therefore, the joy he demands now ("in that day," Luke 6:23) is not chipper. It is not joy-lite. It is not superficial or marked with levity. This is the mistake of too many people and too many churches. They think that Jesus' demand for joy is a demand to tell jokes or weave slapstick into Christian corporate life. I don't smell the Jerusalem-bound Jesus in that atmosphere. Something has gone wrong.

What's wrong is that the aroma of suffering is missing. For Jesus the demand for joy is a way to live with suffering and to outlast suffering. Therefore, this joy is serious. It's the kind you fight for by cutting off your hand (Matt. 5:30) and selling your possessions (Matt. 13:44) and carrying a cross with Jesus to Calvary (Matt. 10:38-39). It has scars. It sings happy songs with tears. It remembers the dark hours and knows that more are coming. The road to heaven is a hard road, but it is not joyless.

THE ROOT OF HOLINESS

Jesus' demand that we rejoice is the key that unlocks his demand for holiness. What chokes the purifying power of spiritual life and destroys Jesus' would-be disciples is the "cares and riches and pleasures of life" (Luke 8:14). And what severs these strangling vines most decisively is the power of a superior pleasure. Jesus said that it is "in his joy" that the believer sells everything. In other words, it is his joy that cuts the stranglehold of sin.

Many Christians think stoicism is a good antidote to sensuality. It isn't. It is hopelessly weak and ineffective. Willpower religion usually fails, and even when it succeeds, it gets glory for the will, not for God. It produces legalists, not lovers. Jonathan Edwards saw the powerlessness of this approach and said:

> We come with double forces against the wicked, to persuade them
> to a godly life. . . . The common argument is the profitableness
> of religion, but alas, the wicked man is not in pursuit of [moral]

profit; 'tis pleasure he seeks. Now, then, we will fight with them with their own weapons.[5]

In other words, the pursuit of pleasure in God is not a compromise with the sensual world but is in fact the only power that can defeat the lusts of the age while producing lovers of God.

THE ROOT OF JOY IN SUFFERING IS GREAT REWARD: JESUS

Jesus bases our present joy explicitly on the hope for great reward. "Rejoice in that day, and leap for joy, for behold, *your reward is great in heaven*" (Luke 6:23). He does not define the reward. But in the whole context of his life and message, the essential reward is fellowship with Jesus himself and with God the Father through him (John 17:3, 24).

There are several pointers to this understanding. For example, Jesus says to his disciples just before his death, "You have sorrow now, but *I will see you again* and your hearts will rejoice, and no one will take your joy from you" (John 16:22). The indomitable joy that Jesus promises is based on his own presence: "I will see you again."

Similarly Jesus says, "These things I have spoken to you, that my joy may be in you, and that your joy may be full" (John 15:11). This fullness of joy is mentioned by John the Baptist, and he bases it on the presence of Jesus, comparing Jesus to a bridegroom and himself to his friend: "The friend of the bridegroom, who stands and hears him, *rejoices greatly at the bridegroom's voice*. Therefore this joy of mine is now complete" (John 3:29).[6] John's "complete" joy is based on the presence of Jesus.

---

[5] Ibid. The preceding and following paragraphs are adapted from John Piper, "A God-Entranced Vision of All Things: Why We Need Jonathan Edwards 300 Years Later," in *A God-Entranced Vision of All Things: The Legacy of Jonathan Edwards*, ed. John Piper and Justin Taylor (Wheaton, Ill.: Crossway Books, 2004), 29.

[6] The word "complete" (πεπλήρωται) translates the same Greek word (πληρόω) that is used in John 15:11 (πληρωθῇ), 16:24 (πεπληρωμένη), and 17:13 (πεπληρωμένην). Each refers to the joy of the disciples being full. Since John 3:29 and 16:24 base that joy on the presence of Jesus, we may assume the other two very likely refer to that as well.

Therefore, I conclude that the essence of the reward that we count on to complete our joy is the fullness of the presence of Jesus experienced in the age to come. The reason that we can rejoice *now* is not only that we taste that future fellowship in hope, but also that Jesus is with us now by his Spirit. He promised us, as he left to return to the Father, "I will not leave you as orphans; I will come to you" (John 14:18). "I am with you always, to the end of the age" (Matt. 28:20). He said that the Spirit of truth would come and make Jesus gloriously real to us even though he is physically absent. "When the Spirit of truth comes, he will . . . glorify me, for he will take what is mine and declare it to you" (John 16:13-14). Therefore, even though we can't see Jesus now, we hope in him with great joy, and he sustains that joy by his continual presence.

JESUS PURCHASES AND PROVIDES OUR JOY

How then shall we obey this demand of Jesus to "rejoice . . . and leap for joy"? We will take heart from the fact that Jesus offered himself to die for the forgiveness of our sins—the forgiveness of our failures to rejoice in him as we ought. At the Last Supper he took the cup of wine and said, "This is my blood of the covenant, which is poured out for many *for the forgiveness of sins*" (Matt. 26:28). This is why he came in the first place: "The Son of Man came . . . to give his life as a ransom for many" (Mark 10:45). So our joy has this solid foundation: Jesus shed his blood so that our failures to rejoice in him might be forgiven.

Then we take heart that he promised to work for us in such a way that the very love that the Father has for the Son would be the experience of our own hearts. He prayed, "I made known to them your name, and I will continue to make it known, that the love with which you have loved me may be in them, and I in them" (John 17:26). Consider carefully that the love the Father has for the Son is not a merciful, forgiving love. The Son has no sin and no flaw. He needs no mercy. The love the Father has for the Son is nothing but infinitely joyful admiration and fellowship. This is what Jesus says will be in us. Therefore, I take this to be a promise to work in us to make sure that our joy will be the very joy that the Father has in the Son. We are not left to ourselves to rejoice in Jesus as we ought. Jesus is committed to making it happen.

THE DEMAND TO REJOICE IN JESUS AS A MEANS TO GLORIFY JESUS

Finally, I conclude from Jesus' commitment to glorify the Father and the Son (John 17:1) that his intention to sustain our joy in him is part of what it means for us to glorify the Father and the Son. In other words, I conclude that rejoicing in the Father and the Son is essential to glorifying God. If this is true, we have a powerful confirmation of the duty to pursue our joy—namely, because it displays the glory of God.

This truth should make us tremble at the horror of not rejoicing in God. We should quake at the fearful lukewarmness of our hearts. We should waken to the truth that it is a treacherous sin not to pursue our fullest satisfaction in God. There is one final word for finding delight in the creation more than in the Creator: *treason*. What a motivation this should be to obey the demand of Jesus, "Rejoice . . . and leap for joy."

THERE IS NO LIMIT TO THE INTENSITY OF JOY IN JESUS

It is true that a passion for happiness can be misdirected to wrong objects, but it cannot be too strong. Jonathan Edwards argued for this in a sermon that he preached on Song of Solomon 5:1. The text reads, "Eat, friends, drink, and be drunk with love!" Edwards drew out of the text the following doctrine: "Persons need not and ought not to set any bounds to their spiritual and gracious appetites." Instead, he says, they ought

> to be endeavoring by all possible ways to inflame their desires and to obtain more spiritual pleasures. . . . Our hungerings and thirstings after God and Jesus Christ and after holiness can't be too great for the value of these things, for they are things of infinite value. . . . [Therefore] endeavor to promote spiritual appetites by

laying yourself in the way of allurement. . . .[7] There is no such thing as excess in our taking of this spiritual food. There is no such virtue as temperance in spiritual feasting.[8]

Therefore, be encouraged that God made you to rejoice in him. Do not settle for any lesser joy. Lay yourself in the way of allurement. That is, fix your eyes on the all-satisfying treasure of Jesus Christ who loved us and gave his life as a ransom for our everlasting joy.

---

[7] Quoted from an unpublished sermon, "Sacrament Sermon on Canticles 5:1" (circa 1729), edited version by Kenneth Minkema in association with *The Works of Jonathan Edwards*, Yale University.

[8] Jonathan Edwards, "The Spiritual Blessings of the Gospel Represented by a Feast," in *Sermons and Discourses, 1723–1729*, ed. Kenneth Minkema, in *The Works of Jonathan Edwards*, Vol. 14 (New Haven, Conn.: Yale University Press, 1997), 286. The preceding two paragraphs are adapted from "A God-Entranced Vision of All Things," 27-28.

Demand #11

FEAR HIM WHO CAN DESTROY BOTH SOUL AND BODY IN HELL

And do not fear those who kill the body but cannot kill the soul. Rather fear him who can destroy both soul and body in hell. —MATT. 10:28

But as for these enemies of mine, who did not want me to reign over them, bring them here and slaughter them before me. —LUKE 19:27

Then he will say to those on his left, "Depart from me, you cursed, into the eternal fire prepared for the devil and his angels." . . . And these will go away into eternal punishment, but the righteous into eternal life. —MATT. 25:41, 46

THE DESCRIPTIONS JESUS USES FOR HELL

Jesus spoke of hell more than anyone else in the Bible. He referred to it as a place of "outer darkness" where "there will be weeping and gnashing of teeth" (Matt. 8:12). In other words, all the joys that we associate with light will be withdrawn, and all the fears that we associate with darkness will be multiplied. And the result will be an intensity of misery that makes a person grind his teeth in order to bear it.

Jesus also refers to hell as a "fiery furnace" where law-breakers will be thrown at the end of the age when he returns. "The Son of Man will send his angels, and they will gather out of his kingdom all causes of sin and all law-breakers, and throw them into the fiery furnace. In that place there will be weeping and gnashing of teeth" (Matt. 13:41-42). He calls it "the hell of fire" (Matt. 5:22), "eternal fire prepared for the devil and his angels" (Matt. 25:41), "unquenchable fire" (Mark 9:43), "eternal punishment" (Matt. 25:46).

This last description—"eternal punishment"—is especially heartrending and fearful because it is contrasted with "eternal life." "These will go away into eternal punishment, but the righteous into *eternal life*." In this contrast we hear the tragedy of loss as well as suffering and endlessness. Just as "eternal life" will be a never-ending experience of pleasure in God's presence, so "eternal punishment" will be a never-ending experience of misery under God's wrath (John 3:36; 5:24).

HELL IS NOT A MERE NATURAL CONSEQUENCE OF BAD CHOICES

The word *wrath* is important for understanding what Jesus meant by hell. Hell is not simply the natural consequence of rejecting God. Some people say this in order to reject the thought that God sends people there. They say that people send themselves there. That is true. People make choices that lead to hell. But it is not the whole truth. Jesus says these choices are really deserving of hell. "Whoever says, 'You fool!' will be liable to [that is, guilty of, or deserving of] the hell of fire" (Matt. 5:22). That is why he calls hell "punishment" (Matt. 25:46). It is not a mere self-imposed natural consequence (like cigarette smoking leading to lung cancer); it is the penalty of God's wrath (like a judge sentencing a criminal to hard labor).

The images Jesus uses of how people come to be in hell do not suggest natural consequence but the exercise of just wrath. For example, he pictures the servant of a master who has gone on a journey. The servant says, "My master is delayed," and he "begins to beat his fellow servants and eats and drinks with drunkards." Then Jesus says (referring to his own sudden second coming), "The master of that servant will come on a day when he does not expect him and at an hour he does not know and will cut him in pieces and put him with the hypocrites. In that place there will be weeping and gnashing of teeth" (Matt. 24:48-51). This picture represents legitimate and holy rage followed by punishment. Jesus will "put" (θήσει) him with the hypocrites.

Jesus told another story to illustrate his departure from the earth and his return in judgment. He said, "A nobleman went into a far country to receive for himself a kingdom and then return. . . . But his citizens hated him and sent a delegation after him, saying, 'We do not want this man to reign over us'" (Luke 19:12, 14). When the nobleman returned in his kingly power to reward those who had trusted and honored him with their lives, he punished those who rejected his kingship: "As for these enemies of mine, who did not want me to reign over them, bring them here and slaughter them before me" (Luke 19:27). Again the picture is not one of hell as a disease resulting from bad habits, but of a king expressing holy wrath against those who rebuff his gracious rule.

FEAR HIM WHO CAN DESTROY BOTH SOUL AND BODY IN HELL

This is why Jesus said, "Fear him who can destroy both soul and body in hell" (Matt. 10:28). The fear he demands is not fear of hell as a natural consequence of bad habits, but of God as a holy judge who sentences guilty sinners to hell. This demand to fear God as a holy judge seems discouraging at first. It seems as though following Jesus means leading a life of anxiety that God is angry with us and is ready to punish us at the slightest misstep. But that is not what Jesus calls us to experience as we follow him.

It seems amazing to us, perhaps, that immediately following his warning to "fear him who can destroy both soul and body in hell," Jesus says something designed to give us deep peace and full confidence under God's fatherly care. The very next sentence goes like this: "Are not two sparrows sold for a penny? And not one of them will fall to the ground apart from your Father. But even the hairs of your head are all numbered. *Fear not*, therefore; you are of more value than many sparrows" (Matt. 10:29-31).

In the same breath Jesus says, "Fear God who casts into hell" and "Do not fear because God is your Father who values you more than the sparrows and knows your smallest need." In fact, the all-providing fatherly care of God is one of Jesus' sweetest and most pervasive teachings:

> Look at the birds of the air: they neither sow nor reap nor gather into barns, and yet your heavenly Father feeds them. Are you not of more value than they? . . . Therefore do not be anxious, saying, "What shall we eat?" or "What shall we drink?" or "What shall we wear?" For the Gentiles seek after all these things, and your heavenly Father knows that you need them all. (Matt. 6:26, 31-32)

God Is to Be Feared, and God Is to Be Trusted

How does Jesus mean for us to experience these two truths about God—he is to be feared, and he is to be trusted? It won't do to simply say that "fear of God" means "reverence for God" rather than "being afraid of him." That does not fit with the words, "Fear him who, after he has killed, has authority to cast into hell. Yes, I tell you, fear him!" (Luke 12:5). Of course, it is true that we should reverence God, that is, stand in awe of his holiness and power and wisdom. But there is also a real fear of him that can coexist with sweet peace and trust in him.

The key is that God himself is the one who removes his wrath from us. Our peace does not come from our removing the God of wrath from our thinking, but from his removing his wrath from us. He has done that by sending Jesus to die in our place so that, for everyone who believes in Jesus, God's wrath is taken away. "As Moses lifted up the serpent in the wilderness," Jesus said, "so must the Son of Man be lifted up [on the cross to die], that whoever believes in him may have eternal life [not wrath]. . . . Whoever does not obey the Son shall not see life, but the *wrath* of God remains on him" (John 3:14-15, 36). When Jesus cried out on the cross, "My

God, my God, why have you forsaken me?" (Mark 15:34), he was experiencing the wrath of God's abandonment in our place—for he had never done anything to deserve being forsaken by God. And when he said finally from the cross, "It is finished" (John 19:30), he meant that the price of our salvation—our deliverance from God's wrath and into all God's blessings—had been paid in full.

Jesus had said that he came "to give his life as a ransom for many" (Matt. 20:28), and now the full ransom was paid and the work of absorbing and removing the wrath of God was finished. Now, he says, everyone who believes has everlasting fellowship with God and is fully assured that the wrath of the Judge is gone. "He does not come into judgment, but has passed from death to life" (John 5:24).

FEARING UNBELIEF

What then is left to fear? The answer is *unbelief*. For those who follow Jesus, fearing God means fearing the terrible prospect of not trusting the one who paid such a price for our peace. In other words, one of the means that God uses to keep us peacefully trusting in Jesus is the fear of what God would do to us if we did not believe. The reason we do not live in the discomfort of constant fear is because we believe. That is, we rest in the all-sufficient work of Jesus and in our Father's sovereign care. But at those moments when unbelief tempts us, a holy fear rises and warns us what a foolish thing it would be to distrust the one who loved us and gave his Son to die for our anxiety-free joy.

HUGGING GOD'S NECK TAKES AWAY FEAR

One illustration has helped me see how this experience works. When my oldest son Karsten was about eight years old, we went to visit a man who owned a huge dog. When we opened the door, the dog looked at my son almost eye to eye. That's a fearful prospect for a little boy. But we were assured the dog was harmless and that he really liked children. After a while we sent Karsten to the car to get something we forgot. As he ran across the yard, the dog gave a deep growl and loped up behind him. The owner leaned out of the door and called to Karsten, "You better just walk; he doesn't like it when people run away from him."

A huge dog that loves children but does not like people to run away from him is what God is like. If we will trust him and enjoy him and throw our arms around his strong neck, he will be everything we ever hoped for in a friend. But if we decide that there are other things we want more than him and turn to run away, he will get very angry. Jesus said this as clearly as we could wish in Luke 19:27, "But as for these enemies of mine, who did not want me to reign over them, bring them here and slaughter them before me." Fearing God means fearing the terrible prospect of running away from the merciful, all-providing, all-satisfying reign of King Jesus.

HELL MEANS THAT SIN IS UNFATHOMABLY SERIOUS

Jesus' demand that we fear the one who can destroy both soul and body in hell teaches us to see sin as more serious than we ever dreamed. The reason so many people feel that eternal hell is an unjust punishment for our sin is that they do not see sin as it really is. This is because they do not see God as he really is. When Jesus tells us what he will say to those who are going to hell he says, "Then will I declare to them, 'I never knew you; depart from me, you workers of *lawlessness*'" (Matt. 7:23). They are workers of "lawlessness." That is, they break God's law. Sin is against God first, then man.

Therefore, the seriousness of sin arises from what it says about God. God is infinitely worthy and honorable. But sin says the opposite. Sin says that other things are more desirable and more worthy. How serious is this? The seriousness of a crime is determined, in part, by the dignity of the person and the office being dishonored. If the person is infinitely worthy and infinitely honorable and infinitely desirable and holds an office of infinite dignity and authority, then rebuffing him is an infinitely outrageous crime. Therefore, it deserves an infinite punishment. The intensity of Jesus' words about hell are not an overreaction to small offenses. They are a witness to the infinite worth of God and to the outrageous dishonor of human sin.

THE PRECIOUS GIFT OF FEAR

Therefore, give heed to Jesus' clear demand to fear the one who can destroy both soul and body in hell. Hear it as a great mercy. What a wonderful thing it is that Jesus warns us. He does not leave us ignorant of the wrath to come. He not only warns. He rescues. This is the best effect of fear: It wakens us to our need for help and points us to the all-sufficient Redeemer, Jesus. Let it have this effect on you. Let it lead you to Jesus who says to everyone who believes in him, "Fear not, little flock, for it is your Father's good pleasure to give you the kingdom" (Luke 12:32).

Demand #12

WORSHIP GOD IN SPIRIT AND TRUTH

The hour is coming, and is now here, when the true worshipers will worship the Father in spirit and truth, for the Father is seeking such people to worship him. God is spirit, and those who worship him must worship in spirit and truth. —JOHN 4:23-24

Then Jesus said to him, "Be gone, Satan! For it is written, 'You shall worship the Lord your God and him only shall you serve.'" —MATT. 4:10

This people honors me with their lips, but their heart is far from me; in vain do they worship me, teaching as doctrines the commandments of men. —MATT. 15:8-9

No one can serve two masters, for either he will hate the one and love the other, or he will be devoted to the one and despise the other. You cannot serve God and money. —MATT. 6:24

Everyone in the world worships something. From the most religious to the most secular, all people value something high enough to build their lives around it. It may be God, or it may be money. But what makes it worship is the driving power of some cherished treasure that shapes our emotions and will and thought and behavior. Into this universal experience of worship Jesus demanded, "Worship [God] in *spirit* and *truth*" (John 4:24). In other words, bring your experience of worship into conformity with what is *true* about God, and let your *spirit* be authentically awakened and moved by that truth.

The Hour Is Coming and Is Now Here

When he said this, he was talking to a Samaritan woman near her hometown. She had challenged him about the difference between places where Samaritans and Jews worship. She said, "Our fathers worshiped on this mountain, but you say that in Jerusalem is the place where people ought to worship" (John 4:20). Jesus responded by turning her attention away from geography to something astonishing that was happening in her very presence. He said, "Woman, believe me, the hour is coming when neither on this mountain nor in Jerusalem will you worship the Father. . . . The hour is coming, *and is now here*, when the true worshipers will worship the Father in spirit and truth" (John 4:21, 23). This is a radical statement—to say that the hour *is now here* when worship in Jerusalem would cease! What did he mean?

Jesus made the breathtaking claim to be the long-awaited Jewish Messiah. The woman said to him, "I know that Messiah is coming (he who is called Christ). When he comes, he will tell us all things." Jesus responded, "I who speak to you am he" (John 4:25). So when Jesus says that the time "is now here" when we will no longer worship in Jerusalem, he meant that the kingdom of the Messiah has dawned and there was going to be a radical break in the way people worship.

"Destroy This Temple, and in Three Days I Will Raise It Up"

The reason is that Jesus intended to take the place of the temple himself. In other words, the "place" where worship would happen—the "place" where people would meet God from now on—would be Jesus, not the temple in Jerusalem. He communicated this in several ways. For example, he stood in the temple and said, "Destroy this temple, and in three days I will raise it up" (John 2:19). The people were astonished and said, "It has taken forty-six years to build this temple, and will you raise it up in three days?" But the Gospel writer explained, "He was speaking about the temple of his body" (John

2:21). In other words, Jesus meant that when he was raised from the dead, he would be the new "temple"—the new meeting place with God.

Jesus said something almost as startling when he was criticized for letting his disciples pick grain and eat it on the Sabbath. Jesus' response to this criticism was to point out that David, the king of Israel, had fed his band of men with the bread of God's house that was only designed for the priests to eat. He made the connection with himself and his band of men by saying, "I tell you, something greater than the temple is here" (Matt. 12:6). In other words, "The Messiah, the son of David, is here, and he himself is going to take the place of the temple."

Not in This Mountain or in Jerusalem, but in Spirit and in Truth

So when Jesus said to the Samaritan woman, "The hour is coming, and *is now here*, when the true worshipers will worship the Father in spirit and truth," he meant that a whole new approach to God in worship had come with the coming of the Messiah himself. No longer would geography be relevant: "Neither on this mountain nor in Jerusalem will you worship the Father." Instead, what takes the place of external geographic concerns are internal spiritual concerns: "Those who worship him must worship in spirit and truth." The external places of Samaria and Jerusalem are replaced with the spiritual realities of "spirit and truth." What matters now is not where you worship but whether you worship God in accordance with the truth and whether your spirit is authentically awakened and moved by that truth.

All Worship Should Be Through Jesus and of Jesus

The key new truth is that worship now happens through Jesus. He is the temple where we encounter God. This is true first because he poured out his blood "for the forgiveness of sins" (Matt. 26:28) and "gave his life as a ransom for many" (Mark 10:45) and opened the way through his own crucified and risen body for us to be reconciled with God (John 3:16, 36). There is no way that sinners could offer acceptable worship to God without having Jesus' blood as a go-between with God.

It's true that worship now happens through Jesus because he himself is God. He is not simply the mediator of worship between us and the Father; he is also the one to *be* worshiped. He made this claim indirectly and directly. He forgave sins, which only God can do (Mark 2:5-11). He accepted worship from his disciples (Matt. 14:33; 28:9). He claimed eternal preexistence with God: "Truly, truly, I say to you, before Abraham was, I am" (John 8:58). He said he was one with the Father: "Whoever has seen me has seen the Father" (John 14:9). "I and the Father are one" (John 10:30). So all should "honor the Son, just as they honor the Father" (John 5:23). Therefore, all worship "in truth" will be worship of Jesus *and* through Jesus. For "whoever does not honor the Son does not honor the Father who sent him" (John 5:23).

WORSHIP IN SPIRIT

What about the phrase "in spirit"? "The hour is coming, and is now here, when the true worshipers will worship the Father *in spirit*" (John 4:23). Some interpreters take this to refer to God's Holy Spirit. I have taken it to refer to *our* spirit. But probably these two interpretations are not far apart in Jesus' mind. In John 3:6 Jesus connects God's Spirit and our spirit in a remarkable way. He says, "That which is born of the Spirit is spirit." In other words, until the Holy Spirit quickens our spirit with the birth of new life, our spirit is so dead and unresponsive, it does not even qualify as spirit. Only that which is born of the Spirit is (a living) spirit. So when Jesus says that true worshipers worship the Father "in spirit," he means that true worship comes only from spirits made alive and sensitive by the quickening of the Spirit of God.[1]

This "spirit" is essential in worship. Otherwise worship is dead.

---

[1] This paragraph is adapted from John Piper, *Desiring God: Meditations of a Christian Hedonist*, revised and expanded edition (Sisters, Ore.: Multnomah, 2003), 82.

Or to use Jesus' phrase, it is "in vain." "This people honors me with their lips, but their heart is far from me; *in vain* do they worship me" (Matt. 15:8-9). A heart (and spirit) alive and engaged with God is essential. Jesus is contrasting authentic worship in spirit and truth with external worship that focuses on Samaria and Jerusalem. What makes it authentic is not only that the worshiping *mind* grasps the truth of Jesus, but also that the worshiping *spirit* experiences awakening and is moved by the truth that the mind knows. A person who has no affections for God awakened by the truth of Jesus is not worshiping "in spirit and truth."[2] And a person with great affections built on false views of God is not worshiping "in spirit and truth." Jesus demands both: worship in spirit and in truth.

ALL OF LIFE IS WORSHIP

One implication of this vision of worship is that it applies to all of life as well as to services of corporate worship. The essence of worship lies in our mind's true vision of God and our spirit's authentic affections for God. This means that whenever we display the worth of God by words or actions that flow from a spirit that treasures him as he really is, we are worshiping in spirit and in truth. We may be at work or at home or at church. It doesn't matter. What matters is that we see the glory of God in Jesus (truth), and we treasure him above all else (spirit), and then we overflow by treating others with self-sacrificing love for their good. Few things display the beauty of God more. For followers of Jesus, therefore, all of life should be this kind of worship.

This is powerfully illustrated by the connection Jesus makes between worshiping God and serving God. When Satan tempted Jesus to worship him, Jesus responded, "Be gone, Satan! For it is written, 'You shall *worship* the Lord your God and him only shall you *serve*'" (Matt. 4:10). Serving was often attached to worshiping as an outward expression of religious ministry in the temple. But now the temple is Jesus. How is the "service" of worship transformed?

---

[2] See Chapter Three, "Worship: The Feast of Christian Hedonism" in *Desiring God* for a fuller defense of this statement and how it fits with the reality that our feelings are unstable, sometimes high and sometimes low.

You Cannot Serve God and Money

We get a surprising glimpse of what service[3] to God means for Jesus in Matthew 6:24. He said, "No one can serve two masters, for either he will hate the one and love the other, or he will be devoted to the one and despise the other. You cannot serve God and money." The surprising thing here is that serving God is compared to serving money. But how do you serve money? Not by helping money or meeting money's needs. You serve money by treasuring it so much that you shape your whole life to benefit from what money can do for you.

So it is with God in the way Jesus sees the service of worship. We do not help God or meet God's needs ("The Son of Man came *not* to be served," Mark 10:45). Rather we serve God by treasuring him so much that we shape our whole life so as to benefit from what he can do for us. And, unlike money, what God can do for us above all other treasures is *be* for us everything we have ever longed for.

The Infinite Worth of God in Jesus

Therefore, all of life is service to God. That is, all of life is shaped by our passion to maximize our experience of the supreme worth of God in Jesus. So we end where we began. All the world worships something. From the most religious to the most secular, all people value something high enough to build their lives around it—even if unconsciously. Jesus demands that every person in the world build his life around the infinite worth of God in Jesus. Consider what you are worshiping. Then ask Jesus to open your eyes to the *truth* of God's supreme worth and to awaken your *spirit* to treasure him above all.

---

[3] The word for "serve" in Matthew 6:24 (δουλεύω) is not the same as the word for serve in Matthew 4:10 (λατρεύω). The latter usually refers to the religious activity in the temple. The former refers usually to what a slave does for a master. My point is that it is precisely the newness of Jesus' situation that makes plain how even the "slave" kind of service is worship in a new way.

Demand #13

ALWAYS PRAY AND DO NOT LOSE HEART

And he told them a parable to the effect that they ought always to pray and not lose heart. —LUKE 18:1

Pray for those who persecute you. —MATT. 5:44

But when you pray, go into your room and shut the door and pray to your Father who is in secret. —MATT. 6:6

And when you pray, do not heap up empty phrases as the Gentiles do. —MATT. 6:7-8

Pray then like this: "Our Father in heaven, hallowed be your name." —MATT. 6:9

Pray earnestly to the Lord of the harvest to send out laborers into his harvest. —MATT. 9:38

How much more will the heavenly Father give the Holy Spirit to those who ask him! —LUKE 11:13

Ask, and you will receive, that your joy may be full. —JOHN 16:24

Whatever you ask in my name, this I will do, that the Father may be glorified in the Son. —JOHN 14:13

Jesus intends to create a praying people. His demand is clear, and the issue is so important that he tells us *why, how, for whom,* and *what* we are to pray. And though we might think that the Son of

God would be above the need to pray, he sets the example for us, as a perfect human being, by rising early in the morning to pray (Mark 1:35) and seeking times alone to pray (Matt. 14:23) and sometimes spending the whole night in prayer (Luke 6:12) and, in the end, preparing for his suffering by prayer (Luke 22:41-42).

WHY? FOR THE GLORY OF GOD

Why did Jesus think prayer was so important for his followers? The reason is that prayer corresponds with two great purposes of God that Jesus came to accomplish: God's glory and our joy. Jesus said, "Whatever you *ask* in my name, this I will do, that the Father may be *glorified* in the Son" (John 14:13). Prayer is designed by God to display his fullness and our need. Prayer glorifies God because it puts us in the position of the thirsty and God in the position of the all-supplying fountain.[1]

Jesus knew the Psalms and read Psalm 50:15 where God, like Jesus, demands that we pray for help and shows that this gives glory to God: "Call upon me in the day of trouble; I will deliver you, and you shall glorify me." Prayer is designed as a way of relating to God, so that it is clear *we* get the help and *he* gets the glory. Jesus said that he had come to glorify his Father. "I glorified you on earth, having accomplished the work that you gave me to do" (John 17:4). Part of what God had given him to do was to teach his disciples to pray, because when we pray in Jesus' name, "the Father [is] glorified in the Son" (John 14:13).

WHY? FOR OUR JOY

The other purpose Jesus came to accomplish was our joy. Everything he taught was aimed to free us from eternal-joy-killers and fill us with the only joy that lasts—joy in God. "These things I speak in the world, that they may have my joy fulfilled in themselves" (John 17:13). One of his most pervasive teachings for our joy was the

---

[1] I do not mean to imply that prayer is only asking and not also thanking and praising and confessing. But this chapter simply focuses on prayer as petition, which is the main way Jesus talks about it.

teaching on prayer, and he made his motive explicit: our joy. "Ask, and you will receive, that your joy may be full" (John 16:24). The most wonderful thing about prayer, as Jesus demands it, is that it is perfectly suited to secure God's glory and our joy.

These are great incentives for us to obey Jesus' demand that we "always . . . pray and not lose heart" (Luke 18:1). To these he adds other incentives, because he is so eager for us to feel hopeful in our praying. He says, for example, "Your Father knows what you need before you ask him" (Matt. 6:8). The point is that we don't need to multiply pious phrases in prayer hoping that we might awaken God's attention or inclination. He is our caring Father, and he is all-knowing. He will answer. Then Jesus underlines God's readiness to answer by comparing him to a human father, but pointing out that God is far more eager to answer than human fathers.

> Ask, and it will be given to you; seek, and you will find; knock, and it will be opened to you . . . which one of you, if his son asks him for bread, will give him a stone? Or if he asks for a fish, will give him a serpent? If you then, who are evil, know how to give good gifts to your children, how much more will your Father who is in heaven give good things to those who ask him! (Matt. 7:7-11)

So in answer to the question *why* we should pray, Jesus says: because God is very inclined to hear and answer our prayers—which is not surprising, since prayer is designed to magnify God's glory while sustaining our joy in him.

How? Simplicity

How then are we to pray? The readiness of God to answer and his perfect knowledge of what we need before we ask means that we should be simple in our wording and reject anything like a repetitive mantra that would imply God is aroused by our monotonous incantations. "When you pray, do not heap up empty phrases as the Gentiles do, for they think that they will be heard for their many words. Do not be like them, for your Father knows what you need before you ask him" (Matt. 6:7-8).

How? With Perseverance

This does not mean there is no place for perseverance in prayer. In fact, Jesus is explicit in telling us to be persistent in prayer over a long period of time, if necessary, as we seek some crucial break-through in the cause of righteousness for his glory (Luke 11:5-8; 18:1-8). The point is not to finally break God's resistance but to discover, by patient prayer, God's wisdom as to the way and time the prayer should be answered. He is not disinclined to help his children and glorify his name. He simply knows better than we do when and how the answer should come. Therefore, our persistence in prayer shows both our confidence that God is our only hope and that he will act in the best way and the best time in response to our persistent pleas.

How? Through His Death and in His Name

The confidence that we have in prayer is owing to Jesus. He did not just teach us to pray—he died for us and rose again to remove insuperable obstacles to prayer. Without the death of Jesus, our sins would not be forgiven (Matt. 26:28) and the wrath of God would still be against us (John 3:36). In that condition we could expect no answers to prayer from God. Therefore, Jesus is the ground of all our prayers. This is why he taught us to pray in his name. "Whatever you ask *in my name*, this I will do, that the Father may be glorified in the Son" (John 14:13; cf. 16:23-24). Ending our prayers "in Jesus' name, Amen" is not a mere tradition; it is an affirmation of faith in Jesus as the only hope of access to God.

How? With Faith

This implies that Jesus does indeed want us to pray *with faith*. "Whatever you ask in prayer, you will receive, *if you have faith*" (Matt. 21:22; cf. Mark 11:24). Some have taken verses like this and turned them into the power of positive thinking. They believe that if we can be confident that something will happen, it will indeed happen. But that would be faith in our faith. When Jesus teaches us how to "move mountains" by faith, he says explicitly, "Have faith *in God*" (Mark 11:22). There seem to be times when God makes clear to us that his will is to do a particular thing. In that case we may be perfectly confident that very thing will be done. In that sense Jesus says to us, "Whatever you ask in prayer, believe that you have received it, and it will be yours" (Mark 11:24). It is God who does it, and our belief rests on him and his revealed will. Otherwise, we would be God, and he would run the universe according to our will, not his.

Jesus makes it clear that there is a kind of filter that our prayers must pass through in order to be sure that they are according to God's will. "If you abide in me, and my words abide in you, ask whatever you wish, and it will be done for you" (John 15:7). Here Jesus' promise is more clearly qualified than in Mark 11:24.[2] Are we trusting in him as our all-supplying vine? And are his words shaping our minds and hearts so that we discern how to pray according to his wisdom?

Praying in faith does not always mean being sure that the very thing we ask will happen. But it does always mean that because of Jesus we trust God to hear us and help us in the way that seems best to him. It may mean that he gives us just what we ask, or that he gives us something better. Will a father give a son a stone if he asks him for bread? No. But neither will he give him bread if it is moldy. He may give him cake. Sometimes God's answers will overwhelm us with their excess. Other times they taste more

---

[2] Even in the context of Mark 11:24, there is an implied qualification of the promise, "Whatever you ask in prayer, believe that you have received it, and it will be yours." The very next verse says, "And whenever you stand praying, forgive, if you have anything against anyone, so that your Father also who is in heaven may forgive you your trespasses" (Mark 11:25). This means that even if you ask for forgiveness and believe that you have it, you will *not* have it unless you forgive the one who has something against you. This makes it clear that the promise is not as sweeping as it sounds at first. There are limits. You cannot simply manipulate God by the power of being confident in what you ask. There are moral guidelines. This is what Jesus is saying with the condition, "If . . . my words abide in you, ask whatever you wish, and it will be done for you" (John 15:7). The words of Jesus shape the attitude and content of our prayers.

like medicine than food and will test our faith that this medicine is really what we need.

How? Not for the Praise of Others

In view of all this, it should be clear that the reward of prayer comes from God, not man. But Jesus shows us that the human heart is capable of turning the most beautifully Godward act in a manward direction and ruining it. He warns us:

> When you pray, you must not be like the hypocrites. For they love to stand and pray in the synagogues and at the street corners, that they may be seen by others. Truly, I say to you, they have received their reward. But when you pray, go into your room and shut the door and pray to your Father who is in secret. And your Father who sees in secret will reward you. (Matt. 6:5-6)

Jesus hates hypocrisy—like appearing to love God when what you really love is the praise of man. His most disparaging language was reserved for "hypocrites." He called them children of hell, "blind guides," "full of greed and self-indulgence," "whitewashed tombs" (Matt. 23:15, 24, 25, 27). The demand is unmistakable: "Beware of the leaven of the Pharisees, which is hypocrisy" (Luke 12:1). The implication for prayer (and fasting and almsgiving, Matt. 6:1-4, 16-18) is: Treasure God, and all that he will be for you, in prayer; but do not treasure the praise of man. And most of all do not turn a God-treasuring act of prayer into a man-treasuring act of hypocrisy.

For Whom?

For whom does Jesus demand that we pray? Clearly ourselves. Not because we are deserving. Prayer has nothing to do with deserving. It's all mercy. We pray for ourselves because we are weak. We are so prone to sin and utterly dependent on preserving grace to sustain our flawed obedience. "Pray then like this," Jesus said, "lead us not into temptation, but deliver us from evil" (Matt. 6:9, 13). That is a prayer for ourselves first, since we know our own frailty and vulnerability better than anyone. Then it is a prayer for the other followers of Jesus and the world.

No one is to be excluded from our prayers. When Jesus tells us to pray, "Hallowed be your name" (Matt. 6:9), he means that we should pray this for anyone who does not yet hallow God's name. And if our selfish hearts should think of some adversary that we do not like, Jesus is unsparing—these too must be blessed in our prayers. "Love your enemies and pray for those who persecute you" (Matt. 5:44); "bless those who curse you, pray for those who abuse you" (Luke 6:28). None must be excluded from our love, and none may be excluded from our prayers.

WHAT?

Finally, *what* does Jesus demand that we pray? What are we to ask the Father to do? Jesus' summary answer is called the Lord's Prayer (Matt. 6:9-13).

> Our Father in heaven,
> 1) hallowed be your name.
> 2) Your kingdom come,
> 3) your will be done, on earth as it is in heaven.
> 4) Give us this day our daily bread,
> 5) and forgive us our debts, as we also have forgiven our debtors.
> 6) And lead us not into temptation, but deliver us from evil.

We pray for ourselves and for other followers of Jesus and for the world (1) that we would reverence and cherish the name of God above things. This is the first function of prayer—to pray that people would pursue the glory of God. (2) We pray that God's saving, purifying, Jesus-exalting rule would hold sway in our lives and would finally come in universal manifestation and extent. (3) We pray that we would do the will of God the way the angels do it in heaven—namely, without hesitation and full of zeal and thoroughness. (4) We pray for the practical provisions of body and mind that make an earthly life of obedience possible. 5) We pray for forgiveness for our daily failures to honor God as we ought. That is, we ask God to apply to us each day the perfect redemption that Jesus obtained once for all when he died on the cross. 6) We pray that God would protect us from the evil one and from the temptations that would bring us to ruin and weaken our witness for him.

The Lord's Prayer shows us the astonishing nature of prayer. It puts in the position of greatest importance the prayer for God's name to be glorified, God's kingdom to advance and triumph, and God's will to be accomplished on the earth the way it's happening in heaven. This means that God intends to use human prayers to accomplish his most ultimate and universal purposes. For example, Jesus tells us to pray for the workers that will be required to spread the gospel to all the nations. "Pray earnestly to the Lord of the harvest to send out laborers into his harvest" (Matt. 9:38). Yet nothing is more certain than that the kingdom of God will triumph. Jesus said, "I will build my church, and the gates of hell shall not prevail against it . . . this gospel of the kingdom will be proclaimed throughout the whole world as a testimony to all nations, and then the end will come" (Matt. 16:18; 24:14). There is no uncertainty about the triumph of God. Nevertheless, in God's providence it depends on human prayer.

This implies that prayer is not only a duty of man but a gift of God. Jesus will awaken in his people the spirit of prayer that asks for everything it will take to accomplish God's purposes in the world. The prayers of Jesus' followers and the purposes of God will not fail.

Do Not Be Anxious About the Necessities of Daily Life

Do not be anxious about your life, what you will eat or what you will drink, nor about your body, what you will put on. Is not life more than food, and the body more than clothing?— MATT. 6:25

Therefore do not be anxious about tomorrow, for tomorrow will be anxious for itself. Sufficient for the day is its own trouble.— MATT. 6:34

Fear not, little flock, for it is your Father's good pleasure to give you the kingdom.— LUKE 12:32

There have been kings who find it very effective to keep their subjects in constant anxiety. If the people are anxious about their life and worry about where their next meal is coming from, then perhaps they will be more willing to do the king's bidding in order to get the food they need from the king's storehouse. Anxiety keeps them in their place. Fear makes the monarchy firm.

Jesus Does Not Secure His Kingship by Cultivating Anxiety

But one of the greatest things about Jesus is that he does not want his people to be anxious. He does not secure his kingship by cultivating anxiety. On the contrary, the aim of Jesus' kingship[1] is to free us from anxiety. He doesn't need to keep us anxious in order to establish his power and superiority. They are untouchable and invincible. Instead, he exalts his power and superiority by working to take away our anxiety.

When Jesus says, "Do not be anxious about tomorrow," he is demanding the kind of life that everybody would want—no anxiety. No fear of man or menacing circumstances. But how does Jesus expect this demand to come true when we see things all around us that make us anxious? Jesus gives us help in two extended treatments about anxiety and fear, one having to do with anxiety over the basics of life, like food, drink, clothing (Matt. 6:25-34), the other having to do with anxiety over the hurt that men can do to us (Matt. 10:24-31). In the first passage Jesus sustains our ability to press on joyfully when we can't see how all our needs will be met. In the second passage, which I deal with in the next chapter, Jesus motivates us to press on boldly in the cause of truth when people threaten us.

THE ANXIETIES OF DAILY LIFE

Everyone can see plainly Jesus' main point in Matthew 6:25-34. "Do not be anxious." Verse 25: "Do not be anxious about your life." Verse 31: "Do not be anxious, saying , 'What shall we eat?'" Verse 34: "Do not be anxious about tomorrow." But that is the negative way of stating the main point of this passage. There is a positive way found in verse 33—namely, instead of being anxious, "Seek first the kingdom of God." In other words, when you think about your life or your food or your clothes—or your spouse or your job or your mission—don't fret about them. Instead, make God the King in that affair and in that moment. That is, hand over the situation to his kingly power, and do his righteous will with the

---

[1] Jesus claims to be a king, though not the kind people expected. He says in John 18:36, "My kingdom is not of this world. If my kingdom were of this world, my servants would have been fighting, that I might not be delivered over to the Jews. But my kingdom is not from the world." See also Matthew 25:31, 34; John 12:14-15.

confidence that he will work for you and meet all your needs. If we believe in the kingship of our heavenly Father, we do not need to be anxious about anything. Virtually everything else in this text is support for Jesus' demand.

LIFE IS MORE THAN FOOD, AND THE BODY IS MORE THAN CLOTHING

I see at least eight reasons Jesus gives for his disciples not to be anxious. The *first* is given in verse 25. "Do not be anxious about your life, what you shall eat or what you shall drink, nor about your body, what you shall put on." Why? "Because life is more than food, and the body is more than clothing." What does this mean?

Why do we tend to get anxious about food and clothing? Because there are three things that we would lose if we didn't have food and clothing. First, we would lose some pleasures. After all, food tastes good. Second, we would lose some human praise and admiring glances if we didn't have nice clothes. Third, we would possibly lose our life if we had no food at all or weren't protected from the cold. So the reason we get anxious about food and clothing is because we don't want to lose physical pleasures or human praise or life.

To this fear Jesus responds: If you are gripped by anxiety over these things, you have lost sight of the greatness of life. Life was not given primarily for physical pleasures, but for something greater— the enjoyment of God (Luke 12:21). Life was not given primarily for the approval of man but for something greater—the approval of God (John 5:44). Life was not even given primarily for extension on this earth, but for something greater—eternal life with God in the age to come (John 3:16).

We ought not to be anxious about food and clothing because food and clothing cannot provide the *great* things of life—the enjoyment of God, the pursuit of his gracious favor, the hope of eternity in his presence. We get anxious about food and clothing to the same degree that we lose sight of the great purposes of a God-centered life.

Look at the Birds of the Air

The *second* reason Jesus gives for not being anxious is in Matthew 6:26: "Look at the birds of the air: they neither sow nor reap nor gather into barns, and yet your heavenly Father feeds them. Are you not of more value than they?" What we see when we look at the birds is not a lesson in laziness. They dig their worms and snatch their bugs and pad their nests with strings and leaves. But Jesus says it is *God* who feeds them. Birds don't anxiously hoard things as though God will not do the same tomorrow. They go about their work—and we should go about our work—as though, when the sun comes up tomorrow, God will still be God.

You Cannot Add One Cubit to Your Span of Life

The *third* reason not to be anxious is that it's fruitless. "And which of you by being anxious can add one cubit to his span of life?" (Matt. 6:27, rsv). The argument is very pragmatic: Anxiety doesn't get you anywhere. It doesn't do you any good. Whatever problem is causing you to feel anxious, you can be sure your anxiety will not reduce the problem. It will only make you miserable while you try to deal with it. So don't be anxious. It's useless.

Consider the Lilies of the Field

The *fourth* reason Jesus gives for not being anxious is based on the lilies. "And why are you anxious about clothing? Consider the lilies of the field, how they grow; they neither toil nor spin; yet I tell you, even Solomon in all his glory was not arrayed like one of these. But if God so clothes the grass of the field, which today is alive and tomorrow is thrown into the oven, will he not much more clothe you, O you of little faith?" (Matt. 6:28-30).

When you look at a lily, which has no will or instinct of its own to labor and spin, yet is adorned with beautiful form and color, Jesus says you should draw at least this one conclusion: God delights to adorn things. But if his delight finds expression in adorning grass that's here today and gone tomorrow, then surely his delight in adornment will express itself in how he clothes his children!

But someone may protest, "God has not adorned me!" Or: "God has not adorned the poor Christians in many destitute situations around the world." That's true. Very few followers of Jesus are dressed like Solomon. But we couldn't do our work if we were. That's the way Jesus spoke about John the Baptist: "Behold, those who are dressed in splendid clothing and live in luxury are in kings' courts"—but not John the Baptist! He had prophetic work to do and wore "a garment of camel's hair and a leather belt around his waist, and his food was locusts and wild honey" (Luke 7:25; Matt. 3:4). "Among those born of women there has arisen no one greater than John the Baptist" (Matt. 11:11). The adornment Jesus promised does not mean that we will have exorbitant clothes, but that we will have the clothes we need. Where have you ever seen a disciple of Jesus who did not have the adornment he needed to do what God had called him to do?

But let's be careful. We must not measure the perfection of God's provision by some standard below his calling. He does not call us to live in palaces, but to take up our crosses and love people no matter the cost. And when we have finished carrying our crosses—on torn shoulders, if God wills—there will be kingly robes for us all. The promise to meet all our needs does not mean he will make us rich. It does not even mean he will keep us alive ("some of you they will put to death," Luke 21:16). It means he will give us all that we need to do the will of God (see below on Matt. 6:33).

YOUR HEAVENLY FATHER KNOWS THAT YOU NEED THEM ALL

The *fifth* and *sixth* reasons why a follower of Jesus shouldn't be anxious are given in Matthew 6:32. We shouldn't be anxious about what we eat or drink or wear because "[fifth reason] the Gentiles seek after all these things; and [sixth reason] your heavenly Father knows that you need them all." Anxiety about the things of this world puts us on the same level with the world of unbelievers. It shows that we are really very much like the world in what makes us happy. And Jesus assumes that we will not want to be like that. It also shows that we don't think our Father in heaven knows our needs. Or perhaps we don't think he has the heart of a loving Father. Anxiety shows that we are too close to the world and too far from God. So don't be anxious—the world has nothing eternal to offer, and your loving heavenly Father knows your needs now and forever.

ALL THESE THINGS WILL BE ADDED TO YOU

The *seventh* reason not to be anxious is that when you seek the kingdom of God first, he works for you and provides all your needs. "Seek first the kingdom of God and his righteousness, and all these things will be added to you" (Matt. 6:33). "All these things" does not mean everything we *think* we need, but everything we really need. And real needs are determined by what God calls us to do, not what we feel like doing. God will give us "all these things" that we need to fulfill his calling on our lives.

TOMORROW WILL BE ANXIOUS FOR ITSELF

The *last* argument is, "Do not be anxious about tomorrow, for tomorrow will be anxious for itself. Let the day's own trouble be sufficient for the day" (Matt. 6:34). In other words, God has appointed to each day its portion of pleasure and pain, as the old Swedish hymn says, especially in the last two lines of this verse.

> Day by day, and with each passing moment,
> Strength I find, to meet my trials here;
> Trusting in my Father's wise bestowment,
> I've no cause for worry or for fear.
> He Whose heart is kind beyond all measure
> Gives unto each day what He deems best—
> Lovingly, its part of pain and pleasure,
> Mingling toil with peace and rest.[2]

---

[2] Karolina Wilhelmina Sandell-Berg, *Day by Day.*

So don't misappropriate God's allotted troubles for tomorrow. That is, don't bring them forward into today in the form of anxiety. Believe that God will be God tomorrow. Tomorrow there will be grace for tomorrow's troubles. That grace is not given today.

The main point of all this is clear and unmistakable: Jesus does not want his followers to be anxious. He does not secure his kingdom by keeping his subjects in a state of worry. On the contrary, according to Matthew 6:33, the more primary and central his kingship becomes in our lives, the less anxiety we will have.

Since Jesus believes that reasons delivered in words (we have seen eight of them) help to overcome anxiety, it would make sense that we keep these reasons before our minds and seek to make them part of our mental and emotional life. I think this implies that it would be wise to memorize Matthew 6:25-34. I know of no way to weave these eight counter-anxiety realities into the fabric of our minds and hearts that omits remembering them.

Demand #15

DO NOT BE ANXIOUS ABOUT THE THREATS OF MAN

You will be dragged before governors and kings for my sake, to bear witness before them and the Gentiles. When they deliver you over, do not be anxious how you are to speak or what you are to say, for what you are to say will be given to you in that hour. —MATT. 10:18-19

A disciple is not above his teacher, nor a servant above his master. It is enough for the disciple to be like his teacher, and the servant like his master. If they have called the master of the house Beelzebul, how much more will they malign those of his household. So have no fear of them, for nothing is covered that will not be revealed, or hidden that will not be known. What I tell you in the dark, say in the light, and what you hear whispered, proclaim on the housetops. And do not fear those who kill the body but cannot kill the soul. Rather fear him who can destroy both soul and body in hell. Are not two sparrows sold for a penny? And not one of them will fall to the ground apart from your Father. But even the hairs of your head are all numbered. Fear not, therefore; you are of more value than many sparrows. —MATT. 10:24-31

Even if we gain a measure of victory over the fear that all our needs will not be met (dealt with in the previous chapter), there remains the gut-wrenching fear of speaking the truth when it may cost us our lives. That's what Jesus deals with in Matthew 10:24-

31. It is especially relevant in our day as the likelihood increases that tolerance will hold sway for everyone except the person who claims that everyone must give absolute allegiance to Jesus.

The aim of Jesus in Matthew 10:24-31 is to give us the courage to speak his truth with clarity and openness no matter what the cost. As with Matthew 6:25-34, the main point of this text is plain from the three repetitions of the command not to fear. Verse 26: "So have no fear of them." Verse 28: "Do not fear those who kill the body." Verse 31: "Fear not therefore; you are of much more value than many sparrows." Jesus' aim is clear: Be fearlessly courageous. But courageous to do what?

WHAT YOU HEAR WHISPERED, PROCLAIM UPON THE HOUSETOPS

Jesus has something very specific in mind that is threatened by fear and advanced by courage. He says in Matthew 10:27-28, "What I tell you in the dark, speak in the light; and what you hear whispered, proclaim upon the housetops. And do not fear . . ." In other words, the fear Jesus focuses on in this passage is the fear of speaking clearly (in the light) and openly (on the housetops) when that speaking might get you in trouble.

So here's the demand: "Don't be afraid to speak clearly and openly what I have taught you, even if it costs you your life." The rest of Jesus' words here are motivation—five reasons why we should have courage in the cause of truth.

THEY WILL MALIGN YOU LIKE THEY DID JESUS

First, notice the word "so" or "therefore" at the beginning of Matthew 10:26: "*So* [therefore] have no fear of them." In other words, fearlessness flows from what Jesus just said—namely, "If they have called the master of the house Beelzebul, how much more will they malign those of his household." How does that help make us fearless?

Jesus reasoning seems to go like this: "Your mistreatment for speaking the truth is not some unexpected, random, meaningless experience; instead it's the same way they treated me, and so it's a sign that you belong to me. So don't be afraid of the names they call you when you speak out plainly. Those very names bind you and me together."

Nothing Is Covered That Will Not Be Revealed

Second, notice the word "for" in the middle of that same verse 26.[1] "So have no fear of them; *for* [here comes the second reason not to be afraid] nothing is covered that will not be revealed, or hidden that will not be known." How does that help us overcome fear and be courageous in the cause of truth?

It helps us by assuring us that the truth we are speaking will triumph. It will be vindicated in the end. People may reject it now. They may call it demonic. They may cast it out. They may try to bury it and hide it from the world and pretend that it does not exist. But Jesus says, "Take heart in the cause of truth, because in the end all truth will be revealed. All reality will be uncovered. And those who spoke it with clarity and openness will be vindicated."

Fear Not, You Can Only Be Killed!

Third, Jesus says, fear not, you can only be killed! "And do not fear those who kill the body but cannot kill the soul" (Matt. 10:28). In other words, the worst thing your opponents can do to you when you speak the truth is kill your body. And that leaves the soul untouched and happy in God forever. But if you keep silent, if you forsake the path of truth and fall in love with the praise of men, you could lose your very soul. If you want to fear something, fear that (see *Demand #11*). But don't fear what man can do to you. All he can do is dispatch your soul to paradise. Fear not.

---

[1] Some English Bible translations drop these important words because they think it helps the flow of thought. For example, the *New International Version* drops this crucial word "for" (γάρ). It is there in the Greek original, and it is important.

EVEN THE HAIRS OF YOUR HEAD ARE ALL NUMBERED

Fourth, don't fear to speak the truth, but be courageous and speak clearly and openly because God is giving close and intimate attention to all you do. Matthew 10:30 means at least that much. Jesus says, "Even the hairs of your head are all numbered." In other words, the suffering you may undergo in speaking the truth is *not* because God is disinterested in you or unfamiliar with your plight. He is close enough to separate one hair from another and give each one a number. Fear not; he is close. He is interested; he cares. Be of good courage, and speak the truth whatever the cost.

NOT ONE OF THEM WILL FALL TO THE GROUND WITHOUT YOUR FATHER'S WILL

Finally, fear not because God will not let anything happen to you apart from his gracious will. "You are of more value than many sparrows." "Not one of them will fall to the ground without your Father's will" (Matt. 10:29 [RSV], 31). Jesus' point is: God governs the world right down to the smallest events like birds falling to the ground. Therefore, no harm can befall you but what God wills. This confidence has given great courage to the followers of Jesus for centuries. Many have spoken in the words of missionary Henry Martyn, "If [God] has work for me to do, I cannot die."[2] We are immortal until the work God has for us is done.

SO DO NOT FEAR THE FACE OF ANY MAN

Therefore, the demand of Jesus stands, and there is sufficient reason to obey it with joy and courage. Don't be anxious about the ordinary needs of life, and don't fear the threats of man. Don't yield to the spirit of the age that woos us into peaceful silence when the truth is being trampled. "Do not think that I have come to bring peace to

---

[2] *Journal and Letters of Henry Martyn* (New York: Protestant Episcopal Society for the Promotion of Evangelical Knowledge, 1851), 460. The original English edition of 1837 was published in London and edited by the Rev. S. Wilberforce, M. A., Rector of Brighstone.

the earth," Jesus said. "I have not come to bring peace, but a sword" (Matt. 10:34). Not the sword of steel, but the sword of truth that gives life to all who believe. Love the truth, therefore, and what you learn from Jesus in the solitude speak from the housetop. And do not fear the face of any man.

HUMBLE YOURSELF BY MAKING WAR ON PRIDE

Whoever exalts himself will be humbled, and whoever humbles himself will be exalted. —MATT. 23:12

The tax collector, standing far off, would not even lift up his eyes to heaven, but beat his breast, saying, "God, be merciful to me, a sinner!" I tell you, this man went down to his house justified. —LUKE 18:13

Blessed are the poor in spirit, for theirs is the kingdom of heaven. —MATT. 5:3

Beware of the scribes, who like to walk around in long robes, and love greetings in the marketplaces and the best seats in the synagogues and the places of honor at feasts. . . . They will receive the greater condemnation. —LUKE 20:46-47

So you also, when you have done all that you were commanded, say, "We are unworthy servants; we have only done what was our duty." —LUKE 17:10

One of the reasons Jesus reserved his most disparaging descriptions for hypocrites (see *Demand #13*) was that the root of hypocrisy is pride. And Jesus' abomination of pride is evident in the frequency and variety of his calls for humility.

PRIDE: DEFIANCE, DESERT, DELIGHT

Pride is difficult to define because its manifestations are subtle and often do not look like arrogance. We can see this if we compare boasting and self-pity as two forms of pride.

Boasting is the response of pride to success. Self-pity is the response of pride to suffering. Boasting says, "I deserve admiration because I have achieved so much." Self-pity says, "I deserve admiration because I have sacrificed so much." Boasting is the voice of pride in the heart of the strong. Self-pity is the voice of pride in the heart of the weak. Boasting sounds self-sufficient. Self-pity sounds self-sacrificing. The reason self-pity does not look like pride is that it appears to be needy. But the need arises from a wounded ego, and the desire is not really for others to see them as helpless but as heroes. The need that self-pity feels does not come from a sense of unworthiness but from a sense of unrecognized worthiness. It is the response of unapplauded pride.[1]

Jesus dissects the depths of pride. He exposes its multiple layers and manifestations. At the bottom of it is a complex disposition of self-rule, merit, and pleasure in feeling superior to others. Or, to be alliterative, there is a combination of *defiance* (against God as rightful ruler), *desert* (of better treatment than we get), and *delight* (in feeling above others). None of these may be obvious.

A person can be passively defiant while avoiding blatant rebellion, and yet deeply committed to ultimate self-determination. Or a person can seem to feel unworthy by constantly deprecating himself in public, but all the while feel angry that others do not recognize this as a virtue. Or a person can express delight in feeling superior to others by boasting or by craving that others would praise him for not boasting.

PRIDE: A SENSE OF MERIT

Jesus focuses on the visible expressions of pride that he can point to. Luke tells us why he told the parable of the boasting Pharisee and

---

[1] This paragraph comes from John Piper, *Desiring God: Meditations of a Christian Hedonist* (Sisters, Ore.: Multnomah, 2003), 302.

the broken tax collector (see *Demand #20*). "He told this parable to some who trusted in themselves that they were righteous, and treated others with contempt" (Luke 18:9). This is what I meant by the disposition of merit—the sense that one deserves something good from God.

This sense of merit goes hand in hand with boasting that we are superior to others. So the merit-conscious Pharisee says in Luke 18:11-12, "God, I thank you that I am not like other men, extortioners, unjust, adulterers, or even like this tax collector. I fast twice a week; I give tithes of all that I get." The fact that he says he thanks God does not obscure the pleasure that he gets in feeling superior. There is a difference between a humble delight in becoming a better person by God's grace and a proud delight in being able to see yourself as superior to others. Pride does not delight in growing holiness, but in growing ability to feel superior.

CRAVING THE PRAISE OF MEN

Even if we do not have a strong sense of merit, we may crave the same result, namely, the praise of men. Jesus warns us not to give to charity or pray or fast in order to be seen by others. "Beware of practicing your righteousness before other people in order to be seen by them" (Matt. 6:1). "When you pray, you must not be like the hypocrites. For they love to stand and pray in the synagogues and at the street corners, that they may be seen by others" (Matt. 6:5). "And when you fast, do not look gloomy like the hypocrites, for they disfigure their faces that their fasting may be seen by others" (Matt. 6:16). Jesus calls them "hypocrites" because in their praying and fasting they want to appear as if they treasure God, but in fact they treasure the praise of men. That is one dimension of pride.

Praise for piety is not the only kind of praise that pride craves. It also craves praise for power and wealth. So Jesus says to his disciples, "The kings of the Gentiles exercise lordship over them, and those in authority over them are called benefactors. But not so with you" (Luke 22:25-26). In other words, do not delight in having superior power or superior wealth. The pleasures of being "over" or "above" others does not come from humble trust in the grace of God. It comes from a heart of pride.

There are a hundred ways pride positions itself to get the praise of man. It may involve where you sit at a meeting or how you carry yourself in a market or what title you put in front of your name. "[The scribes and Pharisees] love the place of honor at feasts and the best seats in the synagogues and greetings in the marketplaces and being called rabbi by others" (Matt. 23:6-7). The issue here is not that being called rabbi is always wrong or that sitting in a place of honor is always wrong. The issue here is what you love—what you need and crave and treasure. Pride is driven by the desire to be honored by men with places and titles.

PRIDE IS LOVELESS

Then Jesus shows how loveless pride is. Just before saying, "They do all their deeds to be seen by others" (Matt. 23:5), Jesus says, "They tie up heavy burdens, hard to bear, and lay them on people's shoulders, but they themselves are not willing to move them with their finger" (Matt. 23:4). In other words, they teach high moral standards but do not have the mercy or the spiritual wisdom to help people carry the load. They are loveless.

That's no surprise for two reasons: One is that the proud do not really want others to advance beyond them. That would mean losing one of their reasons for feeling superior. The other reason is that the proud do not understand the way that God's grace really works to help sinners make progress in holiness without getting proud. They don't lift a finger to show the repentant sinner how Jesus' yoke is easy and his burden is light (Matt. 11:30), because they do not experience it as easy and light. The moral duty that they strive to fulfill is kept heavy so that there can be a sense of merit and boasting in the achievement. If it were light and easy, where would be the boasting?

WE ARE UNWORTHY SERVANTS

So in Jesus' teaching there is a very close connection between humility and servanthood. To be humble is to be a servant. They are not the same. But humility leads to joyful readiness to do lowly service. The disciple moves from poverty of spirit to childlike trust in God's grace to a heart of servanthood and acts of service.

In Jesus' famous Beatitudes the very first one is, "Blessed are the poor in spirit" (Matt. 5:3). That is, blessed are the people who do not find a basis for merit or desert when they look within themselves. They are the opposite of those "who trusted in themselves that they were righteous" (Luke 18:9). They know that they have nothing in themselves to commend them to God.

They happily assume the place of unworthy servants whom Jesus describes in Luke 17:10—"When you have done all that you were commanded, say, 'We are unworthy servants; we have only done what was our duty.'" This is a profound statement—and utterly devastating to the last vestige of pride. Jesus says, no degree of obedience, from the worst to the best, merits any absolute claim on God. A perfectly obedient human should say—it would be part of his obedience—"I am an unworthy servant." That is, "I do not put you in any absolute sense in debt to reward me." This conviction is the root of humility—that we deserve nothing good from God.

Or to put it positively like the brokenhearted tax collector, everything good that we get from God is mercy. It is undeserved. "God, be merciful to me, a sinner!" (Luke 18:13). "This man went down to his house justified," Jesus said (Luke 18:14). The joy of the humble does not reside in being deserving, but in receiving mercy.

HUMBLE YOURSELF IN CHILDLIKENESS, SERVANTHOOD, AND BROKENHEARTED BOLDNESS

Truly, I say to you, unless you turn and become like children, you will never enter the kingdom of heaven. Whoever humbles himself like this child is the greatest in the kingdom of heaven. —MATT. 18:3-4

Let the greatest among you become as the youngest, and the leader as one who serves. —LUKE 22:26

A disciple is not above his teacher, nor a servant above his master. . . . If they have called the master of the house Beelzebul, how much more will they malign those of his household. So have no fear of them. —MATT. 10:24-26

The key to humility is not merely feeling the absence of merit (as we saw in the last chapter), but feeling the presence of free grace. Humility is not only like the servant who says, "I am an unworthy servant"; humility is also like a child at rest in his father's arms. Jesus said, "Truly, I say to you, unless you turn and become like children, you will never enter the kingdom of heaven. Whoever *humbles himself* like this *child* is the greatest in the kingdom of heaven" (Matt. 18:3-4). We must humble ourselves in both ways: like an unworthy servant and like a trusting child.

What is the point of the comparison with a child? If we stay close to the original context, the focus would fall mainly on three terms: *humility* (or lowliness), *little ones*, and *belief*.

HUMILITY

In Matthew 18:4 Jesus says, "Whoever *humbles* himself like this child is the greatest in the kingdom of heaven." The Greek verb for "humble" did not generally describe a positive virtue in Jesus' day. It meant generally to crush, bring down, afflict, humiliate, and degrade.[1] The word was chosen because Jesus' demand was not a romantic one, as though childlikeness were sweet and easy. For a strong, self-confident, self-sufficient, intelligent, resourceful, controlling person, Jesus' demand was devastating. Jesus knew that children were not models for imitation in his day. The reason he chose them is because of "their powerlessness and their low social standing."[2] His demand is that we end our love affair with power and status and self-sufficiency and rights and control.

LITTLE ONES

This is confirmed by the term "little ones" that he uses to describe childlike disciples. He says, "Whoever causes one of *these little ones* who believe in me to sin, it would be better for him to have a great millstone fastened around his neck and to be drowned in the depth of the sea" (Matt. 18:6). He describes believers as "little ones," and he describes little ones as those who "believe." Both terms are important. "Little ones" emphasizes that they are not great in the eyes of the world. They are not strong. They are not self-sufficient. Instead, what marks them is that they "believe in me." That is, they trust not in themselves but in Jesus.

---

[1] See the article on ταπεινός *(tapeinos)* in *Theological Dictionary of the New Testament*, ed. Gerhard Friedrich, Vol. VIII (Grand Rapids, Mich.: Eerdmans, 1972), 4-9. "[In the Greek and Hellenistic world] men 'exploit,' 'oppress,' . . . 'humble,' 'put down' . . . 'humiliate others by breaking their spirit.'. . . That man should humble himself is rejected" (4).

[2] Ulrich Luz, *Matthew 8–20: A Commentary*, trans. James E. Crouch, ed. Helmut Koester, Hermenia (Minneapolis: Augsburg Fortress, 2001), 428.

Trust

This is probably the main focus in Jesus' comparison between his disciples and children. Children may have all kinds of faults, but in a normal, healthy family they trust their daddy to take care of them. They do not lie awake wondering where the next meal is coming from. They do not fret in the stroller that the sky is turning gray. "The child is, by its very position, lowly . . . and lives by instinctive confidence."[3] They are both lowly and non-great by the standards of worldly acclaim. And they are happy, anxiety-free, and confident that everything they need will be provided. The world does not give honorary degrees to children. It does not write books about their accomplishments. We do not put children in charge of anything. But children are not the least bothered by any of that. They are content to be cared for by their parents.

Of course, Jesus is not calling us to be as unproductive or as immature as children. That's not the point of the comparison. The point is that we not love being stronger or more intelligent or richer than others—that our joy does not reside in a feeling of superiority. The point is that we not begrudge the absence of recognition if the world does not value what Jesus calls us to do. We must not fret over being thought lowly and even foolish by worldly standards. Instead we must "believe" in Jesus the way a child believes. We must find our security and meaning and joy in Jesus and all that our heavenly Father is for us in him (see *Demand #4*).

Lowliness Leads to a Spirit of Servanthood

Jesus emphasizes that this poverty of spirit and this childlike lowliness and trust lead to a spirit and life of servanthood. More than once Jesus' disciples were found to be arguing with each other about which of them was the greatest, or would be the greatest, in the kingdom of heaven. Jesus responded each time with more or less the same demand: "If anyone would be first, he must be last of all

---

[3] Alexander McClaren, *The Gospel According to Matthew: Chapters XVII to XXVII* (London: Hodder and Stoughton, n.d.), 3.

and servant of all" (Mark 9:35). Sometimes he illustrated his point by putting a child in their midst and saying, "Whoever receives one such child in my name receives me, and whoever receives me, receives not me but him who sent me" (Mark 9:37). In other words, if you are willing to work in the nursery and happily take the children onto your lap, you will be "first."

Even at the Last Supper, when he was preparing to give his life in the ultimate demonstration of servant-love, the disciples were arguing about who was the greatest—so deeply engrained in us is this craving. He said, "The kings of the Gentiles exercise lordship over them, and those in authority over them are called benefactors. But not so with you. Rather, let the greatest among you become as the youngest, and the leader as one who serves. For who is the greater, one who reclines at table or one who serves? Is it not the one who reclines at table? But I am among you as the one who serves" (Luke 22:25-27). Jesus cut straight from the desire to be great among men to the alternative lifestyle, namely, lowly (youthlike) service.

How Jesus Served and Will Serve

What does service mean? In Matthew 20:26-28, Jesus connects his demand that we serve others with his own service of us and shows us the kind of thing he has in mind. "Whoever would be great among you must be your servant, and whoever would be first among you must be your slave, even as the Son of Man came not to be served but to serve, and to give his life as a ransom for many." Service means doing things out of love that are costly to ourselves but aim to bring temporal and eternal benefit to others.

Astonishingly, the servant role of Jesus does not end with his earthly life. He portrays his second coming not only as a demonstration of great power and glory (Mark 13:26), but also as a time when he will again take the lowly (but beautiful) role of servant: "Blessed are those servants whom the master finds awake when he comes. Truly, I say to you, he will dress himself for service and have them recline at table, and he will come and serve them" (Luke

12:37). Jesus will never stop serving us. Does this not incline your heart to serve others as you follow the one who loved you and gave himself for you and never stops serving you? The heart of a saved sinner who seeks to follow Jesus does not ask, "How can I have maximum prestige or applause?" It asks, "How can I do the greatest good for people who need my help, no matter what it costs me?"

When Jesus said (repeatedly), "Whoever exalts himself will be humbled, and whoever humbles himself will be exalted" (Matt. 23:12; Luke 14:11; 18:14), he was warning against the great service-killer (self-exalting pride) and calling for the great service-maker (Christ-dependent humility).

Brokenhearted Boldness in the Cause of Truth

One of the crucial roles of servanthood needed in our day is broken-hearted boldness in the proclamation of God's truth. I mention this because the spirit of relativism in our day has created an atmosphere in which speaking the truth with conviction and calling others to believe it is not considered humble. The typical condemnation of Jesus' claim to be the only way to heaven (John 5:23; 14:6) is that it is arrogant.

G. K. Chesterton saw this coming in 1908 when he wrote,

> What we suffer from today is humility in the wrong place. Modesty has moved from the organ of ambition. Modesty has settled upon the organ of conviction; where it was never meant to be. A man was meant to be doubtful about himself, but undoubt-ing about the truth; this has been exactly reversed. Nowadays the part of a man that a man does assert is exactly the part he ought not to assert—himself. The part he doubts is exactly the part he ought not to doubt—the Divine Reason. . . . The new skeptic is so humble that he doubts if he can even learn. . . . There is a real humility typical of our time; but it so happens that it's practically a more poisonous humility than the wildest prostra-tions of the ascetic. . . . The old humility made a man doubt-

ful about his efforts, which might make him work harder. But the new humility makes a man doubtful about his aims, which makes him stop working altogether. . . . We are on the road to producing a race of man too mentally modest to believe in the multiplication table.[4]

If humility is not compliance with the relativism of our day, then what is it? I hope what we have seen in this chapter sheds light on this question and helps us see how, for the sake of Jesus and in the service of others, we should boldly speak what Jesus taught us. Here are at least five implications of what we have said in the last two chapters.

HUMILITY: FIVE IMPLICATIONS FOR BOLD TRUTH-TELLING

First, humility begins with a sense of subordination to God in Jesus. "A disciple is not above his teacher, nor a slave above his master" (Matt. 10:24). Our conviction does not come from exalting ourselves but from submitting ourselves to the one who reveals himself to us in his word and commands us to speak it.

Second, humility does not feel a right to better treatment than Jesus got. "If they have called the head of the house Beelzebul, how much more will they malign the members of his household" (Matt. 10:25). Therefore, humility does not return evil for evil. It is not a life based on perceived rights. It is a life of sacrifice.

Third, humility asserts truth not to bolster ego with control or with triumphs in debate. It speaks truth as a service to Christ and as love to the adversary. "What I [Jesus] tell you in the darkness, speak in the light . . . do not fear" (Matt. 10:27-28).

Fourth, humility knows it is dependent on grace for all knowing and believing and speaking. "Apart from me you can do nothing" (John 15:5). This will create a demeanor that is neither cocky nor timid.

---

[4]G. K. Chesterton, *Orthodoxy* (Garden City, NY: Doubleday and Co., 1957), 31-32.

Fifth, humility knows it is fallible, and so considers criticism and learns from it, but also knows that God has made provision for human conviction and that he calls us to persuade others. Jesus told us that the church should stand ready to correct the wayward member (Matt. 18:15-17). And he told us that even though we are fallible and may need correction, we should unashamedly go and make disciples of all nations, telling them to do everything Jesus commanded (Matt. 28:19-20).

HUMILITY: THE GIFT TO RECEIVE ALL THINGS AS A GIFT

When I contemplate closing this chapter with a section on *how* we obey the command to humble ourselves, I see that the answer lies not in a new technique but in the previous chapters on repenting (*Demand #2*) and coming to Jesus (*Demand #3*) and believing in Jesus (*Demand #4*) and loving Jesus (Demand #5) and abiding in Jesus (*Demand #7*) and taking up our cross with Jesus (*Demand #8*). In all of this, the answer emerges: Humility does not flow directly from the performance of a self-renouncing will. The reason is that as soon as we renounce our will, we are aware of the accomplishment and are caught in the temptation to feel proud of this very act of renouncing. How can we escape this trap?

At the bottom, true humility senses that humility is a gift beyond our reach. If humility is the product of reaching, then we will instinctively feel proud of it. Humility is the gift to receive all things as a gift thankfully and unself-consciously. Perhaps I can end on a personal note about how I (imperfectly) fight this battle. On December 6, 1988, I made the following entry in my journal. It's my own confession of need and my answer to the question of how we humble ourselves.

> Is not the most effective way of bridling my delight in being made much of, to focus on making much of God? Self-denial and crucifixion of the flesh are essential, but O how easy it is to be made much of even for my self-denial! How shall this insidious motive

of pleasure in being made much of be broken except through bending all my faculties to delight in the pleasure of making much of God! Christian Hedonism[5] is the final solution. It is deeper than death to self. You have to go down deeper into the grave of the flesh to find the truly freeing stream of miracle water that ravishes you with the taste of God's glory. Only in that speechless, all-satisfying admiration is the end of self.

---

[5] For what this term refers to more fully see John Piper, *Desiring God: Meditations of a Christian Hedonist* (Sisters, Ore.: Multnomah, 2003). The summary sentence of Christian Hedonism is: God is most glorified in us when we are most satisfied in him. And so a Christian Hedonist is one who makes delighting in Jesus Christ the great pursuit of his life because he believes this pursuit is the best way to show that Jesus is the most glorious Reality in the universe.

DO NOT BE ANGRY—
TRUST GOD'S PROVIDENCE

You have heard that it was said to those of old, "You shall not murder; and whoever murders will be liable to judgment." But I say to you that everyone who is angry with his brother will be liable to judgment; whoever insults his brother will be liable to the council; and whoever says, "You fool!" will be liable to the hell of fire. —MATT. 5:21-22

Again and again we have seen that Jesus demands what we, by ourselves, cannot do. Sometimes, as with the command to love or to believe, we try to make his demands doable by defining them as mere external acts or mere decisions of the will. We think these are more in our control than our emotions are. Perhaps. But when it comes to anger, Jesus explicitly does the opposite of what we try to do in making his commands more external and more doable. He is saying that the external act of murder is wrong and, more radically, that the internal experience of anger behind it is wrong. So he demands (along with the Law of Moses) that we not *do* the external act of murder, but goes further and demands that we not *feel* the internal emotion of anger that lies behind the act.

NO ONE DECIDES TO GET ANGRY

We can feel how radical this is if we stop to ponder that no one *decides* to get angry. We don't see an outrageous act of heartless cruelty and injustice and then ponder whether anger would be a good response and then, after consideration, choose to start feeling the proper level of anger. Nobody lives that way. Anger happens. It's spontaneous. It is not a rational choice. It is an unpremeditated experience.[1] Something happens, and anger rises in our heart. What makes it rise when it does, and with the strength and duration it rises, is a combination of the evil we observe and the condition of our mind and heart. Jesus' demand, therefore, is not that we master the expressions of our anger with self-control, though that is often what duty requires. His demand is that there be a change in our condition. He is calling for a deep inward transformation of mind and heart that does not give rise to the anger we should not have. He described this change in different ways: for example, new birth (*Demand #1*) and repentance (*Demand #2*) and faith (*Demand #4*).

Therefore, what we say in this chapter about the command not to be angry is rooted in the other teachings of Jesus. He is not interested in mere psychological and emotional changes. He is interested in newborn disciples who live by faith in his saving work and present help. *He* shed his blood; *we* experience forgiveness (Matt. 26:28). *He* paid the ransom; *we* are freed from the condemnation and bondage of sin (Mark 10:45; John 8:32). *He* brought the kingdom of God; *we* experience God's transforming rule (Luke 11:20). *He* is the vine; *we* are the branches. Without him we can do nothing (John 15:5). That includes obeying the command not to be angry.

WHAT IS ANGER?

As with all emotions, which exist before words and independently of words, anger is hard to define with words. But we should try because evidently there are different experiences called anger, some of which are sinful and some of which are not. For example, in Mark 3:5 Jesus himself is angered by religious leaders who do not want him to heal a man on the Sabbath. "He looked around at them *with anger*, grieved

---

[1] I don't mean to imply that what we do with our wills has no effect on our anger. You can decide to dwell on an offense and so intensify your anger. You can choose to focus your attention on the mercy of Christ toward you and reduce your anger. But my point is that the actual experience is not controlled immediately by the will the way raising your right hand is.

at their hardness of heart." And Jesus repeatedly referred to *God's* anger either directly as the wrath of God in judgment (John 3:36; Luke 21:23) or indirectly in parables (Matt. 18:34; 22:7; Luke 14:21).

A standard English dictionary defines anger as "a strong feeling of displeasure and usually antagonism." The reason the phrase "a strong feeling of displeasure" can't stand by itself is that we don't think of really bad tasting food as awakening anger, even though there may be strong displeasure. That displeasure needs another component before it is experienced as anger. If someone keeps feeding us terrible food, and we sense that they are doing it intentionally, then we may get angry. Anger seems to be a more or less strong displeasure about something that is happening willfully and, we feel, should not be happening.

Of course, we do sometimes get angry when that is not the case. If we trip over a root, we may turn around and kick the root in anger. If we bump our head on the kitchen cabinet, we may smack the cabinet door in anger. But in our best moments we look at those reactions as foolish. We intuitively sense that we are imputing willfulness to the root and the cabinet, as if they did something to us on purpose.

This is why the young Jonathan Edwards resolved not to get angry at inanimate objects. His Resolution #15 said, "*Resolved, Never to suffer the least motions of anger towards irrational beings.*"[2] Therefore, the difference between anger and other emotions of displeasure is that anger involves strong displeasure with something that is happening intentionally that we think should not be happening.

JESUS' ANGER AND OURS

If Jesus, as the ideal human being, could feel and express anger, we are compelled to ask what he is prohibiting in Matthew 5:22 when he said, "Everyone who is angry with his brother will be liable to judgment." In his human perfection he wove a whip and turned over the

---

[2] Jonathan Edwards, *Memoirs of Jonathan Edwards, A. M.,* in *The Works of Jonathan Edwards,* ed. Edward Hickman, 2 vols. (Edinburgh: Banner of Truth, 1974), I:xxi.

tables of the money-changers in the temple (John 2:15; Matt. 21:12). He felt anger and grief in the synagogue (Mark 3:5). He called the scribes and Pharisees children of hell (Matt. 23:15) and "blind fools" (Matt. 23:17) and "whitewashed tombs" (Matt. 23:27).

I do not assume that Jesus alone is permitted to experience anger because he is the Son of God and that no other humans may. The Bible that he read and affirmed (John 10:35; Matt. 5:18) described the anger of holy men of old (Exod. 32:19; Num. 16:15; Neh. 5:6; Ps. 4:4). I think the solution is found rather in trying to define what makes anger good and what makes it bad. He helps us do this both in the context of Matthew 5:22 and in the other things that he said. Let's look first at the other things he said, then come back to the context of Matthew 5:22.

I see at least five factors in Jesus' teaching that govern whether an experience of anger is legitimate or not. They can be described with five key words. In this chapter, we will deal with three of them: *love*, *proportion*, and *providence*. In the next chapter we will deal with *mercy* and *servanthood* as they relate to anger.

LOVE AND ANGER

For human anger to be good, it must be governed by love for those who make us angry. Jesus said, "Love your enemies and pray for those who persecute you . . . do good to those who hate you, bless those who curse you" (Matt. 5:44; Luke 6:27-28). These commands exert a controlling effect on the nature of our anger. They tell us that legitimate anger may not delight in or desire the damnation of the ones who make us angry. If our anger is going to be good, it must be governed by our obedience to the command to bless and pray for and do good to those who make us angry.

This shapes the very definition of anger. If we assume that anger *always* involves feelings of vindictiveness and vengeance and hostility, then by definition good anger is impossible. But that is not the only way godly people have experienced anger. Jesus' own experience of anger tells us that good anger does exist. Therefore, we should define it so that it may be governed by love. In other words,

we should assume that with Jesus' help we can be angry with someone and at the same time pray for him, bless him, and do good to
him. This anger would be a strong displeasure with what they have
done—and even with the corrupt heart from which the deed came—
but at the same time we would desire their good and pray for it and
work for it. Such anger would not have to be evil.

PROPORTION AND ANGER

Jesus teaches that a holy response to evil should be proportion-
ate to its degrees of moral flagrancy. For example, he illustrates
God's purpose to punish some people worse than others with this
parable:

> That servant who knew his master's will but did not get ready or
> act according to his will, will receive a severe beating. But the one
> who did not know, and did what deserved a beating, will receive
> a light beating. Everyone to whom much was given, of him much
> will be required, and from him to whom they entrusted much,
> they will demand the more. (Luke 12:47-48)

One implication from these words is that if punishment should vary
because of different degrees of evil, then so should the degrees of
anger in response to evil.

In other words, our anger should be governed not only by our
love for the one who makes us angry, but also by the seriousness
of his offense. If our anger is out of proportion to the offense, it is
not good anger. This is more obvious when we think of not being
angrier than the offense deserves. We have all experienced an anger
that is more intense than the offense calls for. A father raging against
a three-year-old son and hitting him uncontrollably would be a clear
example of anger that is out of proportion.

It is less obvious that too little anger might be a fault as well.
The absence of anger in the presence of evil is not necessarily a fault.
Jesus clearly tells us not to be angry with our brother (at least in
some circumstances), which implies that there must be situations in

which anger would seem to be natural, but we should not have it. How that is possible we will see in a moment. But for now we must also say that there are *bad* reasons for not getting angry as well as good ones. A person may be undiscerning or insensible about the seriousness of sin, the offense that it is to God, and the damage it can do to people. The absence of anger in such a case is disproportionate to the seriousness of evil and is not good.

PROVIDENCE AND ANGER

One of the greatest truths that Jesus taught to help us be free from sinful anger is the truth of God's all-encompassing providence—that is, his wise and sovereign control over all things for the good of his children. The rise and strength of our anger should be governed by our trust in God's providence—that he is ruling over the evil that makes us angry and will not let anything befall us that is not ultimately good for us.

The rage that could rise in our hearts when we are treated unjustly and when we watch loved ones treated cruelly would be natural and strong. When dealing with these threats, Jesus spoke directly to our fear, not our anger. But the implications for anger are plain. He said, "Do not fear those who kill the body but cannot kill the soul. Rather fear him who can destroy both soul and body in hell. Are not two sparrows sold for a penny? And not one of them will fall to the ground apart from your Father. But even the hairs of your head are all numbered. Fear not, therefore; you are of more value than many sparrows" (Matt. 10:28-31).

The point is, first, that the smallest details of life on earth are governed by God—not a bird falls to the ground apart from him. And the second point is that God is near, and his acquaintance with our situation is total—even the hairs of your head are all numbered. Conclusion: Nothing will befall you apart from his wise and loving providence over your circumstances. Don't fear. And, by implication, don't be angry in a way that contradicts your confidence in God's care over your life. God's providence should change the way we experience circumstances that would otherwise be totally infuriating.

When he was predicting what would befall his disciples in the future Jesus said, "You will be delivered up even by parents and brothers and relatives and friends, and some of you they will put to death. You will be hated by all for my name's sake. But not a hair of your head will perish" (Luke 21:16-18). Here again we are assured in a shocking way that even if we are killed for Christ ("some of you they will put to death"), nevertheless we will be totally safe—"not a hair of your head will perish." God's providence will govern all the evil that comes against us so that his good purposes are fulfilled. This will have an effect on the way we experience anger. Evil is being done, but it does not have the last say, and in the end even serves God's hidden designs. There may be anger, but the bitterness and sting and hostility of it will be removed by this confidence.

REJOICE IN PERSECUTION

One of the clearest illustrations of how God's providence overcomes the controlling effect of anger is Jesus' command that we rejoice when we are persecuted unjustly. He says, "Blessed are you when others revile you and persecute you and utter all kinds of evil against you falsely on my account. Rejoice and be glad, for your reward is great in heaven, for so they persecuted the prophets who were before you" (Matt. 5:11-12). Few things would ordinarily make us angrier than such unjust treatment. Not only are we being hurt by this reviling and persecution, but Jesus emphasizes that it is "evil" and it is "false." These factors tend to infuriate us.

But Jesus utterly transforms that ordinary, understandable emotional experience of anger. Instead of saying, "Be legitimately angry," or "Try to control your anger," he says the most incredible thing imaginable: "Rejoice and be glad." The language in Luke 6:23 is even more extraordinary. He says, "Rejoice in that day, and *leap* for joy." Anger at being persecuted unjustly cannot be unaffected by this command. Our rage at unjust treatment cannot remain untransformed if we rejoice over the same treatment.

Rejoicing does not mean that we approve of the treatment. It does not mean that we stop thinking it is unjust. It probably does not mean there is *no* anger whatsoever. Some kind of holy anger—strong emotional disapproval—may be emotionally compatible with joy. The human soul in the image of God is that complex. And we know, from all that Jesus taught us about God, that God experiences anger and joy simultaneously because he sees and responds perfectly to all evil and all good at the same time.[3]

Our joy in the presence of persecution is possible because of God's providence. Not a hair of your head will perish (when they kill you). Not a bird (or a hateful blow to your head) falls without the will of your Father. Providence governs your suffering. And in the end, "Your reward is great in heaven." This is Jesus' argument why joy and not anger can dominate our experience of persecution: "Rejoice and be glad, *for your reward is great in heaven*" (Matt. 5:12). Therefore, good anger is governed by faith in the all-wise, all-powerful, merciful providence of God.

---

[3] Jesus, for example, taught us that God feeds all the birds and clothes all the lilies in the world (Matt. 6:26-30), and that no bird falls to the ground apart from his attention (Matt. 10:29), and that every hair of our head is known and numbered (Matt. 10:30), and that in all the hostilities of life not a hair of our head perishes (Luke 21:18). In other words, God is perfectly aware of every micro-detail of what happens in the world, and his wrath (John 3:36) and joy (Luke 15:7) happen in perfect proportion to what he sees. Since there is unbelief and repentance happening simultaneously all the time, he is able to respond to both with different emotions simultaneously all the time.

DO NOT BE ANGRY—
EMBRACE MERCY AND
FORGIVENESS

*"Lord, how often will my brother sin against me, and I forgive
him? As many as seven times?" Jesus said to him, "I do not say to
you seven times, but seventy times seven."*—MATT. 18:21-22

*First take the log out of your own eye, and then you will see clearly
to take the speck out of your brother's eye.*—MATT. 7:5

MERCY AND ANGER

Anger is not only influenced by God's providence assuring us of his
present care and future reward (as we saw in the previous chapter), it is also governed by the heartfelt memory that the forgiveness
of our sins is owing to mammoth mercy. Jesus teaches that living
with the awareness that we are forgiven felons (because of assaults
on God's honor) will break the power of unrighteous anger in our
lives. He illustrates this when his disciples ask about how often they
should forgive people.

Jesus' disciples are aware of how maddening it can be when
someone sins against us not just once, but over and over. Few things
make us angrier. So Jesus' disciple, Peter, said to him, "Lord, how
often will my brother sin against me, and I forgive him? As many as
seven times?" Jesus said to him, "I do not say to you seven times,
but seventy times seven" (Matt. 18:21-22). The question cries out to
be asked, how in the world is that possible when someone has hurt
us for the hundredth time?

Jesus answers with a parable about the kingdom of heaven that shows how closely the kingdom is tied to the power to forgive. He says to Peter and the others who can hear, "Therefore the kingdom of heaven may be compared to a king who wished to settle accounts with his servants" (Matt. 18:23). It is significant that he calls this parable a comparison to the kingdom of heaven. That means that the triumph over anger through forgiveness is a part of God's rule (kingdom) in the lives of his people. Forgiveness is not simply a psychological technique for managing human relationships—it is the work of God and the fruit of the forgiveness that Jesus said he would obtain with his own blood (Matt. 26:28).

How We Forgive Seventy Times Seven

The parable says that a king had a servant who owed him the staggering amount of ten thousand talents (Matt. 18:24). "The giant size of this amount is illuminated by the fact that King Herod had a yearly income of about 900 talents, and that Galilee and Peraea [the 'land beyond the Jordan'], in the year 4 BC brought in 200 talents in taxes."[1] So it appears that either this amount is an intentional exaggeration (as when we say "zillions" of dollars), or this servant was a high-ranking official who had the connections to embezzle huge amounts from the king's treasury over many years. In any case, Jesus describes his debt as virtually incalculable.

The king threatened to sell him and his family. But "the servant fell on his knees, imploring him, 'Have patience with me, and I will pay you everything' [an impossibility, it seems, in view of the amount]. And out of pity for him, the master of that servant released him and forgave him the debt" (Matt. 18:26-27). This forgiveness is as spectacular as the size of the debt. That is the point. Jesus wants us to realize that sin is an incalculable debt to God. We could never pay it back. We can never settle accounts with God. No amount of

---

[1] Walter Grundman, *Das Evangelium Nach Matthäus* (Berlin: Evangelische Verlagsanstalt, 1968), 423.

penance or good works or apologies can pay the debt of dishonor
we have heaped upon God by our sins.

But this servant did not receive this forgiveness for what it
was—stunning, undeserved, heart-humbling, mercy-awakening.
Jesus reports no word of gratitude and no word of amazement from
this servant. Incredible! He simply tells the incomprehensible events
that happened next: "When that same servant went out, he found
one of his fellow servants who owed him a hundred denarii [one
denarius was a day's wage for a laborer], and seizing him, he began
to choke him, saying, 'Pay what you owe.' So his fellow servant fell
down and pleaded with him, 'Have patience with me, and I will pay
you.' He refused and went and put him in prison until he should pay
the debt" (Matt. 18:28-30). In other words, this man's experience
of "forgiveness" from the king did not change his anger. He seized
and choked his fellow servant.

The king heard of it and was (legitimately!) angry (Matt. 18:34).
He said to him, "You wicked servant! I forgave you all that debt
because you pleaded with me. And should not you have had mercy
on your fellow servant, as I had mercy on you?" The king "delivered
him to the jailers, until he should pay all his debt" (Matt. 18:32-33).
The conclusion to the parable goes straight to the heart of the issue
of anger and forgiveness. Jesus says, "So also my heavenly Father
will do to every one of you, if you do not forgive your brother from
your heart" (Matt. 18:35).

The point of this parable is that God has no obligation to save
a person who claims to be his disciple if that professing disciple has
not received the gift of forgiveness for what it really is—infinitely
precious, amazing, undeserved, heart-humbling, mercy-awakening.
If we claim to be forgiven by Jesus, but there is no sweetness of
forgiveness in our hearts for other people, God's forgiveness is not
there (cf. Matt. 6:14-15; Mark 11:25).[2]

---

[2] The point of Jesus' parable is not to address the larger issue of whether we can truly experience the forgiveness of God and then lose that forgiveness. We have seen in *Demand #7* that Jesus teaches that he will not let any of his true disciples fall away. The point of this parable is that divinely offered forgiveness that does not transform our lives into forgiving people will not save us.

Remember, this parable was told to help Peter deal with Jesus' demand to forgive seventy times seven (Matt. 18:22). That is, it was told to help us deal with the anger that naturally arises in our hearts when someone hurts us for the hundredth time. The solution, Jesus says, is to live in the overwhelmingly amazed awareness that we have been forgiven a debt larger than all the wrongs ever done against us. Or to put it another way: We should live in the astonished awareness that God's anger against us has been removed, though we have sinned against him far more than seventy times seven. The effect of this awareness is a broken, contrite, tenderhearted joy. And this brokenhearted joy governs our anger. The only good anger is the kind that is shaped by this humble heart.

"First Take the Log Out of Your Own Eye"

One other saying of Jesus confirms how he designs mercy as a way of governing our experience of anger. One of the ways that anger expresses itself is in judging others. Jesus gave us a demand in this regard:

> Judge not, that you be not judged. For with the judgment you pronounce you will be judged, and with the measure you use it will be measured to you. Why do you see the speck that is in your brother's eye, but do not notice the log that is in your own eye? Or how can you say to your brother, "Let me take the speck out of your eye," when there is the log in your own eye? You hypocrite, first take the log out of your own eye, and then you will see clearly to take the speck out of your brother's eye. (Matt. 7:1-5)

The command not to judge sounds as absolute as the command not to be angry. "Judge not, that you be not judged." But what follows the command shows us that there is a kind of judging that is bad and a kind of judging that is necessary and good—just like there is good and bad anger. When Jesus says, "First take the log out of your own eye, and then you will see clearly to take the speck out of your brother's eye," he shows that it is necessary to make judgments about the speck in a brother's eye. What turns this kind, caring, healing judgment into the judgmentalism that Jesus forbids is the failure to see the log in our own eye.

It is the same as the unforgiving servant failing to live in the awareness of the "log-debt" that he had been forgiven (ten thousand talents), so that he could gladly forgive the "speck-debt" of his brother (one hundred denarii). Jesus assumes that when we see the log in our own eye, we know how to remove it—that is, we know how to find forgiveness and help from Jesus. Otherwise the delicate procedure of removing the speck from the eye of our brother would not be possible. You can't do delicate, loving eye surgery with a log hanging out of your eye.

So the point of Jesus' words about judging are to show us how the anger of judgmentalism can be broken. It is broken by a broken heart. We live in the consciousness of our own great sinfulness and in the awareness that only the mercy of Jesus can take the log out of our eye with forgiveness and healing. This awareness turns angry judgment into patient and loving forbearance and delicate correction. Legitimate anger may remain because we are displeased that eye-specks bedevil people we love. But that anger is not the anger of judgmentalism. Good anger is governed by the experience of mercy.

SERVANTHOOD AND ANGER

We are tempted to be angry not only when we are repeatedly hurt, but when we are told what to do by others—especially if we don't want to do it. This anger is often rooted in the kind of pride that does not feel any duty or joy in servanthood. But everything Jesus teaches about serving others leads us to experience servanthood another way (cf. *Demand #17*). Central to being a disciple of Jesus is the willingness to embrace self-denial and cross-bearing: "If anyone would come after me, let him deny himself and take up his cross and follow me" (Matt. 16:24).

Jesus goes to the cross to die for others. He calls us to go with him and, if necessary, die for others. This readiness to suffer as a part of following Jesus gives rise to a spirit of servanthood that does not get angry when demands are put upon us. Jesus used an amazing phrase to express this: "slave of all." He said, "Whoever would be first among you must be *slave of all*. For even the Son of Man came not to be served but to serve, and to give his life as a ransom for many" (Mark 10:44-45).

Jesus does not mean that following him is a begrudging, joyless affair. "These things I have spoken to you, that my *joy* may be in you, and that your joy may be full" (John 15:11). Martin Luther captured the joyful spirit of Christian "slavery" when he said in 1520, "A Christian man is the most free lord of all, and subject to none;[3] a Christian man is the most dutiful servant of all, and subject to every one."[4] We are not our own. We belong to Jesus. What he bids us do, we do—lest we hear him say, "Why do you call me 'Lord, Lord,' and not do what I tell you?" (Luke 6:46).

This spirit of submission transforms the experience of anger. As "slaves of all," the emotional experience of being required to do things we didn't plan to do is not the same as it would be if we were *lords of all*. For Jesus' sake the slave rejoices to serve the good of others. He says with his Master, "My food is to do the will of him who sent me and to accomplish his work" (John 4:34). What we were sent to do is serve. Good anger is governed by the contentment Jesus gives in serving others, even those who do not deserve it.

WHAT KIND OF ANGER IS JESUS PROHIBITING?

We return now to Jesus' prohibition of anger. "You have heard that it was said to those of old, 'You shall not murder; and whoever murders will be liable to judgment.' But I say to you that everyone who is angry with his brother will be liable to judgment" (Matt. 5:21-22). In view of all we have seen, I would make the observation

---

[3] This is what Jesus meant when he said to Simon Peter, "'What do you think, Simon? From whom do kings of the earth take toll or tax? From their sons or from others?' And when he said, 'From others,' Jesus said to him, 'Then the sons are free'" (Matt. 17:25-26). Then to show that the free sons (disciples) are also servants, he told Peter to pay anyway (Matt. 17:27).
[4] Martin Luther, "The Freedom of a Christian," in *Three Treatises* (Philadelphia: Fortress, 1960), 277.

here that the anger Jesus is forbidding is the anger behind murder. In other words, he is intensifying the command not to murder. He is pointing out that it is not only the act of murder but the feeling behind it that is worthy of condemnation. In other words, he is not prohibiting all anger but the kind that leads toward murder.

This focus of his prohibition is confirmed by the two illustrations he gives next: "Whoever insults his brother will be liable to the council; and whoever says, 'You fool!' will be liable to the hell of fire" (Matt. 5:22). These refer to *external* actions, not just internal anger. Therefore, they reveal the kind of anger Jesus has in mind. In his mind, as he condemns anger, anger is a strong feeling of displeasure *including* feelings of contempt and hostility that seek expression in murder or pejorative name-calling. All *such* anger he forbids. But I do not assume from this that Jesus would condemn *all* anger, especially his own (Mark 3:5). All of his other teachings guide us in discerning whether our anger is justified, especially the teachings we dealt with under the headings of love, proportion, providence, mercy, and servanthood.

The Vine Is the Source for Stilling the Force of Anger

Nevertheless, the demand not to be angry is radical and devastating. It puts us face to face with the impossibility of saving ourselves. Jesus' demand is not something we can do in our own power. Becoming angry is not a choice we make. It is a fruit on the branch of our lives. The question is: What vine are we a part of? And whose fruit will we bear? The demand of Jesus not to be angry is, therefore, also a demand that we abide in him as our vine. "Whoever abides in me and I in him, he it is that bears much fruit, for apart from me you can do nothing" (John 15:5).

Do the Will of My Father Who Is in Heaven—Be Justified by Trusting Jesus

Not everyone who says to me, "Lord, Lord," will enter the king-dom of heaven, but the one who does the will of my Father who is in heaven.—Matt. 7:21

If you would enter life, keep the commandments.—Matt. 19:17

The tax collector, standing far off, would not even lift up his eyes to heaven, but beat his breast, saying, "God, be merciful to me, a sinner!" I tell you, this man went down to his house justified, rather than the other. For everyone who exalts himself will be humbled, but the one who humbles himself will be exalted.—Luke 18:13-14

External Conformity to Laws Is Not Enough

A wealthy man asked Jesus, "Good Teacher, what must I do to inherit eternal life?" (Mark 10:17). Jesus answered his question in two steps. First, he said, "You know the commandments: 'Do not murder, Do not commit adultery, Do not steal, Do not bear false witness, Do not defraud, Honor your father and mother'" (Mark 10:19). In other words, he connected eternal life with keeping God's law. "If you would enter life, keep the commandments" (Matt. 19:17).

The man responded, "Teacher, all these I have kept from my youth" (Mark 10:20). Was this true? Maybe at one level it was. Perhaps there were no external behaviors that contradicted God's laws. But what about his heart? Jesus had said in another place, "Unless your righteousness exceeds that of the scribes and Pharisees, you will never enter the kingdom of heaven" (Matt. 5:20; see *Demands #25-27*). The problem with these rigorous law-keepers was that they focused on externals alone: "Woe to you, scribes and Pharisees, hypocrites! For you clean the outside of the cup and the plate, but inside they are full of greed and self-indulgence" (Matt. 23:25). Was that true of this wealthy man?

The second step in Jesus' answer to the man's question reveals a serious problem in his heart. Jesus said, "You lack one thing: go, sell all that you have and give to the poor, and you will have treasure in heaven; and come, follow me" (Mark 10:21). This is amazing. He says he only lacks "one thing." Presumably if he had that one thing, then he would be perfect. In fact, that's the way Matthew records Jesus words, "If you would *be perfect*, go, sell what you possess and give to the poor, and you will have treasure in heaven; and come, follow me" (Matt. 19:21). So he is *not* perfect. He has not kept God's law perfectly. And therefore he will not inherit eternal life unless this "one thing" happens that he is missing.

"You Lack One Thing"

What is this "one thing"? It sounds like three things: Sell what you possess, give it to the poor, follow me. How are these three demands really one? These demands may be summed up like this: "Your attachment to your possessions needs to be replaced by an attachment to me." It is as though the man stood there with his hands full of money and Jesus said, "You lack one thing; reach out and take my hands." To do this the man must open his fingers and let the money fall. The "one thing" is not what falls out of his hands, but what he takes into his hands.

When a person treasures Jesus above money, the poor are always the beneficiaries. That's why Jesus mentions the poor. But the main point concerns what is happening between this man and Jesus. "You lack one thing. You lack me. Stop treasuring money, and start treasuring me. You want to inherit eternal life. You want to enter the kingdom of heaven. I am the treasure of heaven. If you would have treasure in heaven, you must have me. If you prefer money over me now, you will not enter heaven where I am the treasure. But if you treasure me now above your money, 'you will have treasure in heaven.' I will be there. Only by your attachment to me will you inherit eternal life. If you would be perfect—which is the only way into God's kingdom—follow me."

PERFECTION THROUGH JESUS

This is a critical lesson for us. Jesus does not scorn the law of God. He does not say that keeping the commandments is unimportant. He says, "If you depend on keeping the commandments alone, you will not inherit eternal life. There will always be something lacking." The standards of the law are perfection. "You therefore must be perfect," Jesus said, "as your heavenly Father is perfect" (Matt. 5:48). He does not lower that standard. Instead, he demands it from the whole world. And then he offers it through attachment with himself. "If you would be perfect . . . come, follow me." Jesus is the only path to perfect obedience. And perfect obedience is required for eternal life.

The crucial question is: *How* is Jesus the path to perfection? One historic answer is that Jesus himself is our perfection. That is, when we are connected with him by faith, God counts us to be perfect because of Jesus, even though in ourselves we are not. Another historic answer is that Jesus, by his presence and power within us, transforms us so that we really begin to love like he does and move toward perfection, which we finally obtain in heaven. It seems to me that Jesus gives us good reason to believe that both of these answers are true.

Jesus said that he came "to give his life as a ransom for many" (Mark 10:45) and that his blood would be "poured out for many for the forgiveness of sins" (Matt. 26:28) and that believing in him as he was lifted up on the cross would give eternal life to undeserv-ing sinners (John 3:14-15). All of this implies that Jesus' life and death are our only hope of escaping wrath (John 3:36) and obtain-ing heaven. Jesus said concerning the most intentional law-keepers in Israel, "None of you keeps the law" (John 7:19). And he very bluntly called even his disciples "evil." "If you then, *who are evil*, know how to give good gifts to your children, how much more will your Father who is in heaven give good things to those who ask him!" (Matt. 7:11). In other words, all humans are sinners under God's holy wrath with no hope of eternal life based on their own obedience. Jesus came to solve that problem.

Jesus solves it by removing the wrath of God. He removes it by enduring the punishment we deserved and paying the debt we could never pay (see *Demand #11*). Therefore, because of Jesus' shed blood, all our sins are canceled and God does not see us as sinful or imperfect anymore. This is owing to our attachment to Jesus by faith.

"This Man Went Down to His House Justified"

But Jesus teaches that there is more to our perfection than the absence of guilt. He tells a parable of a Pharisee and a tax collector who went up to the temple to pray. These two men represent the groups that were popularly viewed as most righteous (the Pharisees) and most sinful (the Jewish tax collectors, who compromised them-selves by working for the Romans and fleeced their own people to line their pockets).

The Pharisee highlighted his obedience to the law: "I am not like other men, extortioners, unjust, adulterers, or even like this tax collector. I fast twice a week; I give tithes of all that I get" (Luke 18:11-12). But the tax collector, Jesus says, "standing far off, would not even lift up his eyes to heaven, but beat his breast, saying, 'God, be merciful to me, a sinner!' I tell you, this man went down to his house *justified*, rather than the other" (Luke 18:13-14).

The word "justified" is crucial. It captures the very purpose of the parable. Luke introduced this parable by saying: "He also told this parable to some *who trusted in themselves that they were righteous*, and treated others with contempt" (Luke 18:9). Therefore, the parable is dealing with the question of how to be "righteous" before God.

The word "justified" and the word "righteous" are built on the same word in the original Greek. The verb means to "declare righteous" the way a judge does in a courtroom. He does not *make* a defendant righteous. He *recognizes and declares* him as righteous. This is the way the verb is used in Luke 7:29. "When all the people heard this . . . they *declared God just* [literally, they justified God]." Justifying God cannot mean *making* God just or righteous. It means declaring him to be righteous. That is what God does to the tax collector in Luke 18:14: "This man went down to his house *justified*"—that is, this man was declared by God to be righteous.

So the parable dramatically contrasts those who "trusted in themselves that they were righteous" (because of their extensive law-keeping) with those who despaired of their own righteousness and looked away from themselves to the mercy of God to declare them righteous even though they were not. Note carefully that in this parable those "who trusted in themselves that they were righteous" were even willing to give God the credit for the ability to produce this righteousness: "God, *I thank you* that I am not like other men" (Luke 18:11). But that was to no avail. Our own righteousness, even if produced by God's grace, is not a sufficient foundation for vindication in God's holy presence.

THE RICH MAN NEEDS JESUS FOR HIS RIGHTEOUSNESS

Jesus does not go into detail about how his own obedience and death provides the foundation for justification, but we have good reason to think God's declaration of righteousness is given to sinners who look to Jesus as their only hope of acceptance with God. Jesus said to the wealthy man, "Your law-keeping will not get you into the kingdom. You are not perfect. 'You lack one thing.' Come to *me*."

Jesus was what he lacked. If being declared righteous, though he was not, was the man's only hope (as the parable of the tax collector shows[1]), then Jesus is the foundation of that declaration. That is why the man must let go of his money and come to Jesus.

So in one sense the perfection that the rich man lacked is found in Jesus. God will count the man as perfect if he stops depending on his money and starts depending on Jesus. That is the first historic answer to the question, how is Jesus the path to perfection? In relationship to him we are counted as perfect, even though we are still sinners. This is what it means to be justified. We will deal with the second answer in the next chapter, namely, that Jesus, by his presence and power within us, transforms us so that we really begin to love like he does and move toward perfection.

---

[1] It is significant that Luke weaves together first the parable of the Pharisee and the tax collector (Luke 18:9-14), with a word about needing to receive the kingdom like a child (Luke 18:15-17), with the story of the rich ruler who lacks one thing, namely, Jesus, to complete his obedience (Luke 18:18-23). It is as though the truth of the justification of the ungodly by faith is being illustrated in the following stories.

Do the Will of My Father Who Is in Heaven—Be Transformed by Trusting Jesus

Whoever does the will of God, he is my brother and sister and mother. —MARK 3:35

Blessed rather are those who hear the word of God and keep it! —LUKE 11:28

Not everyone who says to me, "Lord, Lord," will enter the kingdom of heaven, but the one who does the will of my Father who is in heaven. —MATT. 7:21

We saw in the previous chapter that the rich man who was seeking eternal life "lacked one thing." If he "would be perfect," he needed Jesus (Matt. 19:21). Jesus is the path to perfection. But *how* is he the path to perfection? The last chapter answered: by being the basis of our perfection before God as we trust him. Now we turn to another answer, which is also true: Jesus, by his presence and power within us, transforms us so that we really begin to love like he does and move toward perfection.

SOME MEASURE OF REAL, LIVED-OUT OBEDIENCE
IS REQUIRED

The answer of the last chapter by itself does not account fully for Jesus speaking the way he does about doing the will of God. Jesus says that doing the will of God really is necessary for our final entrance into the kingdom of heaven. "Not everyone who says to me, 'Lord, Lord,' will enter the kingdom of heaven, but the one who does the will of my Father who is in heaven" (Matt. 7:21). He says that on the day of judgment he really will reject people because they are "workers of lawlessness." "Then will I declare to them, 'I never knew you; depart from me, you workers of lawlessness'" (Matt. 7:23). He says people will "go away into eternal punishment" because they really failed to love their fellow believers: "As you did not do it to one of the least of these, you did not do it to me" (Matt. 25:45-46).

There is no doubt that Jesus saw some measure of real, lived-out obedience to the will of God as necessary for final salvation. "Whoever does the will of God, he is my brother and sister and mother" (Mark 3:35). So the second historic answer to the question, how is Jesus the path to perfection? has been that he enables us to change. He transforms us so that we really begin to love like he does and thus move toward perfection that we finally obtain in heaven.

I say it that way because Jesus does not give us any indication that we can be perfected in this present age. He teaches us to pray the Lord's Prayer, and he puts right beside the petition "Give us this day our daily bread," the petition "Forgive us our debts, as we also have forgiven our debtors" (Matt. 6:11-12). In other words, just as we pray daily for bread, we should pray daily for forgiveness. Therefore, Jesus does not anticipate a time in this age when we will not need daily forgiveness.

That is why I say Jesus transforms us so that we really *begin* to love like he does so that we move *toward* perfection that we *finally obtain in heaven*. But though our lived-out perfection only comes in heaven, Jesus really does transform us now, and this transformation is really necessary for final salvation. But the *way* our new behavior is necessary is different from the way trusting Jesus for our perfection is necessary. Trusting Jesus connects us with him. Then, because of Jesus' work alone, God counts us righteous, even before our behavior is transformed. The tax collector who cried out, "God, be merciful to me, a sinner!" (Luke 18:13) would not dare point to any righteous behavior in himself as the basis of his justification. He looked away from what he was and pled for mercy. God declared him righteous before his behavior changed. Therefore, trusting Jesus is necessary in order to be connected to Jesus who is the foundation of our justification. But new, transformed behavior is necessary as the *fruit* and *evidence* of this connection with Jesus.

EVERY HEALTHY TREE BEARS GOOD FRUIT

We saw in *Demand #7* that being connected with Jesus by faith results in a new life of love. That's the fruit Jesus produces as he works within us: "I am the vine; you are the branches. Whoever abides in me and I in him, he it is that bears much fruit, for apart from me you can do nothing" (John 15:5). In another place he makes it clear that being a "healthy tree"—that is, being a person who truly believes in him—will bear good fruit: "Every healthy tree bears good fruit, but the diseased tree bears bad fruit" (Matt. 7:17).

The fruit does not make the tree good. The tree makes the fruit good. Good deeds do not attach us to Jesus. They are not the ground of our being declared righteous. Trusting Jesus connects us with Jesus. This connection results in God's declaration that we are perfect, and this same connection releases the power that produces fruit. The reason Jesus can say, "Every tree that does not bear good fruit is cut down and thrown into the fire" (Matt. 7:19) is not because the fruit is the basis of our acceptance with God—the tax collector had no fruit to offer—but because the absence of fruit shows we are not connected to Jesus.[1]

---

[1] Though it may cause confusion, it is possible to use the word "justify" to describe how the fruit of good behavior works in the day of judgment. The fruits can "justify" us in the sense of proving that we are believers and belong to Jesus and have a right standing with God in him. That is how I understand Matthew 12:37, "By your words you will be *justified*, and by your words you will be condemned." It is as though the Judge said, "The evidence is compelling: Your words warrant the judgment that you are a true believer in my Son and have rested your case with him and banked on his righteousness for acceptance in this court." Or: "Your words justify [warrant, validate] the conclusion of this court that you have trusted in the righteousness of Jesus Christ for your justification in this court."

Therefore, when Jesus demands that we do the will of his Father who is in heaven, he means two things. First, he means, "Believe in me as your only hope for a perfect righteousness that is not your own. This perfection is the foundation of your acceptance with God and your inheritance of eternal life." This is why, when people asked him, "What must we do, to be doing the works of God?" he could simply answer, "This is the work of God, that you *believe* in him whom he has sent" (John 6:28-29). Believing in Jesus is the first and most essential aspect of God's will for us. Second, he means, "This same faith that attaches you to me for justification also attaches you to me the way a branch relies on a vine, and in this way you bear the fruit of love that fulfills the law of God in real, lived-out behavior."

IS GOD'S WILL TODAY EXPRESSED IN THE OLD TESTAMENT LAW?

Looking back now to the wealthy man who came to Jesus and asked, "Good Teacher, what must I do to inherit eternal life?" (Mark 10:17), how does the keeping of the law fit into Jesus' answer? Jesus' first answer to the man was, "If you would enter life, keep the commandments" (Matt. 19:17). We have seen that even though commandment-keeping will never provide a righteousness good enough to gain acceptance with God, nevertheless, the effort to do God's will is essential. The question now is, is God's will today expressed in the Old Testament law? A simple yes would be misleading. And a simple no would be misleading. Rather we must say something like: Yes, provided the law is filtered through the sieve of all the changes brought about by Jesus, who is the goal and fulfillment of the law.

Jesus said, "Everything written about me in the Law of Moses and the Prophets and the Psalms must be fulfilled" (Luke 24: 44). The Law and the Prophets were all aiming toward Jesus. Not surprisingly, when he came they would be fulfilled and changed. Jesus spoke about this change carefully and respectfully: "Do not think that I have come to abolish the Law or the Prophets; I have not come to abolish them but to fulfill them. For truly, I say to you, until heaven and earth pass away, not an iota, not a dot, will pass from the Law until all is accomplished" (Matt. 5:17-18).

Abolition is not Jesus' purpose. Fulfillment is. And when the law is fulfilled in Jesus, its original use changes dramatically. A new era has dawned, and Jesus' followers will relate to the law differently than Israel did. That's why Jesus said, "The Law and the Prophets were until John [the Baptist]; since then the good news of the kingdom of God is preached, and everyone forces his way into it" (Luke 16:16).

HOW OUR EXPERIENCE OF THE LAW CHANGES WITH THE COMING OF JESUS

Here is a simple sketch of the changes that have happened in our experience of the law since Jesus has come.

First, when Jesus taught that "whatever goes into a person from outside cannot defile him" (Mark 7:18), he virtually nullified the Old Testament ceremonial laws. Mark makes this simple comment, "Thus he declared all foods clean" (Mark 7:19). "On his own authority alone, Jesus set aside the principle of ceremonial purity embodied in much of the Mosaic legislation."[2] From now on "the sons are free" (Matt. 17:26), and we may eat or not eat according to what love demands.

Second, I mention love as the central criterion of our behavior because this is a second thing Jesus did in regard to changing how we experience the law: He said that it was all summed up in love. "So whatever you wish that others would do to you, do also to them, for this is the Law and the Prophets" (Matt. 7:12). In saying this, Jesus directed us away from a focus on the commandments per se and toward a relationship with himself that bears the law-fulfilling fruit of love (see *Demand #32*).

Third, Jesus told a parable about the owner of a vineyard whose tenants would not give him his produce. He repeatedly sent them servants whom the tenants beat. Finally, he sent his son whom they

---

[2] George Ladd, *The Presence of the Future* (Grand Rapids, Mich.: Eerdmans, 1974), 285.

killed. All this represented God's relation to Israel as a people. The great majority of them did not render the fruit of worship and obedience, and finally they killed the Son of God (Matt. 21:33-41). Jesus asked his listeners what the owner should do. They said, "He will put those wretches to a miserable death and let out the vineyard to other tenants who will give him the fruits in their seasons" (Matt. 21:41). Jesus applied this correct answer to his Jewish listeners in a cataclysmic way, signifying a huge change in the law.

He said, "Therefore I tell you, the kingdom of God will be taken away from you [Israel] and given to a people producing its fruits" (Matt. 21:43). In other words, God is turning his primary redemptive focus from Israel to the Gentile nations (see *Demand #50*). The people of God would no longer be defined by ethnicity or by participation in the theocratic system of kings and priests and judges and all the ceremonial and civic laws that held that system together. The people would be defined by faith in Jesus and the fruit of love.

The implications of this change were huge. No longer is it God's will that his people take vengeance in his name on the wicked, as in the case of the conquest of Canaan (Deut. 9:3-6). No longer do God's people (the followers of Jesus) govern themselves by putting to death blasphemers (Lev. 24:14) or adulterers (Lev. 20:10) or fornicators (Deut. 22:21) or Sabbath-breakers (Exod. 31:14) or sorceresses (Exod. 22:18) or false witnesses (Deut. 19:16, 19) or those who disobey their parents (Exod. 21:15, 17). Such commands of the law were woven together with the theocratic, civic government of an ethnic people that no longer applies to a people of God with no ethnic or political identity but rather is scattered through all the ethnic and political groups of the world (Matt. 28:19).

Fourth, the entire religious system involving priests and temple and sacrifices reached its goal and end in Jesus. We saw in *Demand #12* that Jesus himself, by his death and resurrection, took the place of the temple and the sacrifices for sin. Therefore, the laws governing how one was reconciled with God through that system are fulfilled and ended with the death and resurrection of Jesus.

BELIEVE ON HIS SON, AND BEAR THE FRUIT OF LOVE

I conclude therefore that Jesus' demand that we do the will of his Father and that we keep the commandments is a demand that we do what Jesus required of the wealthy man who asked how to inherit eternal life. Jesus' most urgent demand is that we stop treasuring money and start treasuring himself as our only hope of having the "one thing" that we lack—perfect righteousness. Yes, we should keep the commandments, but only as they come through the filter of their fulfillment in Jesus. Practically, this means we should look to Jesus himself, revealed in his life and death and teaching, for the guidance we need. We must depend on Jesus' power to do that the way a branch depends on a vine. In this way Christ, not Moses, gets all the glory for the purchase and the performance of the new covenant.

But even with this divinely enabled transformation (Mark 10:27), our righteousness is not perfect in this life, and it will not suffice for our right standing before God. Therefore, Jesus' demand that we do the will of his Father and that we keep his commandments is also a demand that we despair of making our obedience the ground of God's acceptance. Our transformation is the fruit of our union with Jesus. That union is where the ground of our acceptance lies. And that union is established by believing in Jesus. The fruit demonstrates the reality of the union and the authenticity of faith. This is God's will—that we believe on his Son, that we enjoy our union with him, that we rest in God's merciful declaration of our perfection and acceptance, and that we bear the fruit of love.

Strive to Enter through the Narrow Door, for All of Life Is War

And someone said to him, "Lord, will those who are saved be few?" And he said to them, "Strive to enter through the narrow door. For many, I tell you, will seek to enter and will not be able." —Luke 13:23-24

Jesus taught us that life is war. When he said, "*Strive* to enter through the narrow door" (Luke 13:24), the Greek word behind the English *strive* is recognizable in English transliteration: *agōnizesthe* (ἀγωνίζεσθε). You can see the word *agonize* in that Greek word. The implication is that we must struggle, wrestle, and exert ourselves. But the most important fact about the word "strive" is that the one other place where we find it on Jesus' lips is John 18:36, where he says his disciples would be "fighting" if his kingdom were of this world. "My kingdom is not of this world. If my kingdom were of this world, my servants *would have been fighting* [*egōnizonto*, ἠγωνίζοντο], that I might not be delivered over to the Jews." So here the phrase "strive to enter" means that entering is a battle.

Strive to Enter What?

Entering what? The kingdom of God. This is plain from the following context. After saying that we should "strive to enter through the narrow door," he refers to a master of a house who rises and shuts the door so that no one else can enter (Luke 13:25). Those outside knock and say, "Lord, open to us," but the master says, "I do not know where you come from." Then they say, "We ate and drank in your presence, and you taught in our streets." But he responds, "Depart from me, all you workers of evil!" (Luke 13:25-27).

Then Jesus applies this picture to the real situation of some who will be excluded from the kingdom of God while Gentiles from all over the world will "recline at table in the kingdom of God." "In that place there will be weeping and gnashing of teeth, when you see Abraham and Isaac and Jacob and all the prophets *in the kingdom of God* but you yourselves cast out. And people will come from east and west, and from north and south, and recline at table *in the kingdom of God*" (Luke 13:28-29).

So the "narrow door" through which we must "strive" to enter is the door to the kingdom of God. Outside there is "weeping and gnashing of teeth" (Luke 13:28). This is one of the ways Jesus refers to hell: "Throw them into the fiery furnace. In that place there will be weeping and gnashing of teeth" (Matt. 13:50). The alternative to entering by the narrow gate is destruction. "Enter by the narrow gate. For the gate is wide and the way is easy that leads to *destruction*" (Matt. 7:13). In other words, what is at stake when Jesus demands that we "strive to enter" is heaven and hell. It is an ultimate issue.

THE GREATEST THREAT IS OUR OWN SIN EVERY DAY

But what does Jesus want us to strive against so that we can enter through the narrow door? What are the obstacles? If life is war, who is the enemy? In our striving, the aim is not to hurt anyone. Jesus is clear that we are to love our enemies and do good to those who hate us (Luke 6:27). Saying that life is war does not mean that we make war on people, but on sin, especially our own. In fact, it is only our own sin that can keep us from entering the kingdom, not anyone else's. The sin of others can hurt us, even kill us. But that does not keep us from entering the kingdom of God. Our own sin is the greatest threat to entering the kingdom of God. But temptation to sin comes from an amazing variety of sources.

Jesus is demanding serious personal vigilance. The command to "watch" is one of his most frequent commands. The idea is that we must be awake and alert and ready, lest the temptations of life take us off guard and we be overcome and ruined. Jesus said to his disciples in the Garden of Gethsemane, "Watch and pray that you may not enter into temptation. The spirit indeed is willing, but the flesh is weak" (Mark 14:38). This command is relevant to all of life. Temptations abound, and Jesus does not take them lightly. The watchword of all of life is, watch, be alert.

I say *all of life* because Jesus warned that the days just before his second coming would be in many ways very normal. It will be, Jesus says, like the days of Noah before the flood came and swept people away who were utterly unsuspecting. They were not watchful. Life seemed too normal, so they were not vigilant. "As in those days before the flood they were eating and drinking, marrying and giving in marriage, until the day when Noah entered the ark . . . so will be the coming of the Son of Man. . . . Therefore, *stay awake*, for you do not know on what day your Lord is coming" (Matt. 24:38-39, 42). Nothing is more normal than eating and drinking and marrying. The point is that we must be vigilant all the time, not just when the times feel perilous. They are always perilous. Soul-destroying temptations to unbelief and sin are present in everyday, normal life. Striving to enter through the narrow door is a lifelong, all-day, every-day calling.

Pain and Pleasure Can Keep Us from Entering Through the Narrow Door

Jesus' demand for vigilance is all-embracing. Both the pleasant parts of life and the painful parts of life present dangers to the soul. In the parable of the four soils he warns about both. The painful and the pleasant threaten to destroy the faith-sustaining work of the word in our lives. When the word falls on rocky ground it sprouts, then dies. This represents those who hear the word, but then "tribulation or persecution arises on account of the word" (Matt. 13:21), and they fall away. They do not enter through the narrow door.

When the word falls on thorny ground it sprouts, then dies. This represents those who hear the word, but then "they are choked by the cares and riches and pleasures of life" (Luke 8:14). They do not enter through the narrow door. One person falls away because of pain (tribulation or persecution); the other person falls away because of pleasure (riches and pleasures of life). The call for vigilance is all-embracing. There is no unembattled place in this life.

Surprising to us perhaps, Jesus' demand for vigilance is directed more often at the pleasures of life than the pain. Some people are driven away from God by their pain, but more are lured away by their pleasures. Pleasures seldom awaken people to their need for God; pain often does. So Jesus is more concerned to warn us about the dangers of prosperity than the dangers of poverty.

THE PERILS OF PRAISE AND PHYSICAL INDULGENCE

One powerful lure away from the kingdom of God is the praise of man. Therefore, Jesus said, "Beware of the scribes, who like to walk around in long robes, and love greetings in the marketplaces and the best seats in the synagogues and the places of honor at feasts" (Luke 20:46). "Beware" means be alert, take care, pay close attention to. This is a call for vigilance against the lure of following those who live for the praises of man. "Beware of practicing your righteousness before other people in order to be seen by them" (Matt. 6:1). We feel good when people speak well of us. It may not be wrong. But it is dangerous. It is a time for vigilance. "Woe to you," Jesus says, "when all people speak well of you, for so their fathers did to the false prophets" (Luke 6:26).

Less subtle is the lure of physical indulgence. Jesus focuses on alcohol and the dissipating effects it has on our minds and bodies. He says, "But watch yourselves lest your hearts be weighed down with dissipation and drunkenness and cares of this life, and that day come upon you suddenly like a trap" (Luke 21:34). There are drugs and foods and practices that "weigh down" the heart. They make the heart sluggish. This is the opposite of vigilance. We will not "strive to enter through the narrow door" if we are self-indulgent and use drugs or food or drink in a way that dulls our spiritual alertness and vigilance.

MONEY IS A MORTAL THREAT TO ENTERING THROUGH THE NARROW DOOR

The danger Jesus warns against most often is the danger of money. It is a mortal danger. Heaven and hell hang in the balance in our vigilance against the lure of money. Jesus made this as clear as possible with the words, "It is easier for a camel to go through the eye of a needle than for a rich person to enter the kingdom of God" (Mark 10:25). The issue is entering the kingdom. Striving for wealth is not the striving that leads to the narrow door.

Over and over Jesus warns us to be vigilant against the lure of riches. "Do not lay up for yourselves treasures on earth" (Matt. 6:19). "You cannot serve God and money" (Matt. 6:24). "Do not be anxious, saying, 'What shall we eat?' or 'What shall we drink?' or 'What shall we wear?'" (Matt. 6:31). "The deceitfulness of riches and the desires for other things enter in and choke the word" (Mark 4:19). "Sell your possessions, and give to the needy" (Luke 12:33). "Where your treasure is, there your heart will be also" (Matt. 6:21). "Any one of you who does not renounce all that he has cannot be my disciple" (Luke 14:33). "But woe to you who are rich, for you have received your consolation" (Luke 6:24). "Blessed are you who are poor, for yours is the kingdom of God" (Luke 6:20).[1] "Take care, and be on your guard against all covetousness, for one's life does not consist in the abundance of his possessions" (Luke 12:15).

---

[1] Even though he pronounces a woe on the rich (Luke 6:24) and pronounces blessedness on the poor (Luke 6:20), he does not mean that mere finances make one blessed or damnable. We know this, first, because he also says, "Woe to you who laugh now" (Luke 6:25) and "Blessed are you who weep now" (Luke 6:21), and we know from this very context that disciples are to rejoice now (Luke 6:23). So Jesus assumes that we are going to qualify his seemingly absolute statements here. The rich and the poor who are blessed are those for whom Jesus is their supreme treasure and therefore seek to use their wealth or poverty to magnify the worth of Jesus above money and what it can buy. We also know Jesus did not pronounce damnation and blessedness on mere financial condition because he told the rich young ruler to sell all that he had (Mark 10:21) but commended Zacchaeus for giving half of his money away (Luke 19:8-9). However, having said all that, it is significant that Jesus considers wealth so dangerous and poverty so auspicious; he simply says woe to the one and blessed be the other.

THE "HEALTHY EYE" WILL HELP US STRIVE TO ENTER THE NARROW DOOR

It appears, then, that striving to enter the kingdom of God through the narrow door is largely a battle about how we relate to money. We should linger here since Jesus did. He is jealous that we "guard against all covetousness." He is deeply concerned with our "eyes" when it comes to the treasure of our lives. We see this in a puzzling statement he made in Matthew 6:22-23, "The eye is the lamp of the body. So, if your eye is healthy, your whole body will be full of light, but if your eye is bad, your whole body will be full of darkness. If then the light in you is darkness, how great is the darkness!" In other words, if the eye is good (literally, "single"), the whole body will be full of light. But if the eye is bad, the body will be full of darkness. In other words, how you see reality determines whether you are in the dark or not.

You will naturally ask, what does that have to do with money? First of all, notice that these words of Jesus are sandwiched between the command to lay up treasures in heaven (6:19-21) and the warning that you can't serve God and money (6:24). Why is this saying about the good and bad eye sandwiched between two teachings on money? I think it's because what makes the eye good is how it sees God in relation to money. That's the issue on either side of this saying. In Matthew 6:19-21 the issue is: You should desire heaven-reward, not earth-reward. Which, in short, means: Desire God, not money. In Matthew 6:24, the question is whether you can serve two masters. Answer: You cannot serve God and money.

This is a double description of light! If you are laying up treasures in heaven, not earth, you are walking in the light. If you are serving God, not money, you are walking in the light. Between these two descriptions of the light Jesus says that the eye is the lamp of the body and that a good eye produces a fullness of this light. So, what is the good eye that gives so much light and the bad eye that leaves us in the dark?

WHAT IS THE GOOD EYE?

One clue is found in Matthew 20:15. Jesus has just said that men who worked one hour will be paid the same as those who worked all day, because the master is merciful and generous. And besides, they all agreed to their wage before they worked. Those who worked all day grumbled that the men who worked one hour were paid too much. Jesus responded with the same words found here in Matthew 6:23, "Is your eye bad because I am good?" (literal translation).

What is bad about their eye? What's bad is that their eye does not see the mercy of the master as beautiful. They see it as ugly. They don't see reality for what it is. They do not have an eye that can see mercy as more precious than money.

Now bring that understanding of the "bad eye" back to Matthew 6:23 and let it help us discern the meaning of the "good eye." What would the good eye be that fills us with light? It would be an eye that sees the Master's generosity as more precious than money. Which means that the good eye sees God and his ways as the great Treasure in life, not money. The good eye sees things as they really are. God is really more valuable than all that money can buy.

You have a good eye if you look to God and love to maximize the reward of his fellowship—that is, lay up treasure in heaven. You have a good eye if you look at Master-money and Master-God and see Master-God as infinitely more valuable. In other words, a "good eye" is a wisely valuing eye, a discerning eye, an astutely treasuring eye. It doesn't just see facts about money and God. It doesn't just perceive what is true and false. It sees beauty and ugliness; it senses value and worthlessness; it discerns what is really desirable and what is undesirable. The seeing of the good eye is not neutral. When it sees God, it sees God-as-beautiful. It sees God-as-desirable.

That is why the good eye leads to the way of light: laying up treasures in heaven and serving God, not money. The good eye is a *single* eye. It has *one* Treasure: God. When that happens in your life, you are full of light. And this is so important that Jesus adds in Luke 11:35, "Therefore *be careful* lest the light in you be darkness." In other words, be vigilant. Don't be casual or slack or careless about this matter. Strive, wrestle, fight to keep your eye good. That is, do what you must to see God, not money, as supremely valuable and desirable.

In the next chapter we will continue to unfold the implications of Jesus' demand to strive to enter by the narrow door. We will see how he calls for vigilance and watchfulness in regard to false prophets and false christs and the suddenness of his second coming. And then we will turn to the question, how does the demand for vigilance fit with his demand that we rest in him? How does the seriousness of watchfulness fit with the sweetness of Jesus' care?

Strive to Enter through the Narrow Door, for Jesus Fulfills the New Covenant

Enter by the narrow gate. For the gate is wide and the way is easy that leads to destruction, and those who enter by it are many. For the gate is narrow and the way is hard that leads to life, and those who find it are few. —Matt. 7:13-14

This cup that is poured out for you is the new covenant in my blood. —Luke 22:20

J esus' demand for vigilance—"strive to enter through the narrow door"—is owing to the many dangers that threaten our souls. One of the most frequent imperatives on Jesus' lips is, "Look out!" "Watch!" "Be alert!" We have seen in the previous chapter the need for striving against the perils of pain and pleasure: the deceit of money, the praise of man, the lure of physical indulgence. We turn now to the perils of false prophets and false christs and the danger of nostalgia for the days when the cost of discipleship was not so high. Then we turn to the crucial question: Is all this vigilance and all this striving to enter through the narrow door consistent with the sweet invitations of Jesus to come to him and find rest?

THE PERILS OF FALSE PROPHETS AND FALSE CHRISTS

Jesus warns us that false prophets and even false christs will abound. In fact, the first warning he gives us after saying, "The gate is narrow and the way is hard that leads to life" is this: "Beware of false prophets, who come to you in sheep's clothing but inwardly are ravenous wolves. You will recognize them by their fruits" (Matt. 7:15-16). This is not a casual remark. It is a life-and-death warning: "False christs and false prophets will arise and perform signs and wonders, to lead astray, if possible, the elect. *But be on guard*; I have told you all things beforehand" (Mark 13:22-23). Be on guard! Keep your eyes open! Watch! Be vigilant! Strive to enter by the narrow door.

Jesus underscores that the door is *narrow* that leads to life. Not every claim will fit through the narrow door of the kingdom of God. There are many false christs. In this context *Christ* means Jewish Messiah—the one who fulfills all God's promises and brings in the kingdom and sits on the throne of David ruling over all the world. There is only one Christ, and the rest are "false christs." Jesus is the only Messiah. Therefore, the door is as narrow as faith in Jesus, the only true Messiah and King of kings.

I have sat in my office with followers of another "christ" and pleaded with them to turn to the true and only Christ, Jesus. They said that the Christ had come in our day and that he was gathering a people now for himself. I read to them Luke 17:24 to show them that Jesus said when he comes it would be globally unmistakable and that anyone who says it has already happened is a pretender: "For as the lightning flashes and lights up the sky from one side to the other, so will the Son of Man be in his day." They said that in order to understand the secret meaning of this verse I would need to read a book written by their leader, the "christ" they believed in. As they left I stood at my window watching them walk across the parking lot and prayed for them. I gave thanks that God had helped me "be on guard." Jesus said this would happen and helped me watch as I sat there in my office. This vigilance is part of what it means to "strive to enter through the narrow door."

You Do Not Know When Your Lord Is Coming

What gives Jesus' demand for vigilance and striving its unusual urgency is the warning that the time of his second coming is unknown to any of us. "*Stay awake*, for you do not know on what day your Lord is coming. . . . Watch therefore, for you know neither the day nor the hour" (Matt. 24:42; 25:13). When Jesus tells us to "watch" or "stay awake" because we do not know the time of his second coming, he does not mean that we skip sleep and look out our windows. We know this because the command to "watch" is the climax of the parable of the ten virgins, five of whom were wise and five of whom were foolish, but all of whom slept. The wise made sure they had oil in their lamps so that when the bridegroom came they might go out with their lamps to greet him. That was their job. Jesus says that all ten of them "became drowsy and slept" (Matt. 25:5). He did not criticize the wise virgins for sleeping.

When the bridegroom came at midnight (representing the second coming of Jesus to earth at an unexpected hour), Jesus said, "Those who were ready [the five wise virgins] went in with him to the marriage feast, and the door was shut" (Matt. 25:10). The foolish virgins had to go get oil because they were unprepared. When they returned they cried out, "Lord, lord, open to us" (Matt. 25:11). But the bridegroom (representing Jesus) answered, "Truly, I say to you, I do not know you" (Matt. 25:12). The lesson Jesus draws out of this parable is, "*Watch* therefore, for you know neither the day nor the hour" (Matt. 25:13). But all ten of the virgins were asleep, including the five wise virgins. That's how we know that when Jesus says, "Watch!" he does not mean skipping sleep and looking out our window.

He means, be watchful over your life. Be watchful over what the Bridegroom has called you to do. The wise virgins had done the will of the Master: Their lamps were fully prepared. Sleeping was just fine because they had done their jobs. Therefore, one way to describe "striving to enter through the narrow door" is: Fulfill your calling. Be vigilant to do what God has called you to do. You will be happy if Jesus comes and finds you heartily engaged in your earthly calling for his glory. "Who then is the faithful and wise manager, whom his master will set over his household, to give them their portion of food at the proper time? Blessed is that servant whom his master will find so doing when he comes" (Luke 12:42-43). Striving to enter the kingdom by the narrow door includes vigilant faithfulness in the work Jesus has left us to do. As he said in one of his parables, "Engage in business until I come" (Luke 19:13)—do with all your might what he has given you to do.

PERSEVERANCE AND THE PERIL OF NOSTALGIA

One of the great temptations to keep us from fulfilling what Jesus calls us to do is that we grow weary in the battle and look back on how easy life was before we started to follow him. Strive to enter through the narrow door means, fight for perseverance. The zeal of many would-be followers of Jesus grows cold, and they drift away. Jesus said, "Because lawlessness will be increased, the love of many will grow cold. But the one who endures to the end will be saved" (Matt. 24:12-13). In other words, one of the factors that makes the door to the kingdom of God narrow is that striving to enter must last to the end.

Therefore, Jesus warns us against nostalgia for the former days of worldliness. He says that the stress of the last days of this age will tempt people to look back. So with stark simplicity he warns, "Remember Lot's wife" (Luke 17:32). This was a reference to a woman in the Old Testament who was leaving her hometown of Sodom because God was about to destroy the city for its sin. Tragically, like so many would-be followers of Jesus who begin to leave the old way of sin, she looked back. "Lot's wife . . . looked back, and she became a pillar of salt" (Gen. 19:26). God saw an idolatrous heart in her backward glance toward Sodom. This was her true love, not God. Striving to enter through the narrow door means taking heed to the warning of Jesus: "No one who puts his hand to the plow and looks back is fit for the kingdom of God" (Luke 9:62).

How Does Striving to Enter by the Narrow Door Relate to Resting in Jesus?

The question must now be asked: Is all this vigilance and all this striving to enter through the narrow door consistent with the sweet invitations of Jesus to come to him and find rest? If this striving and vigilance sounds like a miserable and burdened way to live, keep in mind that Jesus rebuked the lawyers who burdened people with impossible laws without giving any help: "Woe to you lawyers also! For you load people with burdens hard to bear, and you yourselves do not touch the burdens with one of your fingers" (Luke 11:46). And most of all, keep in mind how Jesus invited people into his fellowship: "Come to me, all who labor and are heavy laden, and I will give you rest. Take my yoke upon you, and learn from me, for I am gentle and lowly in heart, and you will find rest for your souls. For my yoke is easy, and my burden is light" (Matt. 11:28-30).

What makes the demands of Jesus to strive and to be vigilant seem burdensome is the assumption that we are left to ourselves. Our natural tendency is to think that if Jesus tells us to do something and makes this a condition for entering the kingdom of God and having eternal life, he will then stand back and merely watch to see if we will do it. We do not naturally think that if he demands something, he will enable us to do it.

Jesus Came to Fulfill the New Covenant in His Blood

But Jesus knew that he had come to fulfill the "new covenant" promised by the prophet Jeremiah. At the end of his life at the Last Supper, he took the cup that represented his blood and said, "This cup that is poured out for you is the *new covenant* in my blood" (Luke 22:20).

What was new about the "new covenant" was that the commands of God would not merely be written on stone (Exod. 24:12), as in the covenant with Moses, but would now be written on the heart of God's people. God promised through Jeremiah, "Behold, the days are coming, declares the LORD, when I will make a new covenant with the house of Israel and the house of Judah, not like the covenant that I made with their fathers on the day when I took them by the hand to bring them out of the land of Egypt. . . . But this is the covenant that I will make with the house of Israel after those days, declares the LORD: *I will put my law within them, and I will write it on their hearts*" (Jer. 31:31-33).

Jesus came to inaugurate this new covenant through his life and death and resurrection and by the sending of the Holy Spirit. The prophet Ezekiel wrote that the way the new covenant would secure the obedience of God's people (the striving to enter through the narrow door) was by God's Spirit being given to them and by their own spirit being made new. God said through Ezekiel, "I will put my Spirit within you, and cause you to walk in my statutes. . . . A new spirit I will put within them. I will remove the heart of stone from their flesh and give them a heart of flesh, that they may walk in my statutes and keep my rules and obey them" (Ezek. 36:27; 11:19-20). God's intention was to give his commands *and* the ability to do them. That is the new covenant.

By his shed blood Jesus purchased this new covenant for all who trust him. Then, on the basis of the forgiveness of sins that he obtained for his people (Matt. 26:28), he gave them the promise of the Holy Spirit. He said:

> I will ask the Father, and he will give you another Helper, to be with you forever, even the Spirit of truth . . . he dwells with you and will be in you. . . . When the Helper comes, whom I will send to you from the Father, the Spirit of truth, who proceeds from the Father, he will bear witness about me. . . . He will glorify me, for he will take what is mine and declare it to you. (John 14:16; 15:26; 16:14)

WITHOUT CHRIST OUR STRIVING WOULD BE LOSING

Therefore, by his death and by the sending of the Spirit, Jesus obtains the new-covenant promises for those who trust him. And the heart of that covenant is that our sins are forgiven and the Spirit of God is given to help us do what Jesus demands, namely, strive to enter by the narrow door. In other words, Jesus' demand that we "strive to enter" does not mean he stands aloof and watches. As Martin Luther wrote in his famous hymn:

> Did we in our own strength confide, our striving would be losing;
> Were not the right Man on our side, the Man of God's own
>   choosing:
> Dost ask who that may be? Christ Jesus, it is He;
> Lord Sabaoth, His Name, from age to age the same,
> And He must win the battle.[1]

We are not left to ourselves in our striving. The command to strive is the command to experience the powerful striving of God on our behalf in fulfillment of his new-covenant promise to cause us to walk in his statutes (Ezek. 36:27). We will see this all the more clearly and forcefully in the next chapter, which deals with the presence of the kingdom of God and the presence of eternal life and the way to maintain hope and joy and peace as we strive to enter through the narrow door.

---

[1] Martin Luther, "A Mighty Fortress Is Our God."

STRIVE TO ENTER THROUGH THE NARROW DOOR, FOR YOU ARE ALREADY IN THE KINGDOM'S POWER

Truly, I say to you, whoever does not receive the kingdom of God like a child shall not enter it. — MARK 10:15

The demand to strive to enter the kingdom of God through the narrow door should be heard in connection with the truth that God has already done something to make that striving full of hope and confidence. We strive not with fretting that we will not enter, but with assurance that not only *will* we enter, but in a decisive sense we have already entered. This may sound paradoxical: Strive to enter, for you have entered. But it is profoundly true for all who trust in Jesus.

THE SECRET OF THE KINGDOM OF GOD: IT IS HERE

At the center of Jesus' message is the claim that both the kingdom of God and eternal life are *present* experiences as well as *future* promises. In other words, when Jesus demands that we strive to enter the kingdom through the narrow door, he is focusing on the future experience of final joy and perfect fellowship with God when the kingdom comes in fullest measure in the future. Strive to enter that.

But the "secret of the kingdom" (Mark 4:11) that Jesus revealed to his disciples was that the kingdom had *already* arrived in his ministry and that his followers enter it *now* and experience its power even before its final consummation.[1] For example, Jesus said, "If it is by the finger of God that I cast out demons, then *the kingdom of God has come upon you . . .* behold, the kingdom of God *is in the midst of you*" (Luke 11:20; 17:21). In his ministry the kingdom of God, which will be consummated in the future, has come near, and its power is in delivering people from bondage to Satan and sin.

Which means, for the followers of Jesus, that our striving to "enter through the narrow door" is done in the power of the kingdom that we have received as a free gift. Recall how Jesus put it: "Truly, I say to you, whoever does not *receive* the kingdom of God like a child shall not *enter* it" (Mark 10:15). We now receive it as a gift by faith and experience its power. By this power of the kingdom we will walk the "hard way" and enter the "narrow door." Paradoxically, we strive to *enter* the kingdom from *inside* the kingdom. The present power of the kingdom is here, and we have entered into that power by faith. The consummation of the kingdom, with its victory over death and disease and all sin, is still future, and we are not yet there.

Eternal Life Is Ours Now

The same interconnection between the future and the present is true of *eternal life*, not just the kingdom of God. On the one hand, Jesus speaks of eternal life as a future inheritance: "Everyone who has left houses or brothers or sisters or father or mother or children or lands, for my name's sake, will receive a hundredfold and *will inherit eternal life*" (Matt. 19:29; cf. 25:46). But on the other hand, he teaches that believing on him means having eternal life now:

---

[1] "The mystery of the Kingdom is the coming of the Kingdom into history in advance of its apocalyptic manifestation. It is, in short, 'fulfillment without consummation.' . . . The new truth, now given by revelation in the person and mission of Jesus, is that *the Kingdom which is to come finally in apocalyptic power, as foreseen in Daniel, has in fact entered into the world in advance in a hidden form to work secretly within and among men.*" George Ladd, *The Presence of the Future* (Grand Rapids, Mich.: Eerdmans, 1974), 222.

"Truly, truly, I say to you, whoever hears my word and believes him who sent me *has* eternal life. He does not come into judgment, but *has passed from death to life*" (John 5:24; cf. 3:36). By trusting Jesus we have eternal life now, but we will come into the fullest experience of it in the future.

THE PRESENCE OF LIFE AND KINGDOM DOES NOT PRODUCE PRESUMPTION BUT JOY

Jesus' teaching about this truth—that entering the kingdom of God and entering eternal life are both present experience and future hope—does not express itself in presumption and carelessness. It does not produce the attitude that says, "I'm already saved; it does not matter how I live. I do not need to be vigilant. I do not need to strive to enter through the narrow door." That is not the way a person talks who has entered eternal life and has been grasped by the power of God's kingdom. Instead this truth expresses itself in joyful striving.

To some people striving does not sound like a joyful way to live. It sounds burdensome. But that is not the way followers of Jesus experience it. Of course, taking up our cross and denying ourselves and becoming the "slave of all" (Mark 10:44) is often painful. But it is not oppressive. There is joy at every turn. This was the point of *Demand #10*, "Rejoice and Leap for Joy" (Luke 6:23). In fact, it is the joy of having eternal life now and being in the kingdom of God now and knowing our sins forgiven now and enjoying the fellowship of Jesus now that sustains our ability to strive toward that future entrance through the narrow door into the consummation of God's kingdom. That is the point of the little parable in Matthew 13:44: "The kingdom of heaven is like treasure hidden in a field, which a man found and covered up. Then in his joy he goes and sells all that he has and buys that field." Joy is the sustaining motive for selling all—for striving to enter through the narrow door.

This is an illustration of how doing something difficult and seemingly oppressive—selling all you have—is carried by joy. "*In his joy* he goes and sells all that he has." That is the banner flying over all our striving as we follow Jesus: *In our joy* we fight off every temptation that would destroy our soul with deceptive pleasures or deceptive pain. We fight as those who *must* fight and *will* win. The striving is essential, and its outcome for Christ's sheep is certain. "My sheep hear my voice, and I know them, and they follow me. I give them eternal life, and they will never perish, and no one will snatch them out of my hand" (John 10:27-28).

Help for the Fainthearted

The demand of Jesus that we "strive to enter through the narrow door" is overarching. It gives a sense of urgency to all his demands. It does not refer to a class of commandments but to all of them. It is a demand that we take all his word seriously. It calls for lifelong, everyday, hour-by-hour vigilance over our thoughts and feelings and actions. Therefore, it troubles some followers of Jesus who are fainthearted. I have tried to help us all take heart. It may be practically useful to close this chapter with a summary list of ways to maintain hope and joy as we strive together to enter through the narrow door.

The Fight Is to Cherish What We Have, Not Earn What We Don't

First, remember that the main battle is the battle to keep seeing Jesus as the supreme treasure of your life. He does not call us to fight for plastic jewels. Following Jesus is the result of finding a treasure hidden in a field—an infinitely valuable treasure. Then in our joy we gladly "let goods and kindred go, this mortal life also"[2] to enjoy that treasure to the full. Striving to enter through the narrow door is only as hard as treasuring Jesus above all things.

The battle is not to do what we don't want, but to want what is infinitely worthy of wanting. The fight is not the oppressive struggle to earn God's final rest, but the satisfying struggle to rest in the peace that Jesus freely gives. "Come to me, all who labor

---

[2] Martin Luther, "A Mighty Fortress Is Our God."

and are heavy laden, and I will give you rest. Take my yoke upon you, and learn from me, for I am gentle and lowly in heart, and you will find rest for your souls. For my yoke is easy, and my burden is light" (Matt. 11:28-30). The demands of Jesus are only as hard to obey as his promises are hard to cherish and his presence is hard to treasure.

JESUS PROMISES TO HELP US DO THE IMPOSSIBLE

Second, remember that Jesus promises to help us obey his demand. "I am the vine; you are the branches. Whoever abides in me and I in him, he it is that bears much fruit, for apart from me you can do nothing" (John 15:5; cf. *Demand #7*, "Abide in Me"). He promised to be with us to the end of the age (Matt. 28:20). He promised not to leave us like orphans when he returned to heaven, but to come to us and help us (John 14:16-18). He acknowledges that what he demands is impossible, but then promises omnipotent help: "With man it is impossible, but not with God. For all things are possible with God" (Mark 10:27). Don't think of striving to get his favor. Think of striving with the favor of his help.

FORGIVENESS AND JUSTIFICATION ARE AT THE BOTTOM OF OUR STRIVING

Third, remember that forgiveness of sins and justification by faith are at the bottom of our striving (see *Demand #20*). We do not strive for them. We strive because we have them. Jesus offers forgiveness in Matthew 26:28 ("This is my blood of the covenant, which is poured out for many for the forgiveness of sins"), and he offers justification in Luke 18:13-14 ("The tax collector, standing far off, would not even lift up his eyes to heaven, but beat his breast, saying, 'God, be merciful to me, a sinner!' I tell you, this man went down to his house justified"). Our standing with God as forgiven and righteous is the ground of our striving, not the goal of our striving. We must strive to enter because that is the mark of the one who belongs to Christ. If we do not strive, we do not bear the mark of belonging to Jesus. But the striving does not create the relationship. The secure relationship produces the joyful striving.

PERFECTION AWAITS THE AGE TO COME

Fourth, keep in mind that perfection awaits the age to come. We do wish that we could be free from all sinful feelings and thoughts and actions now. That longing and that labor is part of our striving. But we would despair if perfection in this life were a prerequisite for entering through the narrow door. There *is* a perfection required. We saw it in our treatment of *Demand #20* ("If you would be perfect, go, sell what you possess," Matt. 19:21), but no human can achieve it. Only Jesus fulfills all righteousness (Matt. 3:15). This is why he teaches us to pray, not once, but every day, "Forgive us our debts" (Matt. 6:12). Very bluntly Jesus calls his disciples (not would-be disciples, but committed disciples) "evil"—"If you then, *who are evil*, know how to give good gifts to your children . . ." (Matt. 7:11). Let us then take heart that the mark of a true follower of Jesus is not yet perfection but rather unrelenting battle against sin. We fail, but we do not fall away.[3] We stumble, but we do not fall headlong into apostasy.

JESUS PRAYS FOR US THAT WE NOT FAIL

Fifth, remember that the reason we do not fall away is that Jesus is not only helping us by his presence and Spirit, but is also praying for us. Jesus said to Peter who was about to deny him three times, "I have prayed for you that your faith may not fail. And when you have turned again, strengthen your brothers" (Luke 22:32). Jesus knew Peter would sin, and he knew he would turn back from his sinful denial. He said, "*When* you have turned," not "*If* you turn." He did not use his sovereign power to prevent Peter's sin, but he did

---

[3] The term "fall away" can refer to a temporary departure from Christ in fear followed by repentance and restoration. For example, in Matthew 26:31, Jesus said to his disciples, "You will all fall away because of me this night. For it is written, 'I will strike the shepherd, and the sheep of the flock will be scattered.'" But I am using the term here in its more absolute sense. True followers of Jesus will not fall away utterly and finally.

use it to prevent Peter's falling away. There is no reason to think Jesus has stopped praying like that for his loved ones. God will answer his Son when he prays, "Holy Father, keep them in your name, which you have given me, that they may be one, even as we are one" (John 17:11).

WE ARE STRIVING TO ENTER OUR FATHER'S HOUSE

Sixth, remember your position as a true *child* of God. Jesus taught his disciples to know and trust God as their personal *Father* in heaven. Before Jesus came, Israel as a people thought of God as the Father of the nation, but relating to God *individually* as Father was unusual. But Jesus made it central and referred to it again and again. The implication was: God loves you personally as his child and will take care of you. Bank on it.

This did not apply to everyone. For example, he said to some, "If God were your Father, you would love me, for I came from God and I am here. . . . You are of your father the devil, and your will is to do your father's desires" (John 8:42, 44). This is very important for Jesus' followers: If God is our Father, we love Jesus. This means that being a child of God involves having a new nature. The mark of this new nature is a love for Jesus. Therefore, loving Jesus is a sure sign that we are the children of God.

And if we are already children, we may have deep confidence that our striving to enter the narrow door of our Father's house will succeed. He will see to it. He is our Father now. He is not watching to see if we will strive hard enough to become his children. He is actively helping us get home. For example, when we are tested publicly to see if we will testify of Jesus as we ought, Jesus says not to worry: "It is not you who speak, but the Spirit of *your Father* speaking through you" (Matt. 10:20). Not a single sparrow falls to the ground apart from "your Father," Jesus says. "Fear not, therefore; you are of more value than many sparrows" (Matt. 10:29, 31). That's the spirit of confidence that comes from being a child of God.

Your Name Is Written in Heaven

Seventh, remember, as you strive to enter through the narrow door, that your name is written in heaven. Jesus said, "Do not rejoice in this, that the spirits are subject to you, but rejoice that your names are written in heaven" (Luke 10:20). If everybody's name is written in heaven, there is no reason to rejoice, but many are on the way to destruction, not the narrow door: "The way is easy that leads to destruction, and those who enter by it are many" (Matt. 7:13). Not all names are written there. Having your name written in heaven means that God will deliver you from evil and bring you to his kingdom. Jesus had read about this book in a prophet he knew well, Daniel 12:1: "There shall be a time of trouble, such as never has been since there was a nation till that time. But at that time your people shall be delivered, *everyone whose name shall be found written in the book.*"

You Were Chosen by God and Given to Jesus

Eighth, remember that Jesus is not collecting disciples whom God has not known. God knew his own first and wrote them in his book. Now the Father is drawing them to his Son for salvation. "All that the Father gives me will come to me, and whoever comes to me I will never cast out" (John 6:37). The followers of Jesus belonged to God first and then were given to Jesus (John 17:9). If someone comes to Jesus, it is because the Father knew him and gave him to the Son. That's why Jesus said, "No one can come to me unless it is granted him by the Father" (John 6:65). When they come, Jesus reveals the Father to them, and the Father keeps them from falling away: "I have manifested your name to the people whom you gave me out of the world. Yours they were, and you gave them to me" (John 17:6). "My Father, who has given them to me, is greater than all, and no one is able to snatch them out of the Father's hand" (John 10:29). When you remember and rejoice that you are a chosen child of God, your striving will not be oppressive or slavish.

JESUS SUSTAINS OUR STRIVING BY HIS JOY

Ninth, remember that joy in God is the key way that Jesus enables us to strive to enter through the narrow door. First, Jesus says, "I am the vine; you are the branches . . . apart from me you can do nothing" (John 15:5). Then he says, "These things I have spoken to you, that my joy may be in you, and that your joy may be full" (John 15:11). In other words, the way Jesus enables us to strive successfully to enter through the narrow door is by imparting to us his joy. Then later he adds, "No one will take your joy from you" (John 16:22). This joy in Jesus and all that God is for us in him sustains lifelong striving to enter though the narrow door.

OUR STRIVING WILL NOT BE IN VAIN

Vigilance is the mark of the followers of Jesus. They know that "the gate is wide and the way is easy that leads to destruction" (Matt. 7:13). They are serious about life. Heaven and hell are at stake. Therefore, they are seriously joyful. The Son of God has rescued them from the guilt and power of sin. They are children of God. Their names are written in heaven. They have received the Helper, the Spirit of truth. They have the promise of Jesus to be with them to the end of the age. They know that he is praying for them. They rejoice that they stand righteous before God because of Jesus. They have received the kingdom. They have eternal life as a present possession. And they marvel that no one can snatch them out of God's hand. In this joy they are energized to strive to enter by the narrow door. And they are confident their striving will not be in vain.

YOUR RIGHTEOUSNESS MUST EXCEED THAT OF THE PHARISEES, FOR IT WAS HYPOCRITICAL AND UGLY

For I tell you, unless your righteousness exceeds that of the scribes and Pharisees, you will never enter the kingdom of heaven. —MATT. 5:20

Woe to you, scribes and Pharisees, hypocrites! For you are like whitewashed tombs, which outwardly appear beautiful, but within are full of dead people's bones and all uncleanness. So you also outwardly appear righteous to others, but within you are full of hypocrisy and lawlessness. —MATT. 23:27-28

For from within, out of the heart of man, come evil thoughts, sexual immorality, theft, murder, adultery, coveting, wickedness, deceit, sensuality, envy, slander, pride, foolishness. All these evil things come from within, and they defile a person. —MARK 7:21-23

Blessed are the pure in heart, for they shall see God. —MATT. 5:8

Jesus said that we cannot enter the kingdom of heaven if our righteousness does not exceed that of the scribes and Pharisees (Matt. 5:20). Someone might take this to mean that we must out-Pharisee the Pharisees. They were the most meticulous Jewish students of the Mosaic law and the most rigorous enforcers of its details. The tradition had grown up that there were 246 positive commandments in the Law (the first five books of the Bible) and 365 prohibitions.[1] Getting these right and keeping them meticulously was the vocation of the Pharisees. So does Jesus mean that we are to be even more meticulous in tallying up the laws and shaping our behavior around them?

John Stott answers:

> It is not so much, shall we say, that Christians succeed in keeping some 240 commandments when the best Pharisees may only have scored 230. No. Christian righteousness is greater than pharisaic righteousness because it is deeper, being a righteousness of the heart. . . . The righteousness which is pleasing to [God] is an inward righteousness of mind and motive. For "the Lord looks on the heart."[2]

This is the right answer. But to see it clearly we need to take a look at what Jesus saw when he looked at the righteousness of the scribes and Pharisees. It is not a pretty picture.

JESUS AND THE PHARISEES: ANGER AND ENTREATY

No group awakened anger and aching in the heart of Jesus like the Pharisees. Matthew 23 is the most severe chapter in all four Gospels. It is unremitting criticism of the Pharisees. Yet it ends with an echo of the aching in Jesus' heart: "O Jerusalem, Jerusalem, the city that

---

[1] Maimonides (1135–1204) was a Spanish-born Jewish philosopher and physician, probably the greatest medieval Jewish scholar. He published a definitive list of the laws of the Pentateuch (the first five books of the Bible). He put the number at 613, two more than the traditional number because he treated, "I am the LORD your God" (Exod. 20:1) and "Hear, O Israel: The LORD our God, the LORD is one" (Deut. 6:4) as positive commandments. "He reckoned that since there were 248 distinct parts of the human body, one was to remember to obey God's positive commands with 'all one's self,' and since there were 365 days of the year, one was to remember not to disobey God's commands each day of the year. Since the time of Maimonides, his count of 613 laws has been accepted as the traditional number." John Sailhamer, *The Pentateuch as Narrative* (Grand Rapids, Mich.: Zondervan, 1992), 481. All 613 commandments are listed in Sailhamer, 482-516.

[2] John R. W. Stott, *The Message of the Sermon on the Mount* (Leicester, England: Inter-Varsity, 1978), 75. The reference to God looking on the heart is from 1 Samuel 16:7; see also Luke 16:15.

kills the prophets and stones those who are sent to it! How often would I have gathered your children together as a hen gathers her brood under her wings, and you would not!" (Matt. 23:37). And this longing for the Pharisees is also expressed in the parable of the prodigal son and the attitude of the elder brother of the prodigal. He represents the Pharisees and scribes who criticized Jesus for eating with sinners. "The Pharisees and the scribes grumbled, saying, 'This man receives sinners and eats with them'" (Luke 15:2).

Jesus told the parable of the prodigal son in answer to this criticism. The point of the parable was that Jesus' eating with sinners was not God's complicity with sin but God's pursuit of sinners. But at the end of the parable Jesus reaches out to the Pharisees. He describes the father (who represents God) as coming out and entreating the pharisaic older son to join the celebration of his lost brother's being back home. In other words, the parable is a merciful offer to the Pharisees to join the celebration of grace in Jesus' life and ministry.

But the elder son will not leave his angry position of self-righteous *servant* to join the joyful position of being a son: "Look, these many years I have *served* you, and I never disobeyed your command, yet you never gave me a young goat, that I might celebrate with my friends" (Luke 15:29). He sees himself as a deserving servant, not a freely loved son. The father's last words to this elder brother are full of the ache Jesus felt for the Pharisees: "Son, you are always with me, and all that is mine is yours.[3] It was fitting to celebrate and be glad, for this your brother was dead, and is alive; he was

---

[3] This does not mean that the Pharisees are saved. We know that Jesus expects that they will be cast out of the kingdom if they do not repent. He said in Matthew 8:11-12, "I tell you, many will come from east and west [that is, Gentiles] and recline at table with Abraham, Isaac, and Jacob in the kingdom of heaven, while the sons of the kingdom will be thrown into the outer darkness. In that place there will be weeping and gnashing of teeth." What Jesus means is that his kinsmen, the Jewish people (represented in their leaders by the Pharisees and the elder brother), were in a position of extraordinary privilege. God had given them the law and the covenant and the promises and had come in the flesh as the Jewish Messiah. The kingdom of God belonged to the Jewish people, so to speak, as a natural inheritance. But the ministry of Jesus revealed that many in Israel did not love the God of Israel and were proving themselves unsuited to receive the inheritance. As long as the elder brother insists on being not a joyful son but an angry servant, he will not be able to receive the blessing of what is happening in the house. This is the meaning of the ominous words of Jesus in Matthew 21:43, "Therefore I tell you, the kingdom of God will be taken away from you [the Jewish leaders who oppose Jesus] and given to a people producing its fruits [Jews and Gentiles who have faith in Jesus and follow him on the Calvary road of love]."

lost, and is found" (Luke 15:31). The brother, it seems, will not do what is fitting. He will not love mercy. He wants to be treated for his own merit, not his father's mercy. The parable is open-ended. The Pharisees who are listening should hear an invitation to them. Jesus will welcome them into the celebration of grace and salvation if they will lay down their judgmental self-righteousness and delight in mercy.

But very few of the Pharisees, as far as we know, made that move. Apparently Nicodemus did. He was the Pharisee who came to Jesus with questions at night and heard Jesus say, "Unless one is born again he cannot see the kingdom of God" (John 3:3). We find Nicodemus after the death of Jesus making an extremely risky move for "a ruler of the Jews" (John 3:1). He brought seventy-five pounds of spices to honor Jesus' dead body (John 19:39) and joined with Joseph of Arimathea to give Jesus a proper burial. The Bible does not say he had become a disciple, though it calls Joseph one (Matt. 27:57). But it is hard to imagine a Pharisee taking such a risk if he had not come to faith in Jesus. But that was rare. For the most part, the Pharisees were entrenched in enmity toward Jesus to the end.

WHAT THE PHARISEES LOVED: PRAISE, MONEY, SEX

The picture Jesus paints of them is tragic and ugly. The root problem is that their hearts are far from God. He said to them in Matthew 15:7-8, "Well did Isaiah prophesy of you, when he said: 'This people honors me with their lips, but their heart is far from me.'" Their hearts do not treasure God; they treasure money, praise, and sex.

After Jesus told a parable about the right use of money in Luke 16:1-9, the Pharisees ridiculed him. Luke says that the reason was that they "were lovers of money" (Luke 16:14). Later Jesus said, "Beware of the scribes . . . who devour widows' houses" (Luke 20:46-47). That is, they create rules and preserve traditions that make temple-giving a substitute for caring for the poor, even your own parents (Mark 7:9-13). And when Jesus described what was in the heart of the Pharisees he said they were "full of greed and self-indulgence" (Matt. 23:25). In all their thoroughgoing religiosity, they did not love God; they loved money.

And they loved the praise of man. The reward they sought for what they did was not the enjoyment of God's fellowship, but the admiration of others. Jesus said, "They do all their deeds to be seen by others. For they make their phylacteries broad and their fringes long, and they love the place of honor at feasts and the best seats in the synagogues and greetings in the marketplaces and being called rabbi by others" (Matt. 23:5-7). This love affair with the praise of man made genuine faith in the self-sacrificing Christ impossible. So Jesus said to them,[4] "How can you believe, when you receive glory from one another and do not seek the glory that comes from the only God?" (John 5:44). Their hearts were not drawn to God as their reward, but to the praise of man.

And as is usually the case with those who are driven by the love of money and human praise, the Pharisees were also, it seems, often involved in illicit sex. Jesus calls them a "wicked and *adulterous* generation." "Then some of the scribes and Pharisees answered him, saying, 'Teacher, we wish to see a sign from you.' But he answered them, 'An evil and *adulterous* generation seeks for a sign'" (Matt. 12:38-39). I argued in *Demand #9* that this refers at least in part to the *spiritual* adultery of Israel's not wanting to have Jesus as their true husband. But it is natural to assume that the word "adulterous" implies that the alternative "husbands" include not just money and human praise, but also illicit sex. When the heart is not deeply entranced by the glory of God, it is usually driven along by the pitiful powers of money and the praise of man.

HYPOCRISY: THE CLOAK OF LAW-KEEPING EXACTITUDE

What made this idolatry so ugly to Jesus was that it all came in clean religious clothing. This was the essence of what he called hypocrisy. "Woe to you, scribes and Pharisees, hypocrites! For

---

[4] The Pharisees are not explicitly mentioned in John 5, but "the Jews" mentioned in John 5:10, 15, 16, 18 are probably the spokesmen for the people, namely, the scribes and Pharisees. The role they play is identical to what the Pharisees play elsewhere.

you clean the outside of the cup and the plate, but inside they are full of greed and self-indulgence" (Matt. 23:25). Cleaning the outside of the cup refers to using the law of God to conceal the rejection of God. This made Jesus more angry than anything else. "Woe to you, scribes and Pharisees, hypocrites! For you are like whitewashed tombs, which outwardly appear beautiful, but within are full of dead people's bones and all uncleanness. So you also outwardly appear righteous to others, but within you are full of hypocrisy and lawlessness" (Matt. 23:27-28). These are strong words to describe the hearts of the Pharisees: greed, self-indulgence, dead bones, unclean, hypocrisy, and lawlessness. All of that cloaked with law-keeping exactitude.

But it gets worse. In the next chapter we will see some of the loveless behaviors this inner corruption produces. It should be clear at this point that the righteousness of the Pharisees will not avail with God. We must have a righteousness that exceeds what we see in the Pharisees.

<hr>

Demand #26

YOUR RIGHTEOUSNESS MUST EXCEED THAT OF THE PHARISEES—CLEAN THE INSIDE OF THE CUP

Watch and beware of the leaven of the Pharisees and Sadducees. —MATT. 16:6

You blind guides, straining out a gnat and swallowing a camel! —MATT. 23:24

Woe to you, scribes and Pharisees, hypocrites! For you clean the outside of the cup and the plate, but inside they are full of greed and self-indulgence. You blind Pharisee! First clean the inside of the cup and the plate, that the outside also may be clean. —MATT. 23:25-26

They tie up heavy burdens, hard to bear, and lay them on people's shoulders, but they themselves are not willing to move them with their finger. —MATT. 23:4

Jesus' description of the heart of the Pharisees, which we saw in the previous chapter, is devastating: greed, self-indulgence, dead bones, uncleanness, hypocrisy, lawlessness. Not surprisingly, when this kind of heart protects and provides for itself by looking "righteous" on the outside, it necessarily majors on the minors of righteousness.

BLIND TO SPIRITUAL PROPORTION

It is easier to tithe than to love justice, mercy, and faithfulness. "Woe to you, scribes and Pharisees, hypocrites! For you tithe mint and dill and cumin,[1] and have neglected the weightier matters of the law: justice and mercy and faithfulness" (Matt. 23:23). They were blind to any sense of spiritual proportion: "You blind guides, straining out a gnat and swallowing a camel!" (Matt. 23:24). And what makes matters worse, when the blind become guides, other people are hurt, even destroyed. "They are blind guides," Jesus said, "and if the blind lead the blind, both will fall into a pit" (Matt. 15:14).

Which means their spiritual blindness and deadness was both suicidal and murderous. They were destroying themselves and others. "Woe to you Pharisees!" Jesus warned. "For you are like unmarked graves, and people walk over them without knowing it" (Luke 11:44). Coming in contact with the dead was viewed as defiling. Ironically, in all their effort to remain ceremonially clean they proved to be not only dead themselves but hurtful to others by their deadness.

THE HELLISH CONDITION OF BEING MERCILESSLY DEMANDING

Nor did they care. As is regularly the case with self-righteous hypocrites, their attitude to others is mercilessly demanding. "They tie up heavy burdens, hard to bear, and lay them on people's shoulders, but they themselves are not willing to move them with their finger" (Matt. 23:4). In other words, their use of the law is merciless. Unlike Jesus, whose yoke is easy and burden is light (Matt. 11:28-30) because he grants what he demands,[2] they only demand and do not lift a finger to help. In this way they not only perish themselves but drag people down with them. "Woe to you, scribes and Pharisees, hypocrites! For you shut the kingdom of heaven in

---

[1] Mint, dill, and cumin are spices and represent the minutiae of their external obedience in contrast to the magnitude of their internal corruption.

[2] See *Demands #7, 21, 23, 24.*

people's faces. For you neither enter yourselves nor allow those who would enter to go in" (Matt. 23:13).

Strictly speaking, this is hellish. Hell-bound hypocrites labor to take others with them. With profound love for lost and vulnerable people, Jesus unleashed his fury against the agents of hell: "Woe to you, scribes and Pharisees, hypocrites! For you travel across sea and land to make a single proselyte, and when he becomes a proselyte, you make him twice as much a child of hell as yourselves" (Matt. 23:15). Jesus is not speaking in vague metaphors here. They are children of hell because the devil is their father, not God. Jesus said to them, "If God were your Father, you would love me, for I came from God and . . . he sent me. . . . You are of your father the devil, and your will is to do your father's desires" (John 8:42-44). In other words, their heart is shaped in its affections and choices by the will of Satan. Their disposition is formed by the fashions of hell.

The Pharisees try to deflect this assessment of themselves by turning the tables and accusing Jesus of working for Satan. They say, "It is only by Beelzebul, the prince of demons, that this man casts out demons" (Matt. 12:24). But Jesus points out that his Satan-defeating ministry cannot be explained by complicity with Satan: "If Satan casts out Satan, he is divided against himself. How then will his kingdom stand?" (Matt. 12:26). No, the fact remains: It is the Pharisees who are the "brood of vipers" who cannot speak good because they *are* evil. "How can you speak good, when you are evil? For out of the abundance of the heart the mouth speaks" (Matt. 12:34).

CLEAN THE INSIDE SO THAT THE OUTSIDE ALSO MAY BE CLEAN

This is the essence of their problem: Their heart is evil and "hard" (Mark 3:5; 10:5). All their religious and moral effort is spent cleaning the outside and guarding what goes into their mouths, not what comes out of their heart. It was absolutely crucial for his disciples that Jesus make plain to them that the Pharisees have this backwards. So he explains to them in private, "Do you not see that whatever goes into the mouth passes into the stomach and is expelled? But what comes out of the mouth proceeds from the heart, and this defiles a person. . . . But to eat with unwashed hands does not defile anyone" (Matt. 15:17–20).

The Pharisees were acting like fools—as though the God who made the outside did not care about the inside even more. "You fools!" Jesus cried out, "Did not he who made the outside make the inside also?" (Luke 11:40). Then he told them as plainly and as straightforwardly as possible what they needed to do: "You blind Pharisee! First clean the inside of the cup and the plate, that the outside also may be clean" (Matt. 23:26). Or in another place he expressed it more indirectly and provocatively. He said, "But give as alms those things that are within, and behold, everything is clean for you" (Luke 11:41).

Contrary to this counsel, the Pharisees gave alms to be seen by men (Matt. 23:5). In other words, their heart was not in it. When they gave to the poor, they did not give their heart. That is, they did not give love. They did not care whether the poor became children of hell or children of heaven. They simply wanted to be admired for their deed. Jesus' remedy for this is: "Clean the inside of the cup and the plate, that the outside also may be clean." First comes the transformation of the inside. Then, as a result ("so that," ἵνα), the outside will be clean. Jesus cares about behavior, but not by itself.

This is why a merely social gospel will never find an advocate in Jesus. "Do good things" is not Jesus' main message. Absolutely indispensable to any God-pleasing, Jesus-obeying deeds is, "First clean the inside of the cup." And the "so that" shows that the only external behavior that counts with Jesus is what grows out of a transformed heart. "First clean the inside of the cup and the plate, *that* [ἵνα] the outside also may be clean." The outside matters, but only as the fruit of the inside.

STOTT WAS RIGHT

Now we are in a position to see how right John Stott was in the quote at the beginning of the previous chapter. What does Jesus mean when he says, "Unless your righteousness exceeds that of the scribes and Pharisees, you will never enter the kingdom of heaven" (Matt. 5:20)? Stott answered, "Christian righteousness is greater than pharisaic righteousness because it is deeper, being a righteousness of the heart. . . . The righteousness which is pleasing to [God] is an inward righteousness of mind and motive. For 'the Lord looks on the heart.'"[3] Of course, Stott believes that this true righteousness will have external, visible expression in life. But the decisive thing is the righteousness of the heart.

An Ugly "Righteousness" Is Easy to Exceed— and Hard

In view of what we have seen, this is exactly what Jesus meant. Jesus' portrayal of the Pharisees' "righteousness" is so ugly, our response may be, that is easy to exceed. That would be true in one sense and false in another. The true part is that Jesus said, "My yoke is easy, and my burden is light" (Matt. 11:30). He does not want to be in the category of those who "load people with burdens hard to bear" but do not "not touch the burdens with one of [their] fingers" (Luke 11:46). Therefore, it is right to think that in one sense the righteousness that Jesus demands is "easy" and his burden is "light."

But in another sense, as we saw in *Demand #18*, it is hard. In fact, it is not just hard but impossible. When the rich man turned away from Jesus and went the way of the Pharisees, in love with his money, Jesus commented about how hard it is to "cleanse the inside of the cup" and stop loving money: "With man it is impossible, but not with God. For all things are possible with God" (Mark 10:27). He meant that, left to himself, this man cannot change his heart. He treasures money more than he treasures Jesus. That is what must be changed. That is the righteousness that the Pharisees do not have.

The righteousness that exceeds the Pharisees' righteousness is

---

[3] Cf. 1 Sam. 16:7; Luke 16:15.

the new heart that trusts Jesus and treasures him above money, praise, sex, and everything else in the world. Treasuring what is infinitely valuable is, in one sense, the easiest thing in the world—like being commanded to enjoy your favorite food. But when our hearts do not treasure Jesus in this way, changing on our own is beyond us.

Six Antitheses Show the Righteousness That Exceeds That of the Pharisees

After saying in Matthew 5:20 that our righteousness must exceed that of the scribes and Pharisees, Jesus goes on in the rest of that chapter of the Sermon on the Mount to show that while true righteousness includes loving deeds, it is decisively and essentially internal. *Decisively* because what is on the inside decides whether the external behavior has value before God. And *essentially* because the essence of the behavior's goodness is its inward motive, not the movements of muscles or the effects on externals. All that Jesus said about the hypocrisy of the Pharisees leads us to this conclusion.

Jesus confirms this in the rest of Matthew 5. He gives six examples of how an external reading of the law must be driven inwardly until the demand of God penetrates the heart and lays claim on the heart's deepest affections. Sometimes these six commands are called *antitheses* because Jesus puts his command in contrast (antithesis) to what the Pharisees were making of the Old Testament law and the temporary accommodations of the law itself.[4]

---

[4] Jesus so strongly affirmed the Mosaic law in Matthew 5:17-18 and elsewhere that it is hard to imagine that his commands in Matthew 5:21-48 should be understood as antithetical to the *true* meaning of the law itself. "Do not think that I have come to abolish the Law or the Prophets; I have not come to abolish them but to fulfill them. For truly, I say to you, until heaven and earth pass away, not an iota, not a dot, will pass from the Law until all is accomplished" (Matt. 5:17-18). This is why I say that Jesus puts his command in antithesis to what the Pharisees were making of the Old Testament law. They were treating the law narrowly and as mainly external. Jesus shows that something far deeper is called for, and far more extensive. I do not mean to imply that Jesus did not ever raise some of the standards that were in the Mosaic law. There were parts of the law that were temporary accommodations to the hardness of man's heart. For example, Jesus said, "Because of your hardness of heart Moses allowed you to divorce your wives, but from the beginning it was not so" (Matt. 19:8). With the appearing of the Messiah and the arrival of the power of God's kingdom and the inauguration of the new covenant (see *Demand #23*) and the giving of the Holy Spirit, Jesus commanded his disciples to pursue a higher standard than Moses did in permitting actions because of the hardness of the human heart.

FROM NO MURDER TO NO ANGER

First, Jesus refers to the commandment not to murder. Over against the mere external application of it, he gives the commandment not to be angry and says that anger, even without the external act, is like murder (Matt. 5:21-26). So we see that the righteousness that exceeds that of the Pharisees is essentially the internal change that does not get angry when wronged (see *Demands #18-19*).

FROM NO ADULTERY TO NO LUST

Second, Jesus refers to the command not to commit adultery, and over against its merely external application he puts the command not to lust: "But I say to you that everyone who looks at a woman with lustful intent has already committed adultery with her in his heart" (Matt. 5:28). So he shows that the righteousness that exceeds that of the Pharisees is essentially the inner change that overcomes the heart's bondage to illicit sexual desire. The righteousness Jesus demands is not just the act, but the purity of heart behind the external chastity.

FROM DIVORCE TO FAITHFULNESS

Third, he refers to the provision for divorce in the Old Testament and puts over against it the higher ideal of not divorcing our wives. "But I say to you that everyone who divorces his wife, except on the ground of sexual immorality, makes her commit adultery. And whoever marries a divorced woman commits adultery" (Matt. 5:32). The righteousness that exceeds that of the scribes and Pharisees is the new ability to find an answer to marriage problems not in the external solution of divorce but in the transformation of the heart.[5]

FROM OATH-KEEPING TO SIMPLE HONESTY

Fourth, Jesus refers to the commandment that we "perform to the Lord what you have sworn" (Matt. 5:33). Over against it he calls

---

[5] For more on Jesus' view of divorce and remarriage see *Demands #40, 41, 42*.

for something more radical and more inward. He demands that our heart be so transparently honest that there is no need for external confirmations (like oaths) to buttress our simple yes and no. The righteousness that exceeds that of the scribes and Pharisees is the inward commitment to total truthfulness that makes "I swear" superfluous.

FROM RETALIATION TO LOVING CONTENTMENT

Fifth, Jesus quotes the law, "An eye for an eye and a tooth for a tooth." Then in contrast, he gives six demands: "But I say to you, [1] Do not resist the one who is evil. [2] But if anyone slaps you on the right cheek, turn to him the other also. [3] And if anyone would sue you and take your tunic, let him have your cloak as well. [4] And if anyone forces you to go one mile, go with him two miles. [5] Give to the one who begs from you, and [6] do not refuse the one who would borrow from you" (Matt. 5:39-42). All of these are behaviors, not just inward dispositions.

Therefore, we should not say that the righteousness that exceeds that of the scribes and Pharisees is merely internal. It clearly involves acts of remarkable patience and self-denial and love. But neither can we miss the fact that these six commands are so radically contrary to natural, human (pharisaic!) selfishness that they are impossible to do without an inner change that puts our contentment and security in something other than what this world offers, namely, in Jesus.

FROM LIMITED LOVE TO LOVING OUR ENEMIES

Finally, Jesus quotes the distortion of the Old Testament law (Lev. 19:18): "You have heard that it was said, 'You shall love your neighbor and hate your enemy'" (Matt. 5:43). Then he contradicts the distortion: "But I say to you, Love your enemies and pray for those who persecute you" (Matt. 5:44). Love becomes visible in sacrificial deeds of service. But love is not first visible. It is first a change in the heart.

This is plain from the command that we "*pray* for those who persecute" us. Prayer means that we really do wish them well.[6] We are praying for their salvation and their everlasting joy and that God's merciful saving will be done in their lives. This will not happen if there is only a raw commitment to act with external courtesy toward our enemies. If we are going to pray for them truly, our hearts will have to be dramatically changed from selfishness to security in Jesus. This change, together with the deeds that flow from it, is the righteousness that exceeds that of the scribes and Pharisees.

In the next chapter we turn to the battle for this inner purity and love that the Pharisees lacked. It is as radical as cutting off your hand and tearing out your eye. But we will also see that the security we enjoy rests not merely on the *demonstration* of a different heart than the Pharisees had, but also on our *location* in the forgiveness, acceptance, love, and eternal life of God.

---

[6] For reflections on the imprecatory psalms that express a will for the enemy's destruction, see the "Excursus on Hating the Wicked" in *Demand #29*.

Your Righteousness Must Exceed That of the Pharisees, for Every Healthy Tree Bears Good Fruit

Blessed are the pure in heart, for they shall see God. — Matt. 5:8

But I say to you that everyone who looks at a woman with lustful intent has already committed adultery with her in his heart. If your right eye causes you to sin, tear it out and throw it away. For it is better that you lose one of your members than that your whole body be thrown into hell. And if your right hand causes you to sin, cut it off and throw it away. For it is better that you lose one of your members than that your whole body go into hell. — Matt. 5:28-30

Every healthy tree bears good fruit, but the diseased tree bears bad fruit. — Matt. 7:17

The failure of the Pharisees was that they focused their moral efforts on cleaning the "outside of the cup" and neglected the purity of the heart. In this chapter we focus on the battle for that purity that goes beyond the Pharisees. As with all battles, the question of triumph looms. Will we win this battle? Therefore, at the end we will turn our attention to the ground of our assurance in God's forgiveness, acceptance, love, and life.

Purity of Heart: To Treasure One Thing

When Jesus says in Matthew 5:8, "Blessed are the pure [καθαροὶ] in heart, for they shall see God," he is describing the righteousness that exceeds that of the scribes and Pharisees. He uses the same word "pure" (καθαρός) in describing what the Pharisees need: "You blind Pharisee! First clean [καθάρισον] the inside of the cup and the plate, that the outside also may be clean [καθαρόν]" (Matt. 23:26). The impurity that Jesus cares about most is our failure to trust and love God. The heart is made for God—to trust him and love him. The meaning of *impure* is anything that takes God's place or lessens the degree of our faith in and our love for God.

Søren Kierkegaard wrote a book entitled *Purity of Heart Is to Will One Thing*.[1] That title comes close to the essence of purity. I would only change the word "will" to "treasure." *Willing* can be taken too easily to mean an act of the soul against our true desires. But willing to have God that way would not be purity of heart. Purity rises to the degree that God is *treasured* supremely in Jesus. This is what the Pharisees failed to do, and what the superior righteousness does.

The change of heart that creates a new treasuring of Jesus is a gift of God that we experience when the eyes of our hearts are opened to see Jesus as more to be desired than any other reality. Jesus refers to that change as new birth (see *Demand #1*) or repentance (see *Demand #2*). It is the assumed summons of Jesus behind all his other demands. Get a new heart. Be born again. That is what we are seeing implicitly here in the demand for a righteousness or a purity that exceeds that of the scribes and the Pharisees. This demand is a call most deeply for the new birth.

This internal change is a gift. God demands it, and God gives it. Jesus says, "You must be born again" (John 3:7), but also says, "The wind blows where it wishes, and you hear its sound, but you do not know where it comes from or where it goes. So it is with everyone who is born of the Spirit" (John 3:8). Jesus gives the

---

[1] Søren Kierkegaard, *Purity of Heart Is to Will One Thing* (San Francisco: Harper Perennial, 1956).

command. The free and unpredictable Spirit gives the gift. *Our* responsibility is to see the Jesus who is really there and trust him for all that he is.

THE LIFE-AND-DEATH BATTLE FOR PURITY OF HEART

What is clear from Jesus' teaching is that keeping and growing the gift of purity and the righteousness that surpasses that of the Pharisees is a life-and-death battle. We are not passive. *Jesus* gives the decisive power, as John 15:5 says, "Apart from me you can do nothing." But *we* experience that power in the willingness to engage in radical and persistent attacks on our own sinfulness. Jesus pronounced a blessing on "those who hunger and thirst for righteousness." They are the ones who "shall be satisfied" (Matt. 5:6). Hunger and thirst are relentless. They never stop. They are signs of life. We will do almost anything in our power to satisfy hunger and thirst. That is how Jesus teaches us to pursue purity.

For example, when dealing with the impurity of inward sexual lust, Jesus demands whatever it takes to defeat it because our souls are at stake.

> If your right eye causes you to sin, tear it out and throw it away. For it is better that you lose one of your members than that your whole body be thrown into hell. And if your right hand causes you to sin, cut it off and throw it away. For it is better that you lose one of your members than that your whole body go into hell. (Matt. 5:29-30)

This may be what Jesus is referring to when he says, "From the days of John the Baptist until now the kingdom of heaven has suffered violence, and the violent take it by force" (Matt. 11:12).[2] Taking the kingdom by force may be a way of repeating what Jesus says about the fight against lust: Tear out your eye or cut off your hand—do

---

[2] See George Ladd, *The Presence of the Future* (Grand Rapids, Mich.: Eerdmans, 1974), 163-164.

whatever it takes—to inherit the kingdom and not go to hell. Take the kingdom by force—force against your sin, not force against God. The battle for righteousness in our hearts is fierce.

THE RADICAL POINT OF TEARING OUT THE RIGHT EYE

Notice three things about this battle. One is that the eye is the first organ to be attacked. "If your right eye causes you to sin, tear it out." Even though the issue is sexual sin, he does not say, "Cut off your sexual organ to avoid the deed." He says, "Tear out your eye to avoid the desire." The battle is for purity of heart before the purity of the bed. Without the purity of heart, everything in the bed is impure.

Second, notice that he says to tear out your *right* eye. The significance of this is that it leaves the left one intact to awaken just as much lust as before. Therefore, Jesus' point is not that literally tearing out the right eye is going to solve anything. The point is not that inward desires can be controlled by external maiming. The point is how enormous the stakes are. They are so great, we must do what we have to do to defeat the bondage of sinful desire. It is astonishing how many people deal with their sin casually. Jesus demands otherwise. Fight for a pure heart with the same urgency as tearing out an eye and cutting off a hand.

Third, notice what is at stake: hell. "It is better that you lose one of your members than that your whole body be thrown into hell." Many Christians who love the truth of justification by grace alone through faith alone—which I love, and which I believe Jesus teaches (see *Demand #20*)—find it difficult to take these threats of Jesus at face value. But there is no way to avoid them. They are strewn throughout the Gospels, and they clearly imply that if we forsake the battle for purity, we will perish.

THE EXPERIENCE OF ASSURANCE RESTS ON OUR LOCATION AND DEMONSTRATION

If we do not have a righteousness that exceeds that of the scribes and Pharisees, Jesus says, we will not enter the kingdom of heaven

(Matt. 5:20). Everything we have seen in this chapter shows that Jesus is not thinking here mainly of his own righteousness that is imputed to us.[3] He is thinking of the kind of internal transformation and external application revealed in the following six antitheses of Matthew 5:21-48.

How then do we enjoy security in Jesus when what he requires is real change of heart and real righteous behavior? I tried to answer this question especially in *Demand #24*. Indeed I am trying to give an answer to it throughout the book. So I close this chapter with another summary statement. Think of our sense of security—our assurance that we are going to enter the final manifestation of the kingdom of God at the end of the age—resting most decisively on our *location* in God's invincible favor, but also on our behavioral *demonstration* that we are truly in that location.

What I mean by *location* in God's invincible favor is at least six glorious truths about those who have trusted in Jesus. (1) We belonged to God before we belonged to Jesus (John 17:6), that is, we were in God's favor before we ever had any righteousness at all. (2) Our names are written in heaven among the citizens whom God intends to bring there (Luke 10:20). (3) We are justified—declared righteous—by faith in God's free mercy because of Christ (Luke 18:14). Jesus assured us that we need not, and dare not, trust in any righteousness of our own as the basis for our location in his favor. Luke tells us that Jesus' parable of the Pharisee and the tax collector was addressed "to some who trusted in themselves that they were righteous, and treated others with contempt" (Luke 18:9). (4) We are ransomed from every enemy that would destroy our souls (Mark 10:45). (5) We are forgiven all our sins through the blood of Christ (Matt. 26:28). (6) We possess now the new life of the Spirit which is eternal (John 5:24).

That is our location. It is complete and perfect: We cannot be any more chosen, written, justified, ransomed, forgiven, or eternal

---

[3] For Jesus' understanding of justification by faith and the imputation of righteousness, see *Demand #20*.

than we are. That is the decisive rock of our security and assurance. It is objective, outside of us, and unchanging.

THE DEMONSTRATION OF OUR LOCATION

What I mean by the *demonstration* is that the way we live shows our location. It does not create the location. God establishes our location through faith alone. But he has ordained that it be fitting for the location to have a demonstration in the world. This is the righteousness that exceeds that of the scribes and Pharisees. It is necessary, not optional. That is, Jesus assumes that if there is no demonstration of our location in God's favor, then the location does not exist. Jesus says this demonstration is necessary for final salvation (as we say, going to heaven), because God wills to be glorified both for the grace of establishing our *location* in his eternal favor once for all *and* for the grace of supplying the help we need to *demonstrate* this location by our conduct. None who is located by faith in God's invincible favor will fail to have all that is necessary to demonstrate this in life.

The assurance that our demonstration will be infallibly enabled by God rests on numerous realities. For example, (1) Jesus promises that nothing can snatch us out of his hand (John 10:28-29). (2) He promises that a Helper will come and not leave us to ourselves in this battle (John 14:16, 26; 15:26). (3) Jesus himself promises to be with us to the end of the age (Matt. 28:20). (4) Jesus prays that our faith will not fail and that the Father will keep us (Luke 22:32; John 17:11, 15). (5) Jesus assumes imperfection and makes provision for it (Matt. 6:12). (6) Jesus taught that what is required of us, even when it is impossible from our side, is not impossible with God (Matt. 19:26). (7) What is required in our demonstration is that there be evidence of God-given life, not flawlessness. These and other truths give us assurance that God's work in our lives will bring about the grace-exalting demonstration required in the last day.

EVERY HEALTHY TREE BEARS GOOD FRUIT

The picture Jesus used to illustrate the necessity of demonstration is the picture of a tree and its fruit. "Every healthy tree bears good fruit, but the diseased tree bears bad fruit. A healthy tree cannot bear bad fruit, nor can a diseased tree bear good fruit. Every tree that does not bear good fruit is cut down and thrown into the fire" (Matt. 7:17-19). When he says that "a healthy tree cannot bear bad fruit," he does not mean that no follower of his ever sins. The natural way of thinking about the present tense of a Greek verb like "bear" is "go on bearing." So Jesus would be saying, "A healthy tree cannot *go on bearing* bad fruit." In other words, a tree is cut down not for bad fruit here and there. It is cut down for producing so much bad fruit that there is no evidence that the tree is good. What God will require at the judgment is not our perfection, but sufficient fruit to show that the tree had life—in our case, divine life.

"I tell you, unless your righteousness exceeds that of the scribes and Pharisees, you will never enter the kingdom of heaven" (Matt. 5:20). May God grant us to trust Christ alone for the security of our location in God's invincible favor and for the help that he promises to change our hearts and lead us in demonstrable acts of love.

Demand #28

LOVE YOUR ENEMIES— LEAD THEM TO THE TRUTH

But I say to you, Love your enemies and pray for those who persecute you. —MATT. 5:44

Love your enemies, do good to those who hate you, bless those who curse you, pray for those who abuse you. —LUKE 6:27-28

If you love those who love you, what benefit is that to you? For even sinners love those who love them. And if you do good to those who do good to you, what benefit is that to you? For even sinners do the same. And if you lend to those from whom you expect to receive, what credit is that to you? Even sinners lend to sinners, to get back the same amount. —LUKE 6:32-34

Sanctify them in the truth; your word is truth. —JOHN 17:17

Jesus' demand that we love our enemies, be merciful, make peace, and forgive assumes that there are people who are hard to love. The demand is expressed in different ways because people are hard to love in different ways. Jesus calls some people our "enemies," which means they are against us. They want to see us fail. Love them, Jesus says (Matt. 5:44; Luke 6:27, 35). Others may not be our personal enemies in this way, but simply people whose character or personality or condition makes them unattractive or even repulsive. Be merciful to them, Jesus says (Matt.

5:7; 18:33; Luke 10:37). Don't base your treatment of them on what they attract or deserve, but on mercy. Others may be our relatives or friends who have taken offense at something we have done—rightly or wrongly—and the relationship is cold or non-existent. Strive to be reconciled to them, Jesus says (Matt. 5:23-26). Others may or may not have anything against you, but you do against them. Forgive them, Jesus says (Matt. 6:14-15). Don't let laziness or pride or anger keep you from the humble work of forgiving, peacemaking, and reconciliation.

HAVING ENEMIES MAY MEAN YOU ARE IN STEP WITH JESUS

Jesus' demand also assumes that we *will* have enemies and that not all will be reconciled to us, no matter what we do. He shows us that having enemies is not necessarily a bad thing but may mean we are keeping in step with him. For example, he pronounced a blessing on those who are persecuted on account of their allegiance to him. "Blessed are you when others revile you and persecute you and utter all kinds of evil against you falsely *on my account*" (Matt. 5:11). In other words, having enemies is to be expected: "If they have called the master of the house Beelzebul, how much more will they malign those of his household. . . . If they persecuted me, they will also persecute you" (Matt. 10:25; John 15:20).

In fact, Jesus warned that if there were no persecution, it may be a sign of being more like a false prophet than like Jesus: "Woe to you, when all people speak well of you, for so their fathers did to the false prophets" (Luke 6:26). Enmity between the world and the followers of Jesus is rooted in the truth that the world rejects him (John 18:37) and in the deep difference Jesus makes when he changes a person: "If you were of the world, the world would love you as its own; but because you are not of the world, but I chose you out of the world, *therefore the world hates you*" (John 15:19; cf. 17:14). Therefore, we should not assume that if we have enemies we must have done something wrong. That may be true, and we should search our hearts for unnecessary offenses and repent, but Jesus said very plainly that *faithful* disciples will have enemies. Expect it.

LOVE THOSE WHO KILL AND THOSE WHO SNUB

It is remarkable that Jesus draws attention to both severe persecution and mere snubbing as the kinds of enmity we must deal with. We might think that he would deal only with the worst kind of enmity and assume the other would take care of itself. But evidently he thinks we need to be told not only to love when our life is threatened, but also to love when our ego is threatened by a mere slight. Consider the range of enmity he mentions.

We are to love those who persecute us (Matt. 5:44), hate us (Luke 6:27), curse us, abuse us (Luke 6:28), strike us on the cheek, take our cloak (Luke 6:29). Those are all behaviors that would typically hurt us deeply, either physically or emotionally or both, and might kill us (Matt. 10:21; Luke 11:49). To all this we are to respond with love. But besides these very painful kinds of enmity, little things can bother us as well. Jesus said, for example, "If you greet only your brothers, what more are you doing than others? Do not even the Gentiles do the same? . . . And if you do good to those who do good to you, what benefit is that to you?" (Matt. 5:47; Luke 6:33). Here Jesus is dealing with simple acts like greeting and doing acts of kindness, and the issue is: How readily do we greet someone or do a kindness to someone who is a mere stranger or who has done nothing for us? They have not hurt us. They show us no enmity. They are just going about their business showing us no attention. We may feel it as a snub. Or we may not feel anything. Jesus says, love them. Don't love just the ones who recognize you and do good things for you. Love the persecutor, and love the person who simply acts as if you are not alive.

All this raises two basic questions. First, what is this love? What does it look like? How much of us does it involve? Second, where does it come from? How does it arise in our hearts, and how is it sustained over time and drawn out of us when all that is natural would seem to say, "No love is required here, or even possible"? Let's take first the question about what this love is.

LOVE PRESERVES THE TRUTH OF THE BIBLE

The first answer to the question of what this love involves is so obvious we may not see it. In commanding us to love our enemies, Jesus is confronting and correcting a bad use of the Bible. "You have heard that it was said, 'You shall love your neighbor and hate your enemy.' But I say to you, Love your enemies and pray for those who persecute you" (Matt. 5:43-44). In the very act of commanding love, he loves us by correcting a false and harmful interpretation of Scripture.

The Jewish Scriptures that Jesus shared with his contemporaries did not say, "You shall hate your enemy." They said, "You shall not take vengeance or bear a grudge against the sons of your own people, but you shall love your neighbor as yourself" (Lev. 19:18). Some had taken these references to "your own people" and to "neighbor" and concluded that the command to love applies only to neighbors—our own kind. The first act of love Jesus calls for in his command is by his own example of how he gives the command: He shows us that love rejects the bad interpretation of God's word and sets forth the truth.

TRUTH IS THE ROOT OF LOVE

I mention Jesus' example of love first not only because it is the first and most immediately present act of love in Jesus' words, but also because in our time in history, love is often contrasted with the defense of truth. That is not what Jesus demonstrates. Not here or anywhere. If someone had said to Jesus the words, "Love unites; doctrine divides," I think Jesus would have looked deep into that person's soul and said, "True doctrine is the root of love. Therefore, whoever opposes it, destroys the root of unity."

Jesus never opposed truth to love. He did the opposite. He said that he himself is the embodiment and sum of truth: "I am the way, and the *truth*, and the life" (John 14:6). Referring to him-self he said, "The one who seeks the glory of him who sent him is *true*, and in him there is no falsehood" (John 7:18). At the end of his life, what prompted Pilate's cynical question, "What is truth?" (John 18:38) was Jesus' comprehensive assertion about why he had come into the world: "For this purpose I was born and for this purpose I have come into the world—to bear witness to the *truth*" (John 18:37). Even his adversaries saw how indifferent Jesus was to people's opinions and how devoted he seemed to be to truth. "Teacher, we know that you are *true* and do not care about any-one's opinion" (Mark 12:14). And when Jesus leaves the world and returns to the Father in heaven, the Spirit he would send in his place would be called "the Spirit of truth." "But when the Helper comes, whom I will send to you from the Father, *the Spirit of truth*, who pro-ceeds from the Father, he will bear witness about me" (John 15:26).

Therefore, unlike so many who compromise the truth to win a following, Jesus did the opposite. Unbelief in his hearers confirmed that a deep change was needed in *them*, not in the truth. "Everyone who is of the truth listens to my voice" (John 18:38). "Whoever is of God hears the words of God. The reason why you do not hear them is that you are not of God" (John 8:47). "Because I tell the truth, you do not believe me" (John 8:45). In other words, when the truth does not produce the response you want—when it does not "work"—you don't abandon the truth. Jesus is not a pragmatist when it comes to loving people with the truth. You speak it, and if it does not win belief, you do not consider changing the truth. You pray that your hearers will be awakened and changed by the truth. "You will know the truth, and the truth will set you free (John 8:32). "Sanctify them in the truth," Jesus prayed; "your word is truth" (John 17:17).

When Jesus prays that people be "sanctified in the truth," he reveals the roots of love. Sanctification, or holiness, as Jesus under-stands it, includes being a loving person. He is praying that we would become loving people and would be merciful and peaceable and for-giving. That is all included in the prayer, "Sanctify them." And all this happens in and by the truth, not separate from the truth. The effort to pit love against truth is like pitting fruit against root. Or like pitting kindling against fire. Or like pitting the foundation of a house against the second-floor bedroom. The house will fall down, and the marriage bed with it, if the foundation crumbles. Love lives by truth and burns by truth and stands on truth. This is why Jesus' first act of love in commanding love is to correct a false interpretation of Scripture.

THE UNLOVING USE OF TRUTH

Of course, it is possible to use truth unlovingly. For example, when a village of Samaria would not receive Jesus "because his face was set toward Jerusalem" (Luke 9:53), James and John knew this was a truth-insulting response. It was an assault on the truth of Jesus. So they said to Jesus, in defense of the truth, "Lord, do you want us to tell fire to come down from heaven and consume them?" (Luke 9:54). The answer was swift and blunt: "He turned and rebuked them" (Luke 9:55).

But the solution to that unloving response was not to stay in the village and alter the truth to get a better response. He did not say to the Samaritans, "Doctrine divides, love unites, so let's put our doctrinal differences aside and have relational unity." No, the solution was, "And they went on to another village" (Luke 9:56). There are many people yet to be loved with our truth. We will keep offering the saving truth in love wherever we can, and we will not be violent with those who reject us. But the truth will not be changed. It is the root of love's life, and the kindling of love's fire, and the foundation of love's strength. When Jesus demanded that we love our enemies by contrasting this with the interpretation that said, "Love your neighbor and hate your enemy," he was lovingly showing us that correcting false interpretations of the Bible is one crucial way to love our enemy.

CHALLENGING THE ABSOLUTENESS OF THE BELOVED

The next obvious implication of Jesus' words for the meaning of love is that it is not unloving to call someone an enemy. We live in an emotionally fragile age. People are easily offended and describe their response to being criticized as being hurt. In fact, we live in a time when emotional offense, or woundedness, often becomes a criterion for deciding if love has been shown. If a person can claim to have been hurt by what you say, it is assumed by many that you did not act in love. In other words, love is not defined by the quality of the act and its motives, but by the subjective response of others. In this way of relating, the wounded one has absolute authority. If he says you hurt him, then you *cannot* have acted lovingly. You are guilty. Jesus will not allow this way of relating to go unchallenged.

Love is not defined by the response of the loved. A person can be genuinely loved and feel hurt or offended or angered or retaliatory or numb without in any way diminishing the beauty and value of the act of love that hurt him. We know this most clearly from the death of Jesus, the greatest act of love ever performed, because the responses to it covered the range from affection (John 19:27) to fury (Matt. 27:41-42). That people were broken, wounded, angered, enraged, and cynical in response to Jesus' death did not alter the fact that what he did was a great act of love.

This truth is shown by the way Jesus lived his life. He loved in a way that was often not felt as love. No one I have ever known in person or in history was as blunt as Jesus in the way he dealt with people. Evidently his love was so authentic it needed few cushions. It is owing to my living with the Jesus of the Gospels for fifty years that makes me so aware of how emotionally fragile and brittle we are today. If Jesus were to speak to us the way he typically spoke

---

[1]To his own disciples he spoke bluntly calling them "evil" (Matt. 7:11) and "of little faith" (Matt. 6:30; 8:26; 14:31; 16:8; 17:20) and a "faithless . . . generation" (Matt. 17:17) and telling a would-be disciple who wanted to go to a funeral to let the dead bury their dead (Luke 9:60). He was blunt with his hosts who invited him to dinner: "You gave me no kiss, but from the time I came in she has not ceased to kiss my feet. You did not anoint my head with oil, but she has anointed my feet with ointment" (Luke 7:45-46). "He said also to the man who had invited him, 'When you give a dinner or a banquet, do not invite your friends or your brothers or your relatives or rich neighbors, lest they also invite you in return and you be repaid. But when you give a feast, invite the poor, the crippled, the lame, the blind'" (Luke 14:12-13). He said he was glad that God had hidden truth from the "wise and understanding": "I thank you, Father, Lord of heaven and earth, that you have hidden these things from the wise and understanding and revealed them to little children" (Matt. 11:25). He would not answer those who played word games with the crowds (Matt. 21:23-27). He called Herod a "fox" (Luke 13:32) and excoriated the Pharisees with "brood of vipers" (Matt. 23:33) and "whitewashed tombs" (Matt. 23:27) and "blind guides" (Matt. 23:16) and "hypocrites" (Matt. 23:13) and "fools" (Matt. 23:17). And of course, he made a whip and drove out the money-changers from the temple (Matt. 21:12). All this, and so much more, would simply put Jesus so far

in his own day, we would be continually offended and hurt. This is true of the way he spoke to his disciples and the way he spoke to his adversaries.[1] People were offended in his day as well. "Do you know," his disciples asked him, "that the Pharisees were *offended* when they heard this saying?" (Matt. 15:12). His response to that information was brief and pointed: "Every plant that my heavenly Father has not planted will be rooted up.[2] Let them alone; they are blind guides" (Matt. 15:13-14). In other words, "They are plants that do not produce the fruit of faith because God has not planted them. They don't see my behavior as love because they are blind, not because I am unloving." These and dozens of other things he said to both friend and foe in ways that would rock us back on our emotional heels and make many of us retreat in self-pity.

The point of this is that the genuineness of an act of love is not determined by the subjective feelings of the one being loved. Jesus uses the word "enemies." That would be offensive to some, especially since he goes on to unpack his point with words like, "And if you greet only your *brothers*, what more are you doing than others?" (Matt. 5:47). He does not fret over the possible criticism that he is not being careful enough to distinguish real enemies from annoying brothers. Jesus seems to expect us to handle tough words like "enemy" mingled with tender family words like "brother."

LOVE IS NOT OBLIVIOUS OR UNCARING ABOUT ITS EFFECTS

I do not mean to say that love is oblivious to the words it uses or the effects they may have on others. Love does care about blessing the loved one. It desires to bring the loved one out of pain and sor-

---

[1] outside the range of emotional tolerance in our day that his behavior would simply not feel loving. All of which goes to show that the criterion of what love is does not reside in the subjective response of the one being loved.

[2] "Those plants his Father had planted were those who had received the revelation of Jesus' character from the Father—a revelation he had concealed from the 'wise and prudent' (11:25-27; 13:11-17; 16:16-17; cf. 14:33)." Craig S. Keener, *A Commentary on the Gospel of Matthew* (Grand Rapids, Mich.: Eerdmans, 1999), 413. The saying is parallel with John 10:26, "You do not believe because you are not part of my flock." Or John 18:37, "Everyone who is of the truth listens to my voice." Or John 8:47, "Whoever is of God hears the words of God. The reason why you do not hear them is that you are not of God."

row and into a deeper experience of joy in God—now and forever. But I am stressing another side of the problem that seems unusually prevalent in our psychologized world. I am simply drawing attention to the fact that *feeling* unloved is not the same as *being* unloved. Jesus is modeling for us in his life the objectivity of love. It has real motives and real actions. And when they are loving, the response of the loved one does not change that fact.

This is good news for the lover, because it means that *God* is God and the loved one is *not* God. The judgment of the wounded loved one is not absolute: It may be right, or it may be wrong. But it is not absolute. God is absolute. We give an account to him. And he alone knows our hearts. The decisive thing about our love when we stand before God is not what others thought of it, but whether it was real. That some people may not like the way we love is not decisive. Most people did not recognize Jesus' love in the end—and still do not today. What matters is not that we are justified before men, but that God knows our hearts as truly (though not perfectly) loving. And he alone can make that final judgment (Luke 16:15).

Demand #29

LOVE YOUR ENEMIES—
PRAY FOR THOSE
WHO ABUSE YOU

Love your enemies and pray for those who persecute you. —MATT. 5:44

Pray for those who abuse you. —LUKE 6:28

Father, forgive them, for they know not what they do. —LUKE 23:34

Before turning to the demand that we pray for those who persecute us and abuse us, we need to draw out one more clarification of Jesus' command, namely, that love hates the evil that destroys the ones we love.

LOVE HATES THE EVIL THAT DESTROYS PERSONS

We cannot claim to desire the good of the beloved and be indifferent to what destroys him. Jesus' demand to love our enemy implies that love must hate the evil that destroys the beloved. If there were a universe in which there was no evil that hurt people or dishonored Jesus, there would be only love and no hate. There would be nothing to hate. But in a world like ours it is necessary not only that we love and hate, but that our love include hate.

EXCURSUS ON HATING THE WICKED

This is perhaps the best place to insert some thoughts on the kind of hatred that Jesus read about in the Psalms that are sometimes called the imprecatory psalms— that is, psalms that express hatred for God's enemies and call down divine curses on them. These would include Psalm 5:10; 10:15; 28:4; 31:17-18; 35:4-6; 40:14-15; 58:6-11; 69:22-28; 109:6-15; 139:19-22; 140:9-10. Psalm 139:19-22 says, "Oh that you would slay the wicked, O God! O men of blood, depart from me! They speak against you with malicious intent; your enemies take your name in vain! Do I not hate those who hate you, O LORD? And do I not loathe those who rise up against you? I hate them with complete hatred; I count them my enemies."

We know that Jesus was aware of these psalms and that he did not criticize them but quoted them as authoritative Scripture. At least one of the most severe of them (Psalm 69) seems to have been a favorite from which Jesus, in his human nature, drew guidance and encouragement and self-understanding (John 15:25=Psalm 69:4, "They hated me without a cause." John 2:17=Psalm 69:9, "Zeal for your house will consume me." Matt. 27:34=Psalm 69:21, "They offered him wine to drink, mixed with gall"). This psalm prays, "Pour out your indignation on them, and let your burning anger overtake them" (69:24).

Consider in some of these psalms that *love* for the enemy has been pursued for a long time. "They repay me evil for good . . . when they were sick—I wore sackcloth" (35:12-13). "In return for my love they accuse me, but I give myself to prayer. So they reward me evil for good, and hatred for my love" (109:4-5). Though unexpressed, this may be the case for all the psalms. The wickedness in view has resisted love.

Consider also that hatred may refer at times (not always) to moral repugnance, not personal vengeance. This is not the same as saying, "Hate the sin and love the sinner" (which can be good counsel, but not all there is to say). There is a kind of hate for the sinner (viewed as morally corrupt and hostile to God) that may coexist with pity and even a desire for his salvation. The hate is moral repugnance, not desire for destruction. The analogy with food may help. You may hate spinach (because of its taste) while affirming its worth and desiring that it have its beneficial effect. So it is possible to hate a person in the sense of finding his character loathsome (say, a cannibalistic murderer and child-abuser) while being willing to lay down your life for his salvation. The hate that Jesus forbids to us is the hate that wills a person's destruction.

However, there may come a point when wickedness is so persistent and high-handed and God-despising that the time of redemption is past and there only remain irremediable wickedness and judgment. For example, Jesus speaks of unforgivable sin (Matt. 12:32). He says of the Pharisees who have evidently crossed the line of no return, "Let them alone; they are blind guides. And if the blind lead the blind, both will fall into a pit" (Matt. 15:14). That is an ominous "Let them alone." Craig Keener compares it to Matthew 7:6, "Do not waste your pearls on swine."[1] It seems that Jesus continues what the Psalms affirm, namely, that there comes a point of such extended, hardened, high-handed lovelessness toward God that it may be appropriate to give a person up to destruction and call down anathema on him. Jesus makes it plain that this will happen at the end of the age. He says that the King "will say to those on his left, 'Depart from me, you *cursed*, into the eternal fire prepared for the devil and his angels'" (Matt. 25:41).

From all this, and from the fact that Jesus affirms the divine inspiration of the Psalms (Matt. 22:43; John 10:35), I conclude that he saw the psalmist speaking under the guidance of the Holy Spirit and foreshadowing the Messiah and Judge, who has the ultimate right to call down judgment on the enemies of God. This is not personal vindictiveness. It is a prophetic execution of what will happen at the last day when God casts all his unrepentant enemies into hell (Luke 12:5; Matt. 22:13; 25:30). We would do well to leave such final assessments to God and realize our own corrupt inability to hate as we ought. While there is unforgivable sin, we are told to love our enemies and pray for those who persecute us and return good for evil (as David did in Psalm 35:12-13; 109:4-5). This is our vocation by faith. Let us tremble and trust God, lest we fail, and find ourselves on the other side of the curse.

To illustrate the truth that in a world like ours it is necessary that our love include hate, consider what Jesus says in John 5:29

---

[1] Craig Keener, *A Commentary on the Gospel of Matthew* (Grand Rapids, Mich.: Eerdmans, 1999), p. 413.

that in the last day when the dead are raised, all people will rise, "those who have done good to the resurrection of life, and those who have done *evil* to the resurrection of judgment." This means that there is *evil* in the world that leads to the final destruction of people we love. How does love feel about that evil? My point is that love hates that evil. We do not hate God's judgment. That is just and wise. But we do hate the evil that leads a person to oppose God and incur his judgment.

There Is No Evil That Hurts Only You

One might be tempted to say at this point that the evil I must hate is only the evil that hurts another person but not the evil that hurts me. In other words, it would not be unloving to *you* if I engage in evil behavior that only involves me. Jesus would say, there is no such behavior. Why not? Because everything I do affects my delight in Jesus and my ability to display him as valuable. That is what we were made for (Matt. 5:16; 10:32). We were made to display the worth of Jesus to others, that they might increasingly awaken to it and enjoy it and reflect it forever. That is the greatest good we can do for them. That is what it means to love them. But if we do things to ourselves that damage our delight in Jesus and damage our display of his worth to others (and that is the very essence of evil—it damages our delight in Jesus and our ability to display his worth), then we rob them of what God made us to give them—a display of his worth. That is the opposite of love. Therefore, love must hate evil, whether it is evil the loved one is doing to his own peril, or the evil I am doing to my own *and his* peril.

I point out the relationship between love and hate simply to waken us from the sentimental slumbers of much love-talk. There are people, especially in our day, whose worldview is so relativistic and whose personality so morally flaccid that they do not even have a category for evil, lest they find themselves offending the demand for tolerance of all views. Jesus would say: Tolerance of all views is the opposite of love. It condones what destroys. We cannot read the words of Jesus with an honest heart and conclude that he denies the existence of evil that destroys and good that leads to everlasting joy. Therefore, to minimize or deny the existence of evil, rather than hating it, makes one partner to the destruction of human persons. This is not the love that Jesus demands.

"Pray for Those Who Persecute You"

Jesus gives numerous examples of the kinds of behaviors involved in loving our enemies. The first mentioned in the Sermon on the Mount after the command to love is prayer. "Love your enemies and *pray* for those who persecute you" (Matt. 5:44). And *"Pray* for those who abuse you" (Luke 6:28). This is enormously important in telling us how Jesus thinks about what love is. First, it tells us that love *really wants* the good of the enemy. This is confirmed by the supplementary command, *"Bless* those who curse you" (Luke 6:28). To bless is to desire someone's well-being and turn it into an expressed longing directed to God. For example, Jesus knew the famous blessing from Numbers 6:24-26, "The LORD bless you and keep you; the LORD make his face to shine upon you and be gracious to you; the LORD lift up his countenance upon you and give you peace." Do this, he says, for your enemy. He needs the light of God's countenance to shine on him and melt his heart.

Therefore, it is clear from this specific command that love is not merely behavior. To be sure, it *is* doing good for the enemy, but not merely that. It is also a heart desire. I base this on the assumption that when we pray for our enemies, we ask for God's blessing *from our heart*. Jesus is not commending hypocritical prayer. He is not calling for show-prayer. He is calling for real prayer, that is, real Godward desire for the good of our enemy. Love really wants the enemy to experience God's best. Doing good things is not enough. The heart must aim at the best we can hope for the enemy.

What to Pray for Our Enemies

Not only that, the demand to pray for our enemy tells us what that best is that we should want for our enemy. Fourteen verses after this command in the Sermon on the Mount Jesus tells us what he expects us to pray. He tells us to pray like this:

> Our Father in heaven,
> hallowed be your name.
> Your kingdom come,
> your will be done, on earth as it is in heaven.
> Give us this day our daily bread,
> and forgive us our debts, as we also have forgiven our debtors.
> And lead us not into temptation, but deliver us from evil.
>
> MATT. 6:9-13

It would be unwarranted to think that the loving prayer for our enemy should ask for less important things than we are told to pray for ourselves. So I assume this prayer is what we should pray for our enemies.

• This means that we should ask God that our enemy first and foremost come to hallow God's name, that he value God above all and reverence him and admire him in proportion to God's worth.

• We should pray that our enemy come under the saving sway of God's kingly rule and that God would exert his kingly power to make our enemy his own loyal subject.

• We should pray that our enemy would love to do the will of God the way the angels do it in heaven with all their might and without reservation and with purest motives and supreme joy.

• We should pray that God would supply our enemy with all the physical resources of food and clothing and shelter and education and health care and transportation, etc. that he needs to fulfill God's calling on his life. We should want this for him the way we want it for ourselves.

• We should pray that his sins would be forgiven and that he would be a forgiving person.

• And finally we should pray that God protect him from temptation and from the destructive powers of the devil.
This is what love prays.

It is pathetic to see love stripped of God. Even some Christians are misled into thinking you can love someone without longing for and praying for and aiming at the exaltation of God in the heart of their enemy. What is so sad about this is that it not only betrays the diminished place of God in the heart of the Christian, but also implies that there can be real love where we don't care if someone perishes eternally, as long as they prospered here on earth. It is true that our love and prayer may not succeed in wakening our enemy to faith in Jesus and to the hallowing of God's name. Love is the *aim* of our sacrifice, not its success. We may or may not succeed in the Jesus-exalting, God-hallowing transformation we aim at. But a heart that does not aim at our enemy's eternal joy in Jesus is not the full-orbed, robust love that Jesus demands. It is a narrow and pathetic substitute, no matter how creative and sacrificial and media-admired the labor is for our enemy's earthly welfare. Love prays for our enemy with all the aims and longings of the Lord's Prayer.

"FATHER, FORGIVE THEM, FOR THEY KNOW NOT WHAT THEY DO"

The most compelling example of praying for one's enemy was the prayer of Jesus on the cross. After the simple, understated fact in Luke 23:33, "There they crucified him," Jesus prayed, "Father, forgive them, for they know not what they do" (Luke 23:34). This prayer draws together three acts of the heart involved in loving our enemies: prayer, forgiveness, and mercy. Jesus is unremitting in demanding that his disciples be forgiving people.

When Peter asked him, "Lord, how often will my brother sin against me, and I forgive him? As many as seven times?" Jesus answered, "I do not say to you seven times, but seventy times seven" (Matt. 18:21-22). In other words, "Don't set limits, Peter. Let the mercy in your heart be as bottomless as mine toward you." "Be merciful, even as your Father is merciful" (Luke 6:36). Mercy and forgiveness are needed when there is real guilt, real offense. The "enemy" has really wronged you, and you "deserve" suitable recompense. That is when mercy and forgiveness become relevant and urgent. Mercy says, "I will treat you better than you deserve." And forgiveness says, "I am willing not to count your offense against you. I want the relationship to be restored."

WHY DO THEY NEED FORGIVENESS IF THEY DON'T KNOW WHAT THEY'RE DOING?

Jesus' prayer illustrates this, even though at first it seems not to. He says, "Father, forgive them, for they know not what they do." "Forgive those who murder me because they don't know what they are doing." This raises the question: Why forgive a person for what he does not know he is doing? Wouldn't we say: "Father, since they don't know what they are doing, they are not guilty and don't need to be forgiven"? Isn't it either-or? Either you know what you are doing and need to be forgiven, or you don't know what you are doing and you don't need to be forgiven? Why does Jesus draw attention to their ignorance of what they are doing *and* ask God to forgive them?

The answer is that they are guilty for not knowing what they are doing. Forgiveness is only needed for the guilty. Nobody can forgive an innocent person. So when Jesus says, "Father, forgive them," he means they are guilty. Then when he says, "For they don't know what they are doing," he must mean, "And they *should* know what they are doing. And they are guilty for not knowing what they are doing." In other words, they have so much evidence of the truth that the only explanation for their ignorance is they don't want to see it. They are hard and resistant and have a guilty blindness. That is why they need to be forgiven.

So here are Gentiles and Jews killing the Son of God, the Messiah of Israel, the most innocent and loving man who ever existed. But they did not know whom they were killing. For this ignorance they were guilty and in need of forgiveness. And amazingly, Jesus is praying for them that his Father would open their eyes and help them to see their sin, repent, and be forgiven. That is the beautiful thing about this prayer of Jesus: It declares guilt and offers forgiveness at the same time. It helps us love our enemies by reminding us that our enemies are really guilty and that this must not stop our love and mercy and forgiveness. Most of all it helps us because we know that Jesus was suffering for *us* and praying for *us*. We are called to love and forgive our enemies because we have been loved and forgiven when we were the enemies of God.

Demand #30

LOVE YOUR ENEMIES—
DO GOOD TO THOSE WHO
HATE YOU, GIVE TO THE
ONE WHO ASKS

Peter came up and said to him, "Lord, how often will my brother sin against me, and I forgive him? As many as seven times?" Jesus said to him, "I do not say to you seven times, but seventy times seven."—MATT. 18:21-22

But I say to you who hear, Love your enemies, do good to those who hate you.—LUKE 6:27

And if you greet only your brothers, what more are you doing than others? Do not even the Gentiles do the same?—MATT. 5:47

We closed the previous chapter by dealing with prayer as a form of love for our enemies. That was clear from Jesus' demand to "Love your enemies and *pray* for those who persecute you" (Matt. 5:44). We took Jesus' prayer for his enemies as one example. His focus was forgiveness: "Father, forgive them" (Luke 23:34). Forgiveness and reconciliation are clearly near the heart of Jesus' life and message. Hence we need to dig into these demands more deeply here, then turn to several other forms of enemy love (greeting those outside our group, doing good to those who hate us, turning the other cheek, and giving to the one who asks). Finally, we will wrestle with the question whether all of these commands, like giving to the one who asks, are absolutely the only way that love responds.

THE OPPOSITE OF FORGIVENESS IS NOT ALIENATION

Forgiveness from the heart—not just the mouth—is demanded by Jesus from his disciples: "So also my heavenly Father will do to every one of you [referring to God's punishment in the parable of the unforgiving servant], if you do not *forgive your brother from your heart*" (Matt. 18:35). The opposite of forgiveness is not alienation. The opposite is holding a grudge. The reason for this clarification is that you may have a forgiving heart and be ready to let a painful wrong go, but the one who wronged you may not be willing to repent or even recognize that a wrong was done. Therefore, even though you offer forgiveness, the relationship may not be healed. We know this because Jesus offered forgiveness continually, but not all were reconciled to him. So the opposite of forgiveness is holding a grudge, not removing alienation. We are responsible for what we do, not for what others do. We are responsible for our hearts, not theirs.

But Jesus makes clear that the *effort* to be reconciled is crucial. We should make all reasonable efforts to be reconciled to those who have taken offense at our words or actions. I say all *reasonable* efforts because not every offense people take is warranted. Jesus would have done nothing else with his life if he had to seek out every individual scribe and Pharisee personally who was angry with him. We must keep this in mind when we read Jesus' demand for reconciliation. He said, "If you are offering your gift at the altar and there remember that your brother has something against you, leave your gift there before the altar and go. First be reconciled to your brother, and then come and offer your gift" (Matt. 5:23–24). I take the words, "if . . . your brother has something against you" to mean: "if . . . your brother has something *legitimate* against you."

Someone always had something against Jesus. There was never a moment of his public ministry when someone was not offended at him. If he had not been allowed to worship before approaching all these people individually to be reconciled, he never would have worshiped. So it is with most of his representatives throughout history. They have always had irreconcilable adversaries. In fact, Jesus warned us that we are probably not being his faithful followers if "all people speak well of you" (Luke 6:26). Rather, "Blessed are you when people hate you and when they exclude you and revile you and spurn your name as evil, on account of the Son of Man!" (Luke 6:22).

Resisting Reconciliation Imperils the Soul

So the point of Matthew 5:23-24 is that if a brother has a true reason to be hurt or offended by something we did, we should move quickly to be reconciled. We can see how crucial this is from the use of the word "so" or "therefore" (οὖν) at the beginning of verse 23: "*So* if you are offering your gift at the altar and there remember that your brother has something against you . . ." This connecting word means that Jesus had just said something that makes the command of verses 23-24 urgent. Here's what he had said: "Everyone who is angry with his brother will be liable to judgment . . . and whoever says, 'You fool!' will be liable to the hell of fire" (Matt. 5:22). In a word, this means: Despising your brother imperils your soul.

"*Therefore* . . ." verses 23 and 24 follow. If contempt for a brother or sister imperils our soul—if it threatens to cut us off from God forever, as verse 22 says (by referring to hell)—then we can't go happily on our way to worship with something like that in our heart. It must be dealt with, Jesus said, and quickly! Since despising a brother brings us into peril with God, it is unlikely that God would receive our worship while we are despising a brother in our heart.

But that is *not quite* what Jesus says in verses 23-24. He does not explicitly focus on our anger, but on the relationship that has been damaged by our sin. The focus of Matthew 5:21-22 was indeed on our anger and contempt. And the word "so" at the beginning of verse 23 shows that this anger is still behind what Jesus is about to say. But what he, in fact, does say moves away from our subjective feelings of anger or contempt to the relationship that has been wrecked by our anger. The demand is, "Leave your gift there before the altar and go. First be reconciled to your brother, and then come and offer your gift" (Matt. 5:24). Jesus assumes that this will involve putting your anger aside. But the focus is on the concrete steps you should take to talk to the offended brother. This will involve confessing your sin and asking for forgiveness. It is one of the hardest things that a proud, fallen human being can do. But when it happens, the doors of heaven are open for the sweetest experience of worship.

LOVE GREETS PEOPLE OUTSIDE OUR GROUP

Loving our enemy includes those who are hard to love, whether a hostile stranger or bad-tempered spouse. And therefore the ways of love that Jesus demands are as varied as self-sacrifice at the one end of the spectrum and a simple greeting at the other end. It is remarkable that in the context of enemy-love Jesus says something as ordinary as, "If you greet only your brothers, what more are you doing than others? Do not even the Gentiles do the same?" (Matt. 5:47). People concerned with global suffering and international injustices might think this is ridiculously individualistic and insignificant. Greetings? Does it really matter in a world like ours whom we say hello to on the street? Jesus knows that the true condition of our heart is revealed not just by the global causes we espouse, but by the daily acts of courtesy we show. Relentlessly he pursues the transformation of our hearts, not just the alteration of our social agendas.

"DO GOOD TO THOSE WHO HATE YOU"

But the change of our hearts will result in radically altered social agendas. One of the examples of loving our enemies that Jesus gives is God's daily mercy on this rebellious world: "He makes his sun rise on the evil and on the good, and sends rain on the just and on the unjust" (Matt. 5:45). Sun and rain are two essential things beyond our human control that are needed for crops to grow. So

Jesus is saying that God reaches down to his enemies and helps meet their needs for food and water. He does not wait for them to repent. He shows mercy. Therefore, loving our enemy means practical acts of helpfulness in the ordinary things of life. God gives his enemies sunshine and rain. You give your enemies food and water. This and many other practical things are included in the simple little phrase "do good." "Do good to those who hate you" (Luke 6:27, cf. vv. 33, 35).

DOING GOOD THROUGH HEALING

One of the commands to do good to others that was prominent in the ministry of the twelve apostles during Jesus' ministry was the command to heal. Behind this command was Jesus' own authority to heal. The ministry of healing was a large and essential part of Jesus' ministry. It was a manifestation of the arrival of the kingdom of God. So preaching the kingdom and healing went hand in hand: "He went throughout all Galilee, teaching in their synagogues and *proclaiming the gospel of the kingdom* and *healing every disease and every affliction* among the people" (Matt. 4:23).

The ministry of healing was also one of the primary attestations of Jesus' messiahship. When John the Baptist, sitting in Herod's prison, began to doubt that Jesus was the Messiah, he sent word to Jesus and asked, "Are you the one who is to come, or shall we look for another?" Jesus answered by pointing to his healing ministry: "Go and tell John what you hear and see: the blind receive their sight and the lame walk, lepers are cleansed and the deaf hear, and the dead are raised up, and the poor have good news preached to them. And blessed is the one who is not offended by me" (Matt. 11:3-6; see also Matt. 9:6).

The miracles of healing that Jesus did were meant to be a witness to his unique role as the Messiah and Son of God. "The works that I do in my Father's name bear witness about me" (John 10:25). Therefore, Jesus called people to believe in him because of his works: "Believe the works, that you may know and understand that the Father is in me and I am in the Father. . . . Believe me that I am in the Father and the Father is in me, or else believe on account of the works themselves" (John 10:38; 14:11).

THE AUTHORITY OF JESUS AND THE COMMAND TO HEAL

Nevertheless, though the miracles of Jesus bore special witness to his unique relation to God and his unique authority, he bestowed a measure of this authority on his disciples. This became the foundation of his command to heal. "He called to him his twelve disciples and *gave them authority* over unclean spirits, to cast them out, and *to heal* every disease and every affliction" (Matt. 10:1). Having given them this authority, he commanded them to extend his own pattern of ministry: "Proclaim as you go, saying, 'The kingdom of heaven is at hand.' Heal the sick, raise the dead, cleanse lepers, cast out demons" (Matt. 10:7).

This was true not only of the Twelve, but also of a wider group of seventy-two. "After this the Lord appointed seventy-two others and sent them on ahead of him" (Luke 10:1). His command to them was, "Heal the sick . . . and say to them, 'The kingdom of God has come near to you'" (Luke 10:9).

HOW SHALL WE OBEY THE COMMAND TO HEAL?

From this, the question rises about our responsibility today to continue the healing ministry of Jesus as a witness to the arrival of the kingdom in his life and work. There are those who say that we should indeed continue the ministry of Jesus today, preaching and performing miraculous healings in the same way he did. Others argue that such miraculous gifts and authority ceased with the disappearance of the apostles and the first generation of believers.

My own view lies between these two positions. I think the first group needs to come to terms with the role that miraculous healings had in bearing witness to the unique person and work of Jesus. In other words, it does seem that the astonishing ministry of miraculous healing that Jesus and some of his first followers had was part of the extraordinary events surrounding the incarnation of God's Son. The consistency and completeness with which Jesus healed was unparalleled in human history. Every ministry of miraculous healing after the events of those first days falls far short of what Jesus actually did. I don't think this is owing to unbelief but to the intended uniqueness of Jesus and those foundational days. What Jesus did in healing and raising the dead was to reveal and anticipate the kind of thing that would happen fully in the age to come.

On the other hand, I do not see any reason to deny that some measure of miraculous healing should accompany the ministry of the gospel today. I suspect there will always be differing judgments as to how prominent that ministry should be. The best way forward, it seems to me, is to have an appreciation *both* for the reality of miraculous healing as a witness to God's compassion and power *and* for the centrality of the word of God in saving sinners and the sovereignty of God in healing as he pleases. Therefore, obedience to Jesus today will for some groups mean a return to the centrality of the word, and for other groups a discovery of the freedom and merciful power of God in healing.

Doing Good When Hated

The miracles of Jesus did not always result in saving faith. Some were more impressed with his power than his person. At one point Jesus' own brothers were more enamored by the public acclaim Jesus was getting than by the spiritual beauty revealed through his miracles. They tried to get him to be more public with his miracles in Jerusalem: "No one works in secret if he seeks to be known openly. If you do these things, show yourself to the world." To which John adds, "For not even his brothers believed in him" (John 7:4-5). And one must ponder with grief the stunning fact that Judas probably did miracles of healing along with the other apostles, but in the end he betrayed Jesus.

Therefore, even the ministry of healing can fall within the command, "Do good to those who hate you." We should pause and let this sink in. *Hate* is a very strong word. Think of what it might look like and feel like to be hated. And then ponder the marvel of doing good for the one who hates you. Jesus certainly knew what it was like to be hated (Luke 19:14; John 7:7; 15:18, 24-25), and he laid his life down for all of his enemies who would receive his love. When Jesus said, "Greater love has no one than this, that someone lays down his life for his *friends*" (John 15:13), he was not measuring the greatness of his love by the fact that he was dying for his *friends*, but by the fact that he was *dying*—and doing it *freely*. By referring to his *friends* he meant that the purpose of his death to remove the wrath of God (John 3:14-15, 36) and forgive sins (Matt. 26:28) would only be experienced by those who are now enemies but lay down their enmity and become his friends.

And Jesus made it clear that just as he was hated, we certainly will be hated if we follow him. "You will be hated by all for my name's sake" (Matt. 10:22). And this will be all the more painful because the hate will sometimes come from former friends: "Many will fall away and betray one another and hate one another" (Matt. 24:10). Think of the kinds of emotions that naturally rise in your heart when someone really hates you and lies about you and wants to hurt you. Most of us have such a strong sense of rights that we feel immediately justified in getting even. Jesus demands that our hearts change. There may be legitimate indignation over the evil, but the heart must want the hater's good and "do good." Our love may bring contrition to the hater's heart, or it may be trampled in the dirt (like the love of Jesus). But that is not our business. Jesus says, "Do good to those who hate you."

TURN THE OTHER CHEEK, AND GIVE TO THE ONE WHO ASKS

He becomes graphic in his illustrations of this demand to return good for evil. "To one who strikes you on the cheek, offer the other also, and from one who takes away your cloak do not withhold your tunic either. Give to everyone who begs from you, and from one who takes away your goods do not demand them back" (Luke 6:29-30). The challenge I feel as I face these radical demands is how to let them have their full impact on my heart and life and yet not take them more absolutely than Jesus intended. My fear is that if I make any qualification I will minimize their intended force. On the other hand, they will also lose their force if they seem so unrealistic that people just pass over them as irrelevant to real life. So I will try to find the middle way of showing that Jesus does not absolutize these illustrations of love, but does not water them down to the irrelevance of mere middle-class morality either.

"The Laborer Deserves His Wages"

There are several overlapping reasons why I believe Jesus means for us to take these commands as illustrative of the kind of thing love *often* does, rather than the exact thing love *always* does. First, the requirement that we always comply with someone's demand, and even give more than what is demanded, would undermine, it seems, the principle of justice in the economic order that Jesus himself approves. On the one hand, Jesus says, "Give to everyone who *asks* from you [the word is general rather than a technical term for "beg"], and from one who takes away your goods do not demand them back" (Luke 6:30). But on the other hand, Jesus approved of giving laborers what was a fair wage, not simply what they wanted their employer to give them (Matt. 20:9-14).

Jesus embraced the economic principle, "The laborer deserves his wages" (Luke 10:7), which seems to imply that the laborer is not bound to give labor without wages, and the employer is not bound to give wages without labor. The economic order, which Jesus supports, would collapse if either labor or management used Jesus' command, "Give to him who asks" as a warrant to demand that the other (in obedience to Jesus!) give without any recompense. Nevertheless, Jesus says to his disciples that in their ministry, "You received without paying; give without pay" (Matt. 10:8). So on the one hand we have the statements that call for radical freedom from the need for recompense ("Give to everyone who asks from you"), and on the other hand we have the statements that affirm the economic order that is built on the principle of a just recompense—even in ministry: "The laborer deserves his wages" (Luke 10:7). It seems to me, therefore, that Jesus' demand to "Give to everyone who asks from you" is not a universal or absolute command for all circumstances, but is one frequent way that love acts.[1]

WHEN DOING GOOD DOES NOT GIVE

Another pointer that these demands are not absolute for every situation is that the two commands—"do good" to those who hate us and "give to everyone who asks"—may not always lead us to the same behavior. We may have a very good plan for what would "do good" for a person that would involve *not* giving him what he asks for. And giving him what he asks for may not do him good. This is easily seen in recovery programs where the plan involves no alcohol during the six months of residency. If the patient demands money for a drink, we will say to him in love, that is not the way we can "do good" to him right now.

Jesus did not always give to the one who asked from him. One example is when the chief priests and the elders asked Jesus, "By what authority are you doing these things, and who gave you this authority?" Jesus tested their authenticity. They failed the test, and he said, "Neither will I tell you by what authority I do these things" (Matt. 21:23, 27). What this means is that "doing good" is not always identical with giving to those who ask.

WHEN CANDIDATES FOR LOVE COMPETE

A third pointer that these demands are not absolute for every situation is that we almost always have competing candidates for our

---

[1] We could pose the same question about three other aspects of the social order besides the economic order: the family, education, and government. In the family, would Jesus support discipline that turns the other cheek to the child who strikes his parent? Would Jesus support education in which the teacher gives grades according to what the students demand? Would Jesus oppose a state use of police force in subduing criminals rather than telling the police to turn the other cheek? I suspect we would find that the principle holds: Jesus endorses the legitimate use of the law of recompense in these spheres of the social order. This would mean that the radical commands we are looking at are not meant to be the only way love acts. Rather, they are valid for believers as one frequent way of loving radically within the generally supported economic order as a witness to the truth that the order of this world is not absolute or ultimate; Jesus is.

love. In other words, what love seems to demand for one person is a behavior that will not be loving to another person. Very simply, what if two people demand from you the same thing at the same time? Or what if the money you have set aside to pay the rent for a poor person is demanded by a beggar? Or what if a thief demands to have the keys to your car when your child is in the backseat? Most of the time, any choice to give our time or money to one person means it cannot go to another person. Therefore, we have no choice but to apply principles *other* than simply the command to give, in order to decide the most loving way to give. So I conclude that Jesus' commands to give to those who ask and lend expecting nothing in return are not ultimate or absolute for every situation. The very command of love that he is illustrating functions to guide how they are applied.[2]

Typically commentators will say that these commands are *hyperbole*—rhetorical overstatements.[3] I would ask them to clarify whether they mean: hyperbole in the *kind* of action that Jesus calls for, or hyperbole in the *frequency* it is required. My own sense is that the latter is correct. In other words, I don't want to deny that any of these commands should be fulfilled literally at times. Rather, I think what is hyperbolic is the impression that these behaviors are the *only* way love acts in response to the situations described. I think

---

[2] This point about competing claimants to our love is part of the foundation for why followers of Jesus may at times support very tough measures against people who are hurting or about to hurt others. The use of force by police and by the military is defended on these grounds in part. If force is not used against one person or group of persons, then they will hurt or kill or enslave others. So, even though using force does not look like "turning the other cheek" (Matt. 5:39; Luke 6:29), it is in fact an effort to love one person or group better than if we simply let aggressive people run over them. In such situations Jesus' demand is that we seek extraordinary wisdom—"Behold, I am sending you out as sheep in the midst of wolves, so be *wise* as serpents and innocent as doves" (Matt. 10:16; cf. Luke 12:42). And besides wisdom he is calling for a radical freedom from the need for earthly riches and security and honor. See more on this below.

[3] Craig Keener, in his *Commentary on the Gospel of Matthew*, gives wise and measured comments in regard to most of these commandments in Matthew 5:38-48. For example, he recognizes that Matthew 5:40 ("And if anyone would sue you and take your tunic, let him have your cloak as well") "if followed literally, would leave most disciples stark naked. . . . To deny that Jesus here literally advocates nudity (an offense to Jewish culture that would surely have called for comment in the other sources!) and living on the street—that is to affirm that Jesus is speaking the language of rhetorical overstatement (5:18-19, 29-32; 6:3)—is not to tone down the seriousness of his demand. Jesus produced hyperbole precisely to challenge his hearers, to force them to think about what they valued. Jesus' words in this case strike at the very core of human selfishness, summoning his disciples to value others above themselves in concrete and consistent ways" (195).

Jesus himself gives us ample indications that he does not mean that. There are times when "doing good" for someone will not include giving whatever he asks.

What then do these radical commands mean? What shall we do in response to them? If they are not absolutely the way to act in every situation, what are they? To that we turn in the next chapter, as well as to the question, how is it possible to love like this?

Love Your Enemies to Show That You Are Children of God

To one who strikes you on the cheek, offer the other also, and from one who takes away your cloak do not withhold your tunic either. Give to everyone who begs from you, and from one who takes away your goods do not demand them back. —Luke 6:29-30

Love your enemies and pray for those who persecute you, so that you may be sons of your Father who is in heaven. —Matt. 5:44-45

Be merciful, even as your Father is merciful. —Luke 6:36

Love your enemies, and do good, and lend, expecting nothing in return, and your reward will be great. —Luke 6:35

At the end of the previous chapter we were wrestling with Jesus' radical demand, "To one who strikes you on the cheek, offer the other also, and from one who takes away your cloak do not withhold your tunic either. Give to everyone who begs from you, and from one who takes away your goods do not demand them back" (Luke 6:29-30). We argued that Jesus does not mean that these responses are the only way love acts. In this chapter we turn to a more positive statement of what is required of us, and then to the question, how are we able to love like this?

JESUS IS OUR TREASURE, OUR SECURITY, AND OUR HONOR

What then is Jesus demanding in the radical commands like those of Luke 6:29-30? I cannot escape the implication that behind and within these commands is the demand to be radically free from the love of money and from the need for earthly security and honor. Turning the other cheek even though the backhanded slap is an infuriating public dishonor, and lending without expecting repayment, and taking the time out of your schedule to carry a soldier's burden twice as far as he demanded[1]—all of these things imply that your treasure and your security and your honor are in heaven and not on the earth. Jesus has become for you radically satisfying. If this were not the case one can only imagine that the heart would be seething with rage while doing good and suffering the indignity. Therefore, I infer that in all these commands, Jesus is calling for a change of heart that looks to Jesus and his reward rather than what this world can give.

But it would be a mistake to stress only that Jesus is calling for a change of heart that treasures Jesus more than money and security and honor. He is also calling for real good to be done for our enemy and that we should really want this good to be done. We have seen this most clearly in the demand that we bless and pray for our enemies (Matt. 5:44; Luke 6:28). The real good that we must aim at, if we love our enemies, is that all the petitions of the Lord's Prayer come true for them. To desire these things from our heart for our enemies, and to lay down our lives to bring them about, that is love.

DEALING WITH A SKILLED LIAR

I would add one more description of what this love looks like. It seems to me that in all the complexity of life that can easily help

---

[1] Matthew 5:41, "And if anyone forces you to go one mile, go with him two miles." "Because tax revenues did not cover all the Roman army's needs, soldiers could requisition what they required . . . and legally demand local inhabitants to provide forced labor (Matt. 27:32)." Craig S. Keener, *Commentary on the Gospel of Matthew* (Grand Rapids, Mich.: Eerdmans, 1999), 199.

us rationalize disobedience to these commands, we should default to literal obedience when we are unsure of what love calls for. For example, should I give to those who ask for money on the street in my context in urban America? How do I "do good" to those who ask? Jesus did not seem to be as concerned about being taken advantage of as I am (Matt. 5:40, 42). I am often angered by the lies I am being told. This anger makes me feel justified in giving nothing. But I do not think this is the spirit of Jesus.

I think the spirit of Jesus would first feel compassion even for a skilled liar. Then it would desire to move into the life of that liar with the good news that Jesus came into the world to save liars. Then it would try, if the other demands of love allow, to engage the person more deeply and, if possible, take him somewhere to eat together and talk. If that is not possible, then love may give freely even knowing the person is probably a con artist. And at times love may say no—for example, if the person has been back many times and has proven to be a liar and consistently refused a relationship of love. But my point is, when these things are less clear, the spirit of Jesus seems to me to call for freehanded giving.

How Can We Love Like This?

The final question I ask now about Jesus' demand to love our enemies is: *How* we can do this? Where does power to love like this come from? Think how astonishing this is when it appears in the real world! It is an amazing thing when a person loves like this. To see it in a high degree in anyone is rare. This should make us sober and strip us of all presumption and set us seeking the power to be like this. If we limit our answer to what we see in the immediate contexts of Matthew 5:38-48 and Luke 6:27-36, there are three interwoven answers.

In the Security and Help of Our Heavenly Father

The first is found in the promise that if we love our enemies we will be sons of God: "Love your enemies and pray for those who perse-

cute you, *so that you may be sons of your Father who is in heaven*"
(Matt. 5:44-45). Someone may take this to mean that you must first
become a person who loves his enemies *before* you can be a child of
God. But it may also mean—as I think it does—love your enemies
and so *prove yourself to be what you are—a child of God*. That is,
show that you are a child of God by acting the way your Father acts.
If you are his, then his character is in you, and you will be inclined to
do what he does. God loves his enemies—the evil and the unjust—in
sending rain and sunshine on them instead of immediate judgment
(Matt. 5:45).

There are several reasons for thinking that Jesus is not saying,
you are not a child of God until you prove you can love your enemy,
but rather is saying, you *show* you are a child of God by loving
your enemy. The first comes from the immediate paragraph and
its parallel in Luke. In Matthew 5:48 Jesus says, "You therefore
must be perfect, as your heavenly Father is perfect." And in Luke
6:36 he says, "Be merciful, even as your Father is merciful." Both
these statements assume that the disciples are being called to love
(perfectly) because they *are* children of God, not in order to *become*
children of God.

Confirming this understanding of Matthew 5:45 ("so that you
may be sons of your Father" = "so that you may prove to be sons
of your Father"), there are other parallels that use similar words.
For example, in John 15:8 Jesus says, "By this my Father is glorified, that you bear much fruit and so *prove to be my disciples*." The
words "prove to be" translate the same verb ($\gamma \acute{\epsilon} \nu \eta \sigma \theta \epsilon$) that is used
in Matthew 5:45. Jesus says fruit-bearing is possible because they
are *already* disciples—that is, they are branches in the vine who is
Jesus (John 15:5)—and now they will prove themselves to be so by
doing what branches do, namely, bear fruit (see also John 8:31).

Another argument that our sonship is proved rather than created by loving our enemies is from the earlier part of Matthew 5,
where Jesus says, "Let your light shine before others, so that they
may see your good works and give glory to your *Father* who is in
heaven" (5:16). Notice two things: one is that Jesus speaks to his

disciples and calls God their Father. He does not say, "He may *become* your Father." He says, "He *is* your Father." Second, notice that when people see the good works of the disciples (like loving their enemies), they give glory *to their Father*. Why? Because their Father is in them helping them and enabling them to do the good works. If they did the good works on their own, so that they could then become children of their Father, the world would see their good works and give *them* the glory. So Jesus not only says that God is *already* the Father of the disciples before they do the good works, but also, by implication, that this is the very reason they can do the loving works they do. The light that shines through them *is* the light of their Father's love within them.

So when Jesus says, "Love your enemies, and pray for those who persecute you, *in order that you may be sons of your Father who is in heaven*," he does not mean that loving our enemies earns us the right to be children of God. You can't earn the status of a child. You can be born into it. You can be adopted into it. You can't work your way into it. Jesus means that loving our enemies shows that God has already become our Father, and that the only reason we are able to love our enemies is because he loves us and has met our needs first.

Therefore, the first answer to *how* we can love our enemies is that being children of God has set us free from anxiety. We do not fear that our treasure or security or honor can be lost by the ill-treatment of our enemy or by the loss of earthly possessions. This is the point of Matthew 6:31-32, "Do not be anxious, saying, 'What shall we eat?' or 'What shall we drink?' or 'What shall we wear?' For the Gentiles seek after all these things, and *your heavenly Father knows that you need them all*." Similarly, that's the point of Matthew 10:29-31, "Are not two sparrows sold for a penny? And not one of them will fall to the ground apart from *your Father*. . . . Fear not, therefore; you are of more value than many sparrows." The intimate knowledge and tender, sovereign care of our omnipotent, all-wise, heavenly Father frees us for the radical kind of risks and losses that enemy-love demands.

"Your Reward Will Be Great"

Interwoven with this empowerment is another one in the immediate context of the commands. Jesus promises "great reward" if we love our enemies—not in this life, but in heaven. "Love your enemies, and do good, and lend, expecting nothing in return, *and your reward will be great*, and you will be sons of the Most High" (Luke 6:35). I say the two sources of power are *interwoven* because the "great reward" is connected to "you will be sons of the Most High." In other words, when you prove yourselves to be sons of God by loving your enemy, your inheritance as sons is secured. Sons are heirs, and heirs of God are heirs of everything. "Blessed are the meek, for they shall inherit *the earth*" (Matt. 5:5).

The reason I say that the reward is *in heaven* and not on the earth is, first, that loving our enemy may cost us our lives (Luke 21:16). Jesus said our joy in the midst of persecution is based on our reward in heaven: "Blessed are you when others revile you and persecute you and utter all kinds of evil against you falsely on my account. Rejoice and be glad, *for your reward is great in heaven*" (Matt. 5:11-12). The joy that sustains us in the midst of persecution, as we endeavor to love our enemies, is not based mainly on what this world can offer, but on what God will be for us as our Father, and what Jesus will be for us as our King, in the age to come (see Luke 14:14).

As You Have Received Mercy Freely, Give It Freely

A third truth that enables us to love our enemy is interwoven with the other two in Luke 6:36, "Be merciful, even as your Father is merciful." The implication here is not only that God is already our Father, and that his inheritance is our joy-sustaining reward in suffering, but also that the mercy of God has already been shown to us through his Son Jesus. This means that the mercy we are called to show is not just modeled on God's mercy but is rooted in the saving experience of God's mercy. Jesus put it like this, "You received without paying; give without pay" (Matt. 10:8).

In other words, God has forgiven our sins freely because of Jesus. "Your sins are forgiven . . . your faith has saved you; go in peace" (Luke 7:48, 50). This forgiveness, Jesus says, is purchased for us by his own blood (Matt. 26:28). We did not deserve it or earn it. We received it by faith. He came "to give his life as a ransom for many" (Mark 10:45). He did not come to call the righteous but sinners (Luke 5:32). Therefore, the stunning news is: Tax collectors and the prostitutes go into the kingdom of God before scribes and elders (Matt. 21:31). Which means that we came into the position of a forgiven disciple of Jesus, a citizen of his kingdom, and a child of God by faith, not by loving our enemy first.

Now that we have received all this "without pay"—without buying it or earning it or deserving it—now we are called: Freely you received love when you were enemies of God; now freely give love to your enemies.

LOVE YOUR NEIGHBOR AS YOURSELF, FOR THIS IS THE LAW AND THE PROPHETS

"Teacher, which is the great commandment in the Law?" And he said to him, "You shall love the Lord your God with all your heart and with all your soul and with all your mind. This is the great and first commandment. And a second is like it: You shall love your neighbor as yourself. On these two commandments depend all the Law and the Prophets."—MATT. 22:36-40

So whatever you wish that others would do to you, do also to them, for this is the Law and the Prophets.—MATT. 7:12

The focus of the "second" commandment—"You shall love your neighbor as yourself" (Matt. 22:39)—is not on whether the receiver of love is an enemy or a friend, but on whether the one who loves desires the neighbor's good as he desires his own. Its importance is seen by the two stupendous things that lie on either side of it. On one side is the greatest commandment in the Word of God—"You shall love the Lord your God with all your heart and with all your soul and with all your mind." On the other side is the assertion that everything[1] written in the Law and the Prophets hangs

---

[1] Matthew 22:40, "On these two commandments depend all the Law and the Prophets."

on these two commandments. We are in the company of incomparable superlatives—the two greatest commandments in the entire Word of God, and all of that Word hanging on them. We should take off our shoes in reverence here. There are few texts of Scripture greater than this.

AN OVERWHELMING AND STAGGERING COMMAND

The second commandment seems to me to be an overwhelming commandment. It seems to demand that I tear the skin off my body and wrap it around another person so that I feel that I am that other person; and all the longings that I have for my own safety and health and success and happiness I now feel for that other person as though he were me. It is an absolutely staggering commandment. If this is what it means, then something unbelievably powerful and earthshaking and reconstructing and overturning and upending will have to happen in our souls. Something supernatural. Something well beyond what self-preserving, self-enhancing, self-exalting, self-esteeming, self-advancing, fallen human beings like me can do on their own.

Underlining the greatness of this commandment is the fact that it is surpassed only by the command to love God with our whole being. I have devoted a chapter to that commandment (*Demand #9*). But also underlining the importance of the second commandment is the sweeping statement that all the Law and the Prophets hang on it when it is linked with the first commandment. "On these two commandments depend all the Law and the Prophets" (Matt. 22:40). This phrase, "Law and Prophets" refers to the whole Old Testament, as we can see in Luke 24:27, "Beginning with Moses and all the Prophets, he interpreted to them in *all the Scriptures* the things concerning himself."

This is an amazing statement. Here we have the authority of the Son of God telling us something utterly crucial about the origin and design of the entire plan and Word of God. First, consider the sheer fact that *Jesus said this*. He didn't have to say it. The lawyer who drew him into this discussion didn't ask about this (Matt.

22:36). Jesus went beyond what he asked ("Which is the great commandment in the Law?") and said more. He seems to want to push the importance and centrality of these commandments as much as he can. He said that the commandment to love God is the great and foremost commandment. He said the commandment to love your neighbor as you love yourself is "like it" (Matt. 22:39). That's enough to raise the stakes here almost as high as they can be raised. We have the greatest commandment in all of God's revelation to humanity (love God); and we have the second greatest, which is like the greatest (love your neighbor as yourself).

But Jesus doesn't stop there. He wants us to be stunned at how important these two commandments are. He wants us to stop and wonder. So he adds, "On these two commandments depend all the Law and the Prophets." They are also the two commandments from which everything else in the Scriptures flows.

On These Two Commandments Hang the Whole Law and the Prophets

What does this mean? Answering this question opens a window into heaven. We will see this if we start by contrasting what Jesus says here in Matthew 22:40 with what he says in Matthew 7:12. This verse is better known as the Golden Rule. One way to see it is as a good commentary on "Love your neighbor as you love yourself." In that context, Jesus has just said that God will give us good things if we ask and seek and knock, because he is a loving Father. Then in Matthew 7:12 he says, "So whatever you wish that others would do to you, do also to them, for this is the Law and the Prophets."

Notice that Jesus refers to the Law and the Prophets as he did in Matthew 22:40. He says, if you do to others what you would have them do to you, then "this is the Law and the Prophets." In Matthew 22:40 he said, "On these two commandments hang the whole Law and the Prophets." Note that the first commandment—loving God with all your being—is not mentioned in Matthew 7:12.

Instead, Jesus simply says that treating others the way we would like to be treated "is the Law and the Prophets."

Does Jesus Sum Up the Old Testament Without God?

We must be careful here. Some people over the centuries have tried to take sentences like the Golden Rule and say that Jesus was mainly a profound teacher of human ethics and that what he taught is not dependent on God or any relationship with God. They say, "See, he can sum up the whole Old Testament, the Law and the Prophets, in practical human relationships that don't even mention God."

I say we must be careful here, because thinking like that not only ignores the great things Jesus said about God elsewhere and the amazing things he said about himself coming from God to give his life as a ransom for many (Mark 10:45), it also ignores the immediate context. Verse 12 begins with the word "so," or in some versions, "therefore." "*So* whatever you wish that others would do to you, do also to them." What this shows is that the Golden Rule depends on what went before—on our relationship to God as our Father who loves us and answers our prayers and gives us good things when we ask him (Matt. 7:7-11).

The immediately preceding verse (Matt. 7:11) says, "If you then, who are evil, know how to give good gifts to your children, how much more will *your Father* who is in heaven give good things to those who ask him! *Therefore* . . . [keep the Golden Rule]." This logical connection means God is upholding the Golden Rule by his fatherly provision. His love for us—and our trusting, prayerful love back to him—is the source of power for living the Golden Rule. So you can't turn Jesus into a mere teacher of ethics. He is here and always God-saturated.

Loving God Becomes Visible in Loving Others

But still, Jesus does say that treating others as you want to be treated "is the Law and the Prophets." He does not say here that two commandments are the Law and the Prophets, but only one. This seems significantly different from Matthew 22:40 where the Law and the Prophets depend on both commandments.

Why does he say it in this way? I think what he means is that when you see people love like that (fulfill the Golden Rule), what you are seeing is the visible expression of the aim of the Law and the Prophets. This behavior among people manifests openly and publicly and practically what the Old Testament is about. It fulfills the Law and the Prophets by making the aim visible. Loving God, however, is *invisible*. It is an internal passion of the soul. But it comes to expression when you love others. So loving others is the outward manifestation, the visible expression, the practical demonstration, and therefore the fulfillment of loving God and therefore of what the Old Testament is about.

So there is a sense in which the second commandment (to love your neighbor) is the visible goal of the whole Word of God. It's not as though loving God is not here, or that loving God is less important; rather, loving God is made visible and manifest and full in our visibly, practically, sacrificially loving others. I think that is why the second commandment stands by itself here as an expression of what the Law and the Prophets are—". . . for this *is* the Law and the Prophets." Loving our neighbor is not the Law and the Prophets independently of loving God. Rather, loving our neighbor is based on our love for God and, as the overflow of it, is what the Law and the Prophets were aiming at.

How Do the Law and Prophets Hang on Love?

Now let's return to Matthew 22:37-40. Here Jesus *does* mention both love for God and love for neighbor; and he explicitly says in verse 40, "On these two commandments depend all the Law and the Prophets." Why? I want to suggest that he is saying something different from, but not contradictory to, Matthew 7:12. Here he does not say that these two commandments "are" the Law and the Prophets. He says that the Law and the Prophets *depend* on these two commandments. "On these two commandments depend all the Law and the Prophets."

Here we are facing the window into heaven that I mentioned earlier. Jesus says here that the Law and the Prophets literally *hang* like a stone around the neck (Matt. 18:6) or a man on a cross (Luke 23:39). What do they hang on? They hang on love. This is the reverse of what Matthew 7:12 says. There Jesus said that the Law and Prophets lead to and find expression in love. But here in Matthew 22:40 Jesus is saying the reverse: Love leads to and finds expression in the Law and the Prophets. The Law and the Prophets are hanging on—depending on—something before them, namely, God's passion that this world, this history of humankind, be a world of love to God and radical, other-oriented love to each other.

Let me try to put this in a picture, so we can see it more plainly. Picture the God-inspired history of redemption from creation to consummation as a scroll. This is the Law and the Prophets (and the New Testament). The story of God's acts and purposes in history are told in this scroll, along with God's commandments and promises. Matthew 7:12 tells us that when the people of God love their neighbor as they love themselves, the purpose of this scroll is being fulfilled. Its aim is being expressed visibly and manifested practically so "that [people] may see your good works and give glory to your Father who is in heaven" (Matt. 5:16). So the scroll is leading to love. Love is flowing from the scroll.

The Window into Heaven

But then Jesus gives us an incomparable perspective. He opens a window into heaven, so to speak. He lifts us out of history and out of the world for a moment and shows us the scroll from a distance. Now we can see it whole—the Law and the Prophets, the Old Testament, the story of redemption, the purposes and acts of God in history. And what we see is that the scroll is *hanging* by two golden chains, one fastened to each end of the scroll handles. Then Jesus lifts our eyes to heaven, and we see the chains run up and disappear into heaven. Then he takes us into heaven, and he shows us the upper ends of the chains. They are fastened to the throne of God. One chain is fastened to the right arm of the throne where the words are inscribed: "You shall love the Lord your God with all your heart and with all your soul and with all your mind." And the other chain is fastened to the left arm of the throne where the words are inscribed, "You shall love your neighbor as yourself."

Jesus turns to us and says, "The whole scroll, the whole Law and the Prophets, the whole history of redemption and all my Father's plans and acts, hang on these two great sovereign purposes of God: that he be loved by his creation, and that they love each other as they love themselves." I believe it would not be too much to say that all of creation and all the work of redemption, including the work of Christ as our suffering, dying, and rising Redeemer, and all of history, hang on these two great purposes: that humans love God with all their heart, and that from the overflow of that love we love each other.

Which means that love is the origin (Matt. 22:40) and the goal (Matt. 7:12) of the Law and the Prophets. It is the beginning and the end of why God inspired the Bible. It's the fountainhead and spring at the one end and the shoreless ocean at the other end of the river of redemptive history—remembered and promised in the Word of God. Surely God's purpose is that we take this commandment with tremendous seriousness. It would be wise in this majestic context that we not assume we yet have seen the fullness of what love is or that it already has the centrality in our lives that it should. Jesus is saying: All of Scripture, all of his plans for history, *hang* on these two great purposes: that he be loved with all our heart, and that we love each other as we love ourselves.[2]

---

[2] Though I have not handled in detail a closely related command of Jesus that he gave in the context of controversy over the law, it should at least be mentioned in this chapter: "Go and learn what this means, 'I desire mercy, and not sacrifice'" (Matt. 9:13; cf. 12:7). In sum, it seems that Jesus is saying that there are clues in the Old Testament, like this quote from Hosea 6:6, that, if we truly understood them, would enable us to see that all the law was pointing beyond the ceremonial and the external to the heartfelt love commanded by Jesus.

Demand #33

LOVE YOUR NEIGHBOR WITH THE SAME COMMITMENT YOU HAVE TO YOUR OWN WELL-BEING

. . . as yourself. —MATT. 22:39

I n this chapter we turn to look more closely into the command itself, especially the devastating phrase "as yourself." "Love your neighbor[1] *as yourself*" is a very radical command. What I mean by "radical" is that it cuts to the *root* of our sinfulness and exposes it and by God's grace severs it.

THE ROOT OF SIN: THE DESIRE TO BE HAPPY APART FROM GOD

The root of our sinfulness is the desire for our own happiness *apart from God* and *apart from the happiness of others in God*. I mean that to be read carefully. Let me say it again: The root of our sinfulness is the desire to be happy *apart from God* and *apart from whether others find their eternal happiness in God*. All sin comes from a desire to be happy cut off from the glory of God and cut off

---

[1] We will see in the following chapter how Jesus defines the scope of the word *neighbor*, but suffice it to say here that any attempt to narrow it along ethnic or family or associational lines would fly into the face of Jesus' intention. The one in need along your path, the one whom you can help, is your neighbor.

from the good of others. The command of Jesus cuts to this root, exposes it, and severs it.

Another name for this root of sinfulness is *pride*. Pride is the presumption that we can be happy without depending on God as the source of our happiness and without caring if others find their happiness in God. Pride is the contaminated and corrupted passion to be happy. It is corrupted by two things: (1) the unwillingness to see God as the only fountain of true and lasting joy, and (2) the unwillingness to see other people as designed by God to share our joy in him. If you take the desire to be happy and strip away from it God as the fountain of your happiness and strip from it people as the ones you hope will share your happiness in God, what you have left is the engine of pride. Pride is the pursuit of happiness anywhere but in the glory of God and the good of other people for God's sake. This is the root of all sin.

WHAT DOES "AS YOURSELF" MEAN?

Now Jesus says, "Love your neighbor as yourself." And with that commandment he cuts to the root of our sinfulness. How so? Jesus says in effect: "I start with your inborn, deep, defining human trait—your love for yourself. My command is, 'You shall love your neighbor *as yourself.*' You love yourselves. This is a given. I don't command it; I assume it.[2] All of you have a powerful instinct of self-preservation and self-fulfillment. You all want to be happy. You all want to live, and to live with satisfaction. You want food for yourself. You want clothes for yourself. You want a place to live for yourself. You want protection from violence against yourself. You want meaningful or pleasant activity to fill your days. You want some friends to like you and spend some time with you. You want your life to count in some way. All this is self-love. Self-love is the deep longing to diminish pain and to increase happiness." That's what Jesus starts with when he says "as yourself."

---

[2] I think the modern effort to see "self-love" here as "positive self-image" and to see a command that we seek this positive image so that we can then love others is profoundly mistaken. See John Piper, "Is Self-Love Biblical?" *Christianity Today* 21 (August 12, 1977): 6-9.

Everyone, without exception, has this human trait. This is what moves us to do this or that. Even suicide is pursued out of this principle of self-love.[3] In the midst of a feeling of utter meaningless and hopelessness and numbness of depression, the soul says, "It can't get any worse than this. So even if I don't know what I will gain through death, I do know what I will escape." And so suicide is an attempt to escape the intolerable. It is a misguided act of self-love.

JESUS STARTS WITH THE GIVEN AND THE GOODNESS OF SELF-LOVE

Now Jesus says, "I start with this self-love. This is what I know about you. This is common to all people. You don't have to learn it. It comes with your humanity. My Father created it. In and of itself it is good." To hunger for food is not evil. To want to be warm in the winter is not evil. To want to be safe in a crisis is not evil. To want to be healthy during a plague is not evil. To want to be liked by others is not evil. To want your life to count in some significant way is not evil. This was a defining human trait before the fall of man into sin, and it is not evil in itself.

Whether it has become evil in your life will be exposed as you hear and respond to Jesus' commandment. He commands, "*As you love yourself*, so love your neighbor." Which means: As you long for food when you are hungry, so long to feed your neighbor when he is hungry. As you long for nice clothes for yourself, so long for nice clothes for your neighbor. As you work for a comfortable place to live, so desire a comfortable place to live for your neighbor. As you seek to be safe and secure from calamity and violence, so seek comfort and security for your neighbor. As you seek friends for yourself, so be a friend to your neighbor. As you want your life to count and be significant, so desire that same significance for your

---

[3] Blaise Pascal, the French mathematician and philosopher, wrote, "All men seek happiness. This is without exception. Whatever different means they employ, they all tend to this end. The cause of some going to war, and of others avoiding it, is the same desire in both, attended with different views. The will never takes the least step but to this object. This is the motive of every action of every man, even of those who hang themselves." *Pensées* (New York: E. P. Dutton, 1958), 113, Thought #425.

neighbor. As you work to make good grades yourself, so work to help your neighbor be able to make good grades. As you like to feel welcome in a new company of people, so seek to make others feel welcome. As you would that men would do to you, do so to them.

YOUR SELF-SEEKING BECOMES THE MEASURE OF YOUR SELF-GIVING

In other words, make your *self-seeking* the measure of your *self-giving*. When Jesus says, "Love your neighbor as yourself," the word "as" is very radical: "Love your neighbor *as* yourself." That's a *big* word: "as!" It means: If you are *energetic* in pursing your own happiness, be energetic in pursuing the happiness of your neighbor. If you are *creative* in pursuing your own happiness, be creative in pursuing the happiness of your neighbor. If you are *persevering* in pursuing your own happiness, then persevere in pursuing the happiness of your neighbor.

In other words, Jesus is not just saying, seek for your neighbor the *same things* you seek for yourself, but also seek them in the *same way*—with the same zeal and energy and creativity and perseverance. And with the same life and death commitment when you are in danger. Make your own self-seeking the measure of your self-giving. Measure your pursuit of the happiness of others, and what it should be, by the pursuit of your own. How do you pursue your own well-being? Pursue your neighbor's well-being that way too.

Now this is very threatening and almost overwhelming, because we feel immediately that if we take Jesus seriously, we will not just have to love others "as we love ourselves," but we will have to love them *instead* of loving ourselves. That's what it seems like. We fear that if we follow Jesus in this and really devote ourselves to pursuing the happiness of others, then our own desire for happiness will always be preempted. The neighbor's claim on my time and energy and creativity will always take priority. So the command to love my neighbor as I love myself really feels like a threat to my own self-love. How is this even possible? If there is born in us a natural desire for our own happiness, and if this is not in itself evil but good, how can we give it up and begin only to seek the happiness of others at the expense of our own?

How the First Commandment Sustains
the Second

I think that is exactly the threat that Jesus wants us to feel, until we realize that this—exactly this—is why the first commandment is the first commandment. It's the first commandment that makes the second commandment doable and takes away the threat that the second commandment is really the suicide of our own happiness. The first commandment is, "Love the Lord your God with all your heart and with all your soul and with all your mind." The first commandment is the basis of the second commandment. The second commandment is a visible expression of the first. Which means this: Before you make your own self-seeking the measure of your self-giving, make God the focus of your self-seeking. This is the point of the first commandment.

"Love God with all your heart" means: Find in God a satisfaction so profound that it fills up all your heart. "Love God with all your soul" means: Find in God a meaning so rich and so deep that it fills up all the aching corners of your soul. "Love God with all your mind" means: Find in God the riches of knowledge and insight and wisdom that guide and satisfy all that the human mind was meant to be.

In other words, take all your self-love—all your longing for joy and hope and love and security and fulfillment and significance—and focus it on God, until he satisfies your heart and soul and mind. You will find that this is not a canceling out of self-love. This is a fulfillment and transformation of self-love. Self-love is the desire for life and satisfaction rather than frustration and death. God says, "Come to me, and I will give you fullness of joy. I will satisfy your heart and soul and mind with my glory." This is the first and great commandment.

And with that great discovery—that God is the never-ending fountain of our joy—the way we love others is forever changed. When Jesus says, "Love your neighbor *as yourself*," we don't respond by saying, "Oh, this is threatening. This means my love for myself is made impossible by all the claims of my neighbor. I could never do this." Instead we say, "Oh, yes, I love myself. I have longings for joy and satisfaction and fulfillment and significance and security. But God has called me—indeed he has commanded me—to come to him first for all these things. He commands that my love for him be the form of my love for me." That's not a misprint. My love for him is the form of my self-love. That is, all the longings that would satisfy me (self-love) I direct to him and find satisfied in him. That is what my self-love now *is*. It is my love for God. They have become one. My quest for happiness is now nothing other than a quest for God. And he has been found in Jesus.

SELF-LOVE, FULFILLED IN GOD-LOVE, BECOMES THE MEASURE OF NEIGHBOR-LOVE

So what then is Jesus commanding in the second commandment (that we love our neighbor as ourselves)? He is commanding that our self-love, which has now discovered its fulfillment in God-love, be the measure and the content of our neighbor-love. Or to put it another way, he is commanding that our inborn self-seeking, which has now been transposed into God-seeking, overflow and extend itself to our neighbor. So, for example:

• If you are longing to see more of God's bounty and liberality through the supply of food and rent and clothing, then seek to show others the greatness of this divine bounty by the generosity you have found in him. Let the fulfillment of your own self-love in God-love overflow into neighbor-love. Or better: Seek that God, who is the fulfillment of your self-love, will overflow through your neighbor-love and become the fulfillment of your neighbor's self-love.

• If you want to enjoy more of God's compassion through the consolations he gives you in sorrow, then seek to show others more of God's compassion through the consolations you extend to them in sorrow.

• If you long to savor more of God's wisdom through the counsel he gives in stressful relationships, then seek to extend more of God's wisdom to others in their stressful relationships.

• If you delight in seeing God's goodness in relaxed times of leisure, then extend that goodness to others by helping them have relaxed, healthy times of leisure.

• If you want to see more of God's saving grace powerfully manifested in your life, then stretch out that grace into the lives of others who need that saving grace.

• If you want to enjoy more of the riches of God's personal friendship through thick and thin, then extend that friendship to the lonely through thick and thin.

In all these ways neighbor-love does not threaten self-love because self-love has become God-love, and God-love is not threatened, diminished, or exhausted by being poured into the lives of others.

Demand #34

LOVE YOUR NEIGHBOR AS YOURSELF AND AS JESUS LOVED US

But he, desiring to justify himself, said to Jesus, "And who is my neighbor?" —LUKE 10:29

Whatever you wish that others would do to you, do also to them, for this is the Law and the Prophets. —MATT. 7:12

A new commandment I give to you, that you love one another: just as I have loved you, you also are to love one another. By this all people will know that you are my disciples, if you have love for one another. —JOHN 13:34-35

I don't presume in the previous chapters to have solved all perplexities in the life of love. There are competing claims on our limited time and resources. There are hard choices about what to give up and what to keep. There are different interpretations of what is good for another person. I don't mean that all of that becomes simple.

RADICAL COMMAND AND RADICAL PROVISION

What I do mean is this: Loving God sustains us through all the joy and pain and perplexity and uncertainty of what loving our neighbor should be. When the sacrifice is great, we remember that God's grace is sufficient. When the fork in the road of love is unmarked, we remember with joy and love that his grace is sufficient. When we are distracted by the world and our hearts give way temporarily to selfishness and we are off the path, we remember that God alone can satisfy, and we repent and love his mercy and patience all the more.

It is a very radical command. It cuts to the root of sin called pride—the passion to be happy (self-love) contaminated and corrupted by two things: 1) the unwillingness to see God as the only fountain of true and lasting joy, and 2) the unwillingness to see other people as designed by God to receive our joy in him. But that is exactly the corruption of self-love that Jesus counteracts in these two commandments. In the first commandment, he focuses the passion to be happy firmly on God and God alone. In the second commandment he opens a whole world of expanding joy in God and says, human beings, everywhere you find them, are designed to receive and enlarge your joy in God. Love them the way you love yourself. Give them—through every practical means available—what you have found for yourself in God.

WARNING: DON'T NARROW THE MEANING OF "NEIGHBOR"

Before we leave the commandment to love our neighbor as ourselves, we need to hear a warning that Jesus sounded. He warned us that when we hear the command, "Love your neighbor as yourself" we should not try to justify our lovelessness by narrowing down who the neighbor is. He sounded this warning with the parable of the Good Samaritan.

Once "a lawyer stood up to put him to the test, saying, 'Teacher, what shall I do to inherit eternal life?'" Jesus answered him, "What is written in the Law? How do you read it?" The lawyer responded with the two great commandments: "You shall love the Lord your God with all your heart and with all your soul and with all your strength and with all your mind, and your neighbor as yourself." Jesus said, "You have answered correctly; do this, and you will live."[1] Then the lawyer said something that Jesus did not like. Luke describes the motive behind the man's next words: "But he, desiring to justify himself, said to Jesus, 'And who is my neighbor?'" (Luke 10:25-29).

Of all the many issues that could be taken up from the parable of the Good Samaritan, I focus only on one. Jesus responds to the lawyer's self-justifying question with a parable that does not answer his question but changes it. He changes the question from *What kind of person is my neighbor?* to *What kind of person am I?* He changes the question from *What status of people are worthy of my love?* to *How can I become the kind of person whose compassion disregards status?*

Jesus exposes the lawyer's duplicity by showing him that he already knew the answer to his question and was only trying to trap Jesus (Luke 10:25). Now the lawyer knows that his motives have been exposed and that he needs to confess or cover his hypocrisy. He chooses to cover it—or to give it another name; he chooses to "justify himself" (Luke 10:29). He does so by saying something like, "Well, you know, Jesus, it's not so easy to figure out who our neighbor is. Life is complicated. Which kind of people do we have to love? Who qualifies for being a neighbor in this command, 'Love your neighbor'? Every race? Every class? Both sexes? All ages? Outcasts? Sinners?"

A Question Jesus Will Not Answer

How does Jesus answer? He does not like this question—carving humanity up into groups some of whom are worthy of our love and others of whom are not. Jesus does not answer the question, "Who is my neighbor?" He tells a parable that changes the question. Between Jerusalem and Jericho a man falls among robbers. Luke 10:30 says they "stripped him and beat him and departed, leaving him half dead." The first two people to pass by are a priest

---

[1] See *Demand #20* for reflections on how this relates to Jesus' understanding of justification by faith alone.

and a Levite[2]—the most religious folks—and they both pass by on the other side of the road (Luke 10:31, 32). Then came a Samaritan, not even a Jew, and the key phrase about this man is at the end of Luke 10:33, "He had compassion."

You see how the focus has shifted. The question about what kind of man is dying is not even in the story anymore. The whole focus is now on the kind of people who are walking by. The first two felt no compassion. The Samaritan was a different kind of person. So when you get to the end, what's the question that Jesus asks? Was it, "So was the wounded man a neighbor?" No. That is not the question. Jesus asked the lawyer, "Which of these three do you think proved to *be* a neighbor to the man who fell among the robbers?"(Luke 10:36). The lawyer answered, "The one who showed him mercy." And Jesus said to him, "You go, and do likewise" (Luke 10:37). Jesus does not give an answer to his question, "Who is my neighbor?" Instead, he says in effect, go become a new kind of person. Go get a compassionate heart.

THE DEATH OF JESUS: PURCHASE AND PATTERN

This is exactly what Jesus died for. This is the promise of the new covenant in Ezekiel 36:26, "I will give you a new heart, and a new spirit I will put within you." And Jesus said at the Last Supper, "This cup that is poured out for you is the new covenant in my blood" (Luke 22:20). Those who follow Jesus all the way to the cross will see him there paying for their new heart with his own blood.

Which brings us to one final point in this chapter: the relationship between Jesus' command that we love our neighbor as ourselves and his command that we love each other as he has loved us. Jesus' death is both guilt-bearing and guidance-giving. It is a death that forgives sin and a death that models love. It is the purchase of our life from perishing and the pattern for a life of love. I close with this focus because of the seeming tension between the two

---

[2] The Levites were descendants of the tribe of Israel named after Levi (Exod. 6:25; Lev. 25:32; Num. 35:2). The name is, however, generally used as the part of the tribe that assisted the priests in the service of the temple (1 Kings 8:4; Ezra 2:70).

commandments: "Love your neighbor as yourself" and the "new commandment."

In John 13:34-35 Jesus said, "A new commandment I give to you, that you love one another: just as I have loved you, you also are to love one another. By this all people will know that you are my disciples, if you have love for one another" (see also John 15:12). Jesus makes the connection between his love and his death when he says, "Greater love has no one than this, that someone *lays down his life* for his friends" (John 15:13). So it is important that we see the connection between the death of Jesus and our fulfillment of the commandment, "Love your neighbor as yourself." On the one hand, the death of Jesus models how we should love, and on the other hand the death of Jesus purchases for us the very transformation that enables us to love.[3] We have discussed the purchasing work of Jesus in previous chapters (see *Demands #10, 23*). Here we need to ponder how the pattern of Jesus' love relates to the command "Love your neighbor as yourself."

Jesus called the commandment to love as he loved "a new commandment" (John 13:34). But the commandment "Love your neighbor as yourself" is an old commandment from Leviticus 19:18. Does that mean that the command to love our neighbor as we love ourselves is now passé and we have a new one—to love as Jesus loved? I don't think so.

What's new is that we had never seen the old commandment of love lived out for us perfectly by the Son of God. Before Jesus, no one had ever been able to say without qualification, "Love as I have loved." Not only that, the newness seems to relate to the purpose of Jesus to have a new people whose mark in the world would be allegiance to him (and his Father) and to each other in love. So he says, "By this all people will know that you are my disciples, if you have

---

[3] See *Demands #20, 21, 27* for the relationship between the transformation that Jesus' death purchases and the location or justification that it purchases. The point there is that Jesus is the basis of a new "location" in God's favor that becomes the basis and hope of the demonstration of that favor through a transformed heart and life.

love for one another" (John 13:35). "Love like mine is the badge of belonging to the new people that I am gathering."

JESUS LOVED US PERFECTLY IN LOVING HIMSELF PERFECTLY

But the essence of what love is—what we have unfolded earlier in this chapter—is not different from what Jesus demands here. When Jesus died for us, he loved us as he loved himself. He perfectly fulfilled the command, "love your neighbor as yourself." Jesus loved himself perfectly in that he desired his happiness with perfectly holy desire. That is, he found his happiness from all eternity in his fellowship with his Father and in being one with the Father (John 10:30). When he laid down his life for us, he did not deny or discard that desire for his own infinite happiness in God; he expressed it. He pursued it.

When Jesus died he purchased for sinners like us everything needed for us to find our joy in God. Since our joy in God magnifies the worth of God, this is exactly what Jesus has delighted in for all eternity. Therefore, in dying for our joy in God he is dying to display and preserve his fullest joy in God's glory. That glory is reflected in our blood-bought joy in God. Therefore, Jesus' love is a perfect expression and fulfillment of the command to "Love your neighbor as yourself."

So whether he says to us, "Love God and love your neighbor as yourself, because on these two hang all the Law and the Prophets," or whether he says, "Love one another as I have loved you so that all will know you are my disciples," he is commanding essentially the same thing. It is a radical command. We must make our own passion for happiness the measure of our passion for the good of others. And we must make the measure of Jesus' suffering and the perfection of his happiness in God the standard of our sacrifice and the focus of the joy we pursue for ourselves and others.

Lay Up for Yourselves Treasures in Heaven by Giving Sacrificially and Generously

Do not lay up for yourselves treasures on earth, where moth and rust destroy and where thieves break in and steal, but lay up for yourselves treasures in heaven, where neither moth nor rust destroys and where thieves do not break in and steal. For where your treasure is, there your heart will be also. —Matt. 6:19-21

You received without paying; give without pay. —Matt. 10:8

One who is faithful in a very little is also faithful in much, and one who is dishonest in a very little is also dishonest in much. If then you have not been faithful in the unrighteous wealth, who will entrust to you the true riches? And if you have not been faithful in that which is another's, who will give you that which is your own? —Luke 16:10-12

The more sacrificially generous you are on earth, the greater will be your enjoyment of heaven. Therefore, since Jesus loves us and summons us to maximize our eternal joy in heaven, he demands radical freedom from the love of money and radical generosity, especially toward the poor.

SACRIFICE IS THE MEASURE OF A GIFT'S SIZE

The reason I say, "the more *sacrificially* generous you are" is because of what Jesus said about the widow's offering. Here's the story:

> [Jesus] sat down opposite the treasury and watched the people put-
> ting money into the offering box. Many rich people put in large
> sums. And a poor widow came and put in two small copper coins,
> which make a penny. And he called his disciples to him and said to
> them, "Truly, I say to you, this poor widow has put in more than
> all those who are contributing to the offering box. For they all con-
> tributed out of their abundance, but she out of her poverty has put
> in everything she had, all she had to live on." (Mark 12:41-44)

The point here is that the value of a gift is not measured by its size but by its sacrifice. She put in "more" than all, Jesus said. Not more in quantity, but more in sacrifice. The reason for this is that sacrifice is a better measure of where your heart is. If you are rich and give much, you have so much left over that your heart may easily rest in the remainder. But if you sacrifice for Jesus and have little left, then the heart has less to rest in. The heart is more likely to be resting in the hope of heaven. It is more likely to be depending on Jesus than on money.

WHY SUCH A HUGE CONCERN WITH OUR MONEY AND POSSESSIONS?

It is astonishing how much Jesus deals with money and what we do with it. Randy Alcorn reckons that "15 percent of everything Christ said relates to this topic—more than his teachings on heaven and hell combined."[1] Consider just a sampling of the kinds of things Jesus says about money and related lifestyle issues:

> You lack one thing: go, sell all that you have and give to the
> poor, and you will have treasure in heaven; and come, follow
> me. (Mark 10:21)

---

[1] Randy Alcorn, *The Treasure Principle* (Sisters, Ore.: Multnomah, 2001), 8. I highly recommend this small book as a way to help people live out the radical call of Jesus concerning money.

Blessed are you who are poor, for yours is the kingdom of heaven. . . . But woe to you who are rich, for you have received your consolation. (Luke 6:20)

Any of you who does not renounce all that he has cannot be my disciple. (Luke 14:33)

It is easier for a camel to go through the eye of a needle than for a rich person to enter the kingdom of God. (Luke 18:25)

One's life does not consist in the abundance of his possessions. (Luke 12:15)

Seek first the kingdom of God and his righteousness, and all these things will be added to you. (Matt. 6:33)

Sell your possessions and give to the needy. Provide yourselves with moneybags that do not grow old. (Luke 12:33)

Zacchaeus . . . said to the Lord, "Behold, Lord, the half of my goods I give to the poor." And Jesus said to him, "Today salvation has come to this house." (Luke 19:8-9)

The kingdom of heaven is like treasure hidden in a field, which a man found and covered up. Then in his joy he goes and sells all that he has and buys that field. (Matt. 13:44)

Jesus . . . saw a poor widow put in two small copper coins. And he said, "Truly, I tell you, this poor widow has put in more than all of them." (Luke 21:1)

But God said to [the man who built even bigger barns], "Fool! This night your soul is required of you, and the things you have prepared, whose will they be?" So is the one who lays up treasure for himself and is not rich toward God. (Luke 12:20-21)

> Foxes have holes, and birds of the air have nests, but the Son of
> Man has nowhere to lay his head. . . . Follow me. (Luke 9:58-59)

Why does Jesus express such a remarkable concern with what we do with our money? The reason for this, it seems, is the basic principle that Jesus laid down: "Where your treasure is, there your heart will be also" (Matt. 6:21; Luke 12:34). In other words, the reason money is so crucial is that what we do with it signals where our heart is. "Where our heart is" means where our worship is. When the heart is set on something, it values it, cherishes it, treasures it. That is what worship means.

YOU CANNOT SERVE TWO MASTERS: GOD AND MONEY

You can see this in Jesus' warning that "No one can serve two masters, for either he will hate the one and love the other, or he will be devoted to the one and despise the other. You cannot serve God and money" (Matt. 6:24). The idea of "serving" here is peculiar. It relates more to worshiping than to providing a service. Jesus said, "You cannot serve God and *money*." How do we serve money?

The answer is not: Provide a service for money. Or, provide help to money, or meet money's needs. Just the opposite: Serving money means looking to money to provide you a service and to provide your help and meet your needs. Serving money means planning and dreaming and strategizing and maneuvering to be in a position to maximize our wealth and what money can provide for us. Money is the giver and the benefactor in this servant-master relationship. You don't do any good for money. You look to money to do good for you.

Now Jesus says, "You cannot serve God and money." The meaning of "serve" would, presumably, be the same in these two relationships. So what Jesus is saying is that we should serve God *not* in the sense of providing a service or giving him help, but the opposite: We look to God to be our helper, our benefactor and treasure. To serve him would be to plan and dream and strategize and maneuver to be in a position to maximize our enjoyment of God and what he alone promises to be for us. God then, not money, becomes the giver and the benefactor in this servant-master relationship. You don't meet God's needs (he has none!). You look to God to meet yours.

So the reason money is so crucial for Jesus is that across all cultures and all ages it represents the alternative to God as the treasure of our hearts, and therefore the object of our worship. It becomes the great threat to our obedience to the first and last of the Ten Commandments: "You shall have no other gods before me" (Exod. 20:3), and "You shall not covet" (Exod. 20:17). Money represents all the other material things and securities and pleasures that it can buy. Therefore, it represents the great alternative to God in our hearts. This is why what we do with our money is so crucial to Jesus.

SELFISHNESS SEPARATES FROM HEAVEN, AND SACRIFICE HEIGHTENS JOY IN IT

Let's return to the main point I made in the first paragraph of this chapter: The more sacrificially generous you are on earth, the greater will be your enjoyment of heaven. There are two things being said here. One is that a selfish spirit will keep us out of heaven. And the other is that there are degrees of reward, or degrees of joy, in heaven, depending on how sacrificially generous we were on earth. Both of these claims are controversial. But in view of what we have seen in the previous chapters, they should not come as a complete surprise. In the next chapter I will take them one at a time and give some evidence from the words of Jesus.

Demand #36

LAY UP FOR YOURSELVES TREASURES IN HEAVEN AND INCREASE YOUR JOY IN JESUS

How difficult it is for those who have wealth to enter the kingdom of God! For it is easier for a camel to go through the eye of a needle than for a rich person to enter the kingdom of God. — Luke 18:24-25

One who is faithful in a very little is also faithful in much, and one who is dishonest in a very little is also dishonest in much. If then you have not been faithful in the unrighteous wealth, who will entrust to you the true riches? And if you have not been faithful in that which is another's, who will give you that which is your own? — Luke 16:10-12

Emerging in the previous chapter were two controversial claims that I will try to support from Jesus' teaching in this chapter. First, the claim that a selfish spirit will keep us out of heaven. Second, the claim that there are degrees of reward, or degrees of joy, in heaven, depending on how sacrificially generous we were on earth.

First, Jesus implies, again and again, that a selfish spirit will keep us out of heaven. Here are five examples to show this truth.

THE RICH RULER AND ETERNAL LIFE

First, when the rich ruler asked Jesus what he must do to inherit eternal life, Jesus responded, "Sell all that you have and distribute to the poor, and you will have treasure in heaven; and come, follow me" (Luke 18:18, 22). This seems to make eternal life dependent on being free from the love of money and being generous to the poor. This is indeed what Jesus is saying, as we can see from the fact that when the man who was "extremely rich" (Luke 18:23) turns away, Jesus says, "How difficult it is for those who have wealth to *enter the kingdom of God*! For it is easier for a camel to go through the eye of a needle than for a rich person to *enter the kingdom of God*" (Luke 18:24-25).

As we can imagine, the disciples are surprised by this statement and ask, "Then who can be saved?" (Luke 18:26). They see that "inheriting eternal life" and "entering the kingdom of God" are terms that refer to "being saved." Jesus' answer is *not* to say, "Salvation is not at stake in this man's selfishness." Rather he says, "What is impossible with men is possible with God" (Luke 18:27). In other words, only God can change the selfishness that keeps a man out of heaven. But it is clear that this man's love for his money kept him out of heaven: "He went away sorrowful, for he had great possessions" (Mark 10:22). (For how this relates to justification by faith alone see *Demand #20*.)

THE RICH MAN, THE BEGGAR, AND TWO DESTINIES

A second example is the story of the rich man and the beggar at his gate. Jesus said, "There was a rich man who was clothed in purple and fine linen and who feasted sumptuously every day. And at his gate was laid a poor man named Lazarus, covered with sores" (Luke 16:19-20). The poor man wanted just a crumb from the rich man's table, but the picture we get is that the rich man was oblivious or disdainful to the poor at his very door. So Jesus describes the death and afterlife of both men: "The poor man died and was carried by the angels to Abraham's side. The rich man also died and was buried, and in Hades, being in torment, he lifted up his eyes and saw Abraham far off and Lazarus at his side" (Luke 16:22-23). In other words, Jesus is saying that the selfish indifference of the rich has landed him in hell.[1]

FAILURE TO LOVE AND FINAL JUDGMENT

Third, similarly, in Matthew 25:31-46 Jesus warns that a professing follower of Jesus who is indifferent to the needs of the poor will endure "eternal punishment." When the king (representing Jesus in the story) pronounces this dreadful sentence over the selfish "disciples," they say, "Lord, when did we see you hungry or thirsty or a stranger or naked or sick or in prison, and did not minister to you?" And the king answers, "Truly, I say to you, as you did not do it to one of the least of these, you did not do it to me." And Jesus gives the final word: "And these will go away into eternal punishment, but the righteous into eternal life" (Matt. 25:44-46). In other words, a selfish spirit will keep us out of heaven.

THE RICH FOOL WHO LOSES HIS SOUL

Fourth, again Jesus tells a parable of a rich fool. The man's fields prosper, and he has more than he can use. Instead of thinking generously he says, "I will tear down my barns and build larger ones, and there I will store all my grain and my goods. And I will say to my soul, Soul, you have ample goods laid up for many years; relax, eat, drink, be merry" (Luke 12:18-19). To this selfish decision Jesus says that God responds with these words: "Fool! This night your soul is required of you, and the things you have prepared, whose will they be?" (Luke 12:20). In other words, his selfish spirit led to the loss of his soul.

HOW TO LOSE TRUE AND LASTING RICHES

Fifth, here is one last illustration of how a selfish spirit keeps us out of heaven. After the parable of the dishonest manager (Luke 16:1-9), Jesus draws out these conclusions:

---

[1] The point is not that poverty lands someone in heaven. The spiritual condition of the poor man is not the focus of the parable. It goes unmentioned. There is no reason to assume he was not a genuine believer. But the focus is on the rich man who perished. The parable is a warning of the danger of riches.

> One who is faithful in a very little is also faithful in much, and one
> who is dishonest in a very little is also dishonest in much. If then
> you have not been faithful in the unrighteous wealth, who will
> entrust to you the true riches? And if you have not been faithful
> in that which is another's, who will give you that which is your
> own? (Luke 16:10-12)

It is fairly clear that "true riches" and "that which is your own"
refer to the treasures of heaven—the pleasures of the age to come
when we enjoy unbroken fellowship with Jesus. Therefore, Jesus
is saying that we will not get these *true riches* if we have not been
faithful with what we were given to use in this fallen world. He is
referring to our money—that is, the material resources at our disposal here. If we have been stingy rather than using our money to
lead people to faith (Luke 16:9), we will not enter heaven with its
true riches of fellowship with Jesus.

The Ground of Our Acceptance with God

That is one implication of what I said in the first sentence of this
chapter: A selfish spirit will keep us out of heaven entirely. I hope it
is plain by now in this book that I do not believe a sacrificially generous spirit is the ground of our acceptance with God. When Jesus
says that a selfish spirit keeps us out of heaven, he does not mean
that God watches to see if we show ourselves to be generous before
he accepts us into his everlasting favor. Before we can be generous,
God receives us into his favor through faith in Jesus (John 3:16).
He takes us into his family as his children (John 1:12). He counts
us righteous (Luke 18:14); he forgives our sins (Matt. 26:28); he
gives us eternal life (John 5:24). None of these is obtained in this
life by first overcoming our selfish spirit. It is the other way around.
We recognize our selfish spirit and despair of overcoming it on our
own and turn to Jesus as our only hope. In this turning to Jesus, we
are justified, forgiven, adopted, secured in his care forever (John
10:28-30). On that basis we now make progress in overcoming our
selfish spirit.

GREATER SACRIFICES OF LOVE LEAD TO GREATER JOY IN HEAVEN

The other controversial claim emerging in the previous chapter and mentioned in the first paragraph of this chapter is that the degree to which we overcome our selfishness determines, in some measure, the degree of our reward—our joy—in heaven. The more sacrificially generous you are on earth, the greater will be your enjoyment of heaven. The first indication that Jesus means this is found in his Parable of the Ten Minas.[2] Jesus compares his departure from this earth to a nobleman who goes to a far country to receive a kingdom and gives his ten servants (representing the followers of Jesus) one mina each, saying, "Engage in business until I come" (Luke 19:13). I take this "business" to include the kind of loving generosity that Jesus repeatedly commanded.

When the king returns, he calls his servants to give an account of how they used their mina. The first came and said he had made ten more minas with his mina. The second said he had made five more. The third made none. To the first Jesus said, "Well done, good servant! Because you have been faithful in a very little, you shall have authority over ten cities." To the second he said, "And you are to be over five cities" (Luke 19:17, 19). I take these two different rewards to represent diversity of rewards in heaven. My point is not how literally to take the promise of cities. My point is simply that this is an indication that in the kingdom there will be different rewards.

THE MEASURE YOU USE WILL BE USED TO MEASURE YOU

Another indication that Jesus thinks this way about heaven is the way he speaks in Luke 6:37-38: "Judge not, and you will not be judged; condemn not, and you will not be condemned; forgive, and you will be forgiven; give, and it will be given to you. Good measure, pressed down, shaken together, running over, will be put into

---

[2] A mina is an amount of money, namely, about three months' wages for a laborer.

your lap. For with the measure you use it will be measured back to you." What does Jesus mean, "With the measure you use it will be measured back to you"?

First, he confirms what we saw before, that a selfish spirit will rob us of all blessing: "Give, and it will be given to you." He is not speaking of mere human relations here. He is speaking of the final reckoning with God. That is the context of judgment and condemnation and forgiveness. It is also implied in the gracious promise that our reward will be "pressed down, shaken together, running over." This is a picture of God's overflowing grace. If we give, God will super-reward. If we do not, we will be condemned for our selfish, unbroken, unredeemed heart.

But what about "the measure" that we use in giving? "With the measure you use it will be measured back to you." This is where I get the idea that there will be varying rewards in heaven for different measures of sacrificial generosity on earth. R. C. H. Lenski seems to me to be especially insightful on this text. He says:

> Jesus explains this return measure by stating the principle on which it is given: "for with what measure you go on measuring it shall be measured to you in return: $\dot{\alpha}\nu\tau\acute{\iota}$ in the verb (*anti*metrēthēsetai) means in turn or back. In other words, by our giving we build the measure that will be used for giving back to us. Our own measure is used to measure back to us. By using it ourselves we declare that we want God to use it for us at the end. . . . It is the measure we bring to God, and all he can do is to fill it. And fill it overflowing he will ("pressed down, shaken together, running over"). . . . Thus they who give nothing will receive even less, and they who give much their lifelong will receive vastly more. This is both justice and grace.[3]

I assume that by "justice" he does not speak strictly, since even our best generosity is imperfect and deserves nothing from God. I take

---

[3] R. C. H. Lenski, *The Interpretation of St. Luke's Gospel* (Minneapolis: Augsburg, 1946), 374-375.

him to mean that it is *fitting* and *proper* and *just* that there be a correspondence between our giving and God's giving to us—not an exact one, but a real one. So he uses the same measure, but he fills it more overflowingly than we ever did for anyone here.

The point I am stressing here is that there are differences in the fullness of delight that each of us enjoys in heaven. Each will be full in heaven, for there are no frustrations there. But the fullness of each will not be the same since the measure that we used to bless others on earth, and that God will use to bless us in heaven, are different for different people. Therefore I say again, the more sacrificially generous we are on earth, the greater will be our enjoyment of heaven.

"LAY UP FOR YOURSELVES TREASURES IN HEAVEN"

Because of this, I take Jesus' command, "Lay up for yourselves treasures in heaven" (Matt. 6:20), to mean: Strive to make the measure of your generosity as large as you can. This is clearly the way Jesus means it in Luke 12:33, "Sell your possessions, and give to the needy. Provide yourselves with moneybags that do not grow old, with a treasure in the heavens that does not fail, where no thief approaches and no moth destroys." In other words, the way you provide yourselves with "moneybags that do not grow old" and with "treasure in the heavens" is to "give to the needy." *Ageless moneybags* and *treasure in heaven* are metaphors for heavenly reward—the fullness of the measure of joy we will be given in heaven. Their measure is determined by the positive command, "Give to the needy." We lay up treasure in heaven by not hoarding here on earth, but by using our possessions sacrificially and generously—that is, lovingly.

We will see in the next chapter that this kind of sacrificial generosity is grounded in the goodness of God to us *before* and *while* we are generous to others. We are able to love and give because he has already given freely to us and promises to meet every need we have in a lifetime of generosity (Matt. 6:33; 7:7-12; Luke 12:32).

LAY UP FOR YOURSELVES TREASURES IN HEAVEN— "IT IS YOUR FATHER'S GOOD PLEASURE TO GIVE YOU THE KINGDOM"

Fear not, little flock, for it is your Father's good pleasure to give you the kingdom. Sell your possessions, and give to the needy. Provide yourselves with moneybags that do not grow old, with a treasure in the heavens that does not fail, where no thief approaches and no moth destroys. For where your treasure is, there will your heart be also. —LUKE 12:32-34

Before looking at the ground of our giving in the goodness of God, there is a pressing question that rises whenever the motivation of rewards is mentioned. I turn first to that question and then to the goodness of God beneath all our giving.

WHY IS THIS NOT PRUDENTIAL SELF-REGARD?

Why would this motivation for giving—to enlarge the measure of our joy in heaven—not turn our giving from an act of love into an act of prudential self-regard? The reason is that in all our giving our aim is that the beneficiaries—whether enemies or brothers—will be helped, by our giving, to see more of the beauty of Jesus so that they are drawn with us into the heavenly reward. No genuine follower of Jesus wants to enjoy Jesus alone. That is not the kind of Jesus who exists. He cannot be enjoyed alone. He lived and died to be "a ransom for *many*" (Mark 10:45). The joy that we want to increase for ourselves is a shared joy. Giving sacrificially and generously enlarges the measure of our joy in heaven not only by the size of our *heart* toward others, but—to shift the emphasis—by the size of our heart toward *others*. We aim that they share our joy and that we share theirs, so that both joys are larger because of being shared.

Or to turn the problem around: What sort of love would it be if in giving generously to others we did not want to share in the joy we want for them? Disinterested giving would send the signal that the gift I am giving you is not worth having. If I have no passion to enjoy what I offer you, then how can my offer be seen as valuable? I think some people entangle themselves in a contradiction here because they think it is loving to give to the needy without regard to the eternal joy of the needy. They think that simply giving to the poor without aiming at their conversion, so that Jesus becomes their treasure, is a loving thing to do. It is not. If we are indifferent to whether our generosity leads the beneficiary to love Christ, we are not acting in love. I do not mean we must succeed in order for our generosity to be love. Our aim may not be attained. They may reject Jesus while accepting our generosity. We will not stop loving them for that—as long as they live. But not to *aim* at their eternal joy in Jesus is not a loving way to give.

GIVING SACRIFICIALLY SHOWS OUR FREEDOM FROM BONDAGE TO THINGS

The giving that Jesus has in mind is as diverse as the possible ways to bless others with what we have and do and say. His demand is that we use what we have to bless others. It may be money (Matt. 19:21) or healing (Matt. 10:8) or a cup of cold water (Mark 9:41) or time and effort like the Good Samaritan's (Luke 10:34-35) or your home and hospitality (Luke 14:13-14). The point of Jesus' demand is that we be radically free from the love of money and what it can buy, and from the fear of losing the security and comforts it affords.

Money enslaves either by greed or fear. We are greedy for more of it and fearful of losing what we have. Jesus wants us free. Sacrificial giving is one evidence that we have been liberated from the idols that money provides. It is also evidence that we have begun to love other people the way we should—that is, we are focusing outwardly on the joy of making others glad, not just the private pleasures that putrefy in the small world of selfishness.

We can see how Jesus thinks about our liberation by the way he links the promise of God's provision with the demand for sacrificial generosity. Here's the link: "Fear not, little flock, for it is your Father's good pleasure to give you the kingdom. Sell your possessions, and give to the needy" (Luke 12:32-33). Surely Jesus intends for us to understand a "therefore" between the promise and the command: "Fear not, little flock, for it is your Father's good pleasure to give you the kingdom. *Therefore*, sell your possessions, and give to the needy."[1]

Luke 12:32 is the key to being liberated from our fearful slavery to possessions. It is the dynamite that can demolish the house of materialism that we live in. Luke 12:32 is a powerful word from Jesus about the nature of God. It's about what kind of heart God has—what makes God glad, not merely what he has or does. Indeed, it is about what God *delights* to do, what he *loves* to do and takes *pleasure* in doing. "Fear not, little flock, for it is your Father's good pleasure to give you the kingdom." These are the words that set us free to sell our possessions and give sacrificially and generously.

---

[1] The same logic is found in numerous places in the teachings of Jesus. For example, Jesus says, "When you give a feast, invite the poor, the crippled, the lame, the blind, and you will be blessed, because they cannot repay you. [*For*] you will be repaid at the resurrection of the just" (Luke 14:13-14). And: "If you then, who are evil, know how to give good gifts to your children, how much more will your Father who is in heaven give good things to those who ask him! *So* whatever you wish that others would do to you, do also to them" (Matt. 7:11-12). And: "Therefore do not be anxious, saying, 'What shall we eat?' or 'What shall we drink?' or 'What shall we wear?' *For* . . . your heavenly Father knows that you need them all" (Matt. 6:31-32).

The Goodness of God Is the Ground of Our Giving

Notice every amazing part of this extravagantly gracious verse: "It is your Father's *good pleasure* to give you the kingdom." In other words, God is not acting in this generous way in order to cloak and hide some malicious motive. The words "good pleasure" utterly rule that out. He is not saying inside, "I will have to be generous for a while even though I don't want to be, because what I really want to do is bring judgment on sinners."

Jesus' meaning is inescapable: God is acting here in freedom. He is not under constraint to do what he doesn't really want to do. At this very point, when he gives his flock the kingdom, he is acting out of his deepest delight. This is what the word means: God's joy, his desire, his want and wish and hope and pleasure and gladness and delight, is to give the kingdom to his flock.

Then consider the phrase *"your Father's."* "Fear not, little flock, it is your Father's good pleasure to give you the kingdom." Jesus does not say, "It is your employer's good pleasure to pay you your salary." He does not say, "It is your slavemaster's good pleasure to provide your lodging." He does not even say, "It is your king's good pleasure to bestow the kingdom." He chooses every word in this sentence to help us get rid of the fear that God is ill-disposed to us. So he calls God our "Father."

God Is the Best of Fathers—Far Better Than the One You Had!

Now, not all of us have had fathers who patterned their lives after God. And so the word *father* may not be full of peace and security the way Jesus means it to be. So let me try to fill the word *father* with two of the meanings Jesus intended it to carry.

First, if the King is our Father, then we are heirs of his kingdom. There is something natural about our receiving it—it's our inheritance. Matthew 25:34 says that in the last day King Jesus will say, "Come, you who are blessed of my Father, *inherit* [note the word!]

the kingdom prepared for you from the foundation of the world." Before the beginning of the world God prepared a kingdom for his children. It is theirs by the right of inheritance. And God does not begrudge his children coming into their inheritance. It is his good pleasure to give them the kingdom.

Second, if the King is our Father, then we are free from being taxed. In Matthew 17:25, Peter wondered if the disciples had to pay the temple tax. Jesus says, "What do you think, Simon? From whom do kings of the earth take toll or tax? From their sons or from others?" And when he said, "From others," Jesus said to him, "Then the sons are free." God does not levy taxes against his children. It is those outside the palace who feel the burden of law, not the children within. The children are free! The fatherhood of God means freedom.

The list of implications of what it means to have God as our Father could go on—and all of them would serve to overcome the fear that God is begrudging in his kindness to us. He is not begrudging. He is eager. He delights to give to his children. He is our Father, and if we who are evil know how to give good things to our children, how much more will our Father in heaven give the kingdom to those who ask him (Matt. 7:7-11).

THE LAVISH AND TENDER GENEROSITY AND CARE OF GOD

Then consider the word "give." "It is your Father's good pleasure to *give* you the kingdom." Jesus does not say *sell* you the kingdom. He does not say *trade* you the kingdom. He says it is the Father's good pleasure to *give* you the kingdom. God is a mountain spring and not a watering trough. He wells up self-replenishingly. He delights to overflow. It is the nature of an eternal fountain of life to give, give, give. The good news is that God does not need a bucket brigade or sweaty pumpers. He demands water drinkers, not water haulers. Following Jesus means getting down on our faces and satisfying our soul-thirst with his perfect love.

He *gives* the kingdom! It cannot be bought or bartered for or earned in any way. There is only one way to have it, and it is the easiest way of all—the way of Luke 18:17: "Truly, I say to you, whoever does not *receive* the kingdom of God like a child shall not enter it." It is God's good pleasure to *give* us the kingdom. (See Luke 8:10.)

Then consider the word "flock." "Fear not, little *flock*, for it is your Father's good pleasure to give you the kingdom." Jesus is piling up the metaphors. God is our Father. And since he gives us a kingdom, he must be a King. And since we are his flock, he must be a Shepherd. Jesus is at pains to choose every word he can to make his point clear: God is not the kind of God who begrudges his blessings.

Calling us his "flock" or his "sheep" reminds us that Jesus said that the good shepherd lays down his life for the sheep. Does he do it begrudgingly or under constraint? No. "No one takes [my life] from me, but I lay it down of my own accord" (John 10:18). The Father did not begrudge the gift of his Son, and the Son did not begrudge the gift of his life. It is the *Shepherd's* good pleasure to give the kingdom to his *flock*.

Then ponder the word "little." "Fear not, *little* flock, for it is your Father's good pleasure to give you the kingdom." Why does he say "*little* flock"? I think this has two effects. First, it's a term of affection and care. If I say to my family when they are in danger, "Don't be afraid, little family," what I mean is, I know you are in danger and that you are small and weak, but I will use all my power to take care of you because you are precious to me. So "*little* flock" carries the connotation of affection and care.

It also implies that God's goodness to us is not dependent on our greatness. We are a little flock—little in size, little in strength, little in wisdom, little in righteousness, little in love. If God's goodness to us depended on our greatness, we would be in big trouble. But that's the point. It doesn't. So we aren't. "Fear not, *little* flock, it is the Father's good pleasure to give us the kingdom."

The Gift of God's Sovereign Rule on Our Behalf

Finally, consider the word "kingdom." There might be one little foothold left for the feeling that God is begrudging and ill-disposed toward us. Someone might say, "OK, God is our Father and not our slavemaster; he enjoys giving instead of selling; he treats us the way a good shepherd treats his flock; he has an affection and pity toward us in our littleness. But what, after all, does he promise to give?"

He doesn't promise to give money. In fact, he says, "It is easier for a camel to go through the eye of a needle than for a rich man to enter the kingdom of God" (Luke 18:25). He doesn't promise popularity or fame or admiration among men. In fact, he says, "Blessed are you when men hate you and when they exclude you and revile you and spurn your name as evil, on account of the Son of Man!" (Luke 6:22). He doesn't even promise security in this life. Instead, he says, "You will be delivered up even by parents and brothers and relatives and friends, and some of you they will put to death. You will be hated by all for my name's sake" (Luke 21:16).

What does he promise to give to his little flock—to prove once and for all that it is not only his good pleasure to give, but that it is his good pleasure to give big? He promises to give them the *kingdom of God*. And what does it mean to be given the sovereign reign and rule of God?

It means simply and staggeringly and unspeakably that the omnipotent rule and authority of the King of the universe will be engaged forever and ever on behalf of the little flock of God. Who can describe what it will be like when that saying comes to pass that Jesus spoke at the Last Supper, "I assign to you as my Father has assigned to me a kingdom, that you may eat and drink at my table in my kingdom" (Luke 22:29-30)?

Jesus knows that the flock of God struggles with fear about selling what we don't need and giving sacrificially and generously to the poor. He knows that one of those fears is that God is the kind of God who is basically angry and delights most of all to judge sinners and only does good out of a sense of constraint and duty, not delight. Therefore, the Lord is at pains in Luke 12:32 to free us from this fear by telling us the truth about God. He has chosen every word to help liberate us from the love of money and satisfy us with all that God promises to be for us in Jesus. Every word counts. Always read it slowly.

> Fear not,
> little
> flock,
> for it is your Father's
> good pleasure
> to give you
> the kingdom!

THE SIMPLICITY AND GENEROSITY OF WILLIAM CAREY

What kind of life will this promise produce for those who really believe it? I close this chapter with one illustration from the life of the missionary to India, William Carey. In October 1795, Carey received a packet of letters in India from his homeland, England. One of the letters criticized him for "engaging in affairs of trade," instead of devoting himself full-time to his missionary work (which would go on to last for over thirty years of amazing fruitfulness, without a furlough). Carey was hurt and angered by the accusation. If he had not worked, he and his family would probably have starved, since the support from England was so slow and small and sporadic in arriving. He wrote back these words that describe the kind of life that I pray you and I will live:

> It is a constant maxim with me that, if my conduct will not vindicate itself, it is not worth vindicating. . . . I only say that, after my family's obtaining a bare allowance, my whole income, and some months, much more, goes for the purposes of the gospel, in supporting persons to assist in the translation of the Bible, write

copies, teach school, and the like. . . . I mention . . . [this] to show
that the love of money has not prompted me to pursue the plan
that I have engaged in. I am indeed poor, and shall always be so till
the Bible is published in Bengali and Hindosthani, and the people
[lack] no further instruction.[2]

That is the kind of sacrificial, generous devotion to the cause of his
kingdom that Jesus meant when he demanded, "Lay up for yourselves treasures in heaven."

---

[2] Mary Drewery, *William Carey: A Biography* (Grand Rapids, Mich.: Zondervan, 1984), 91.

Demand #38

Do Not Take an Oath— Cherish the Truth and Speak It Simply

Again you have heard that it was said to those of old, "You shall not swear falsely, but shall perform to the Lord what you have sworn." But I say to you, Do not take an oath at all, either by heaven, for it is the throne of God, or by the earth, for it is his footstool, or by Jerusalem, for it is the city of the great King. And do not take an oath by your head, for you cannot make one hair white or black. Let what you say be simply "Yes" or "No"; anything more than this comes from evil. —MATT. 5:33-37

Jesus teaches that truth is precious. All of us agree with this when we are being lied about. The most relativistic professor in the university, who scoffs at the concept of truth in the classroom, will be indignant if his electricity bill is false to his disadvantage. He will call the utility company and complain that there is some mistake. He will not think it funny if the voice on the other end says, "It's a mistake in *your* view, but not in *our* view."

For Ordinary People Truth Is Precious

Truth is precious. Did the baby swallow the missing needle or didn't she? Is this water drinkable or isn't it? Are you a friend or a spy? Will you keep your marriage vows to love and cherish me, or are you only interested in money and sex? Do we have enough fuel on this airplane to reach our destination or should we turn back? Will this surgery leave me worse or better than I was before? Did the desperate 911 caller say 11th Avenue or 11th Street?

Those who mock the concept of truth are people with power who do not (at the moment) need to appeal to truth for their lives. Totalitarian despots do not care about truth, because they have power to create the reality they want—for a fleeting moment in history. Tenured professors may not care about truth in the classroom because they have the power and security to entertain their students with academic games without being forced to apply their foolishness to their own real lives after they go home at night. But for most of the world, truth matters. And they know it. It matters ultimately. Their lives depend on it.

"I Have Come to Bear Witness to the Truth"

Jesus loved truth and hated deceit. He confirmed the ninth commandment, "Do not bear false witness" (Mark 10:19). He warned that "deceit" comes out of the heart and defiles a person (Mark 7:21-22). He considered religious hypocrisy a hellish form of lying (Matt. 23:15). He said that those who use their piety to cloak their evil are sons of the devil. "You are of your father the devil, and your will is to do your father's desires. He was a murderer from the beginning, and has nothing to do with the truth, because there is no truth in him. When he lies, he speaks out of his own character, for he is a liar and the father of lies" (John 8:44). Lying originates with the devil, and those who turn away from speaking truth join forces with Satan.

Over against this, Jesus came into the world to reveal the truth about God and man and salvation and what is right and wrong. At the end of his ministry, when he was on trial for his life, he said to Pontius Pilate, "For this purpose I was born and for this purpose I have come into the world—*to bear witness to the truth*. Everyone who is of the truth listens to my voice" (John 18:37). Like many modern cynics, Pilate responded, "What is truth?" and turned to go without waiting for an answer.

"I AM THE TRUTH"

But we know the answer he would have received. Jesus would have said what he had already said, "I *am* . . . the truth" (John 14:6). Jesus himself—in all that he is and all that he does and all that he says—is the criterion of what is real and true and right and beautiful. When he speaks, there is no error or falsehood. He said of himself, "The one who seeks the glory of him who sent him is true, and in him there is no falsehood" (John 7:18). Therefore, when others did not believe what he said, he did not consider changing the message to win a better hearing. If truth was met with unbelief, the problem lay with the unbelieving heart, not the truth. "Because I tell the truth, you do not believe me" (John 8:45). Jesus said that people turn away from the light not because they think it's false, but because they love darkness (John 3:19).

When Jesus left the earth he promised to send a Helper. He called him "the Spirit of truth." "When the Helper comes, whom I will send to you from the Father, the *Spirit of truth*, who proceeds from the Father, he will bear witness about me" (John 15:26). This Spirit of truth will help us know the truth and be changed by the truth. So Jesus prays before he leaves and asks the Father to make the truth effective in our lives: "Sanctify them in the *truth*; your word is truth" (John 17:17). So we can see how supremely important truth is to Jesus, and how destructively evil is the impulse to deceive and mislead and speak in devious ways.

THE FOLLY OF CROSSING YOUR FINGERS AND CROSSING YOUR HEART

Therefore, it is not surprising that in the Sermon on the Mount Jesus overturned one of the subtle practices of his day to avoid truth-telling and promise-keeping. When a promise is not kept, it becomes a lie. And when a promise made with a public oath is not kept, we call it perjury. When I was growing up we joked that if you had your fingers crossed when you made a promise, you didn't have to keep it. We also had our own youthful ways of reinforcing our distrusted word: We said, "Cross my heart and hope to die." What we meant was: I am speaking from my heart, not just my lips, and if what I say is not true let me die.

Jesus was not happy about either of these devices—the crossing of the fingers to escape a promise and the crossing of the heart to reinforce a promise. Here is what he said:

> Again you have heard that it was said to those of old, "You shall not swear falsely, but shall perform to the Lord what you have sworn." But I say to you, Do not take an oath at all, either by heaven, for it is the throne of God, or by the earth, for it is his footstool, or by Jerusalem, for it is the city of the great King. And do not take an oath by your head, for you cannot make one hair white or black. Let what you say be simply "Yes" or "No";[1] anything more than this comes from evil. (Matt. 5:33-37)

Jesus is demanding two things here: First, he demands that we not use verbal evasions to escape promise-keeping; second, he demands that we be so truthful that oaths are superfluous.

TECHNICAL EVASIONS OF PROMISE-KEEPING

The verbal evasions Jesus cites are in reference to heaven and earth and Jerusalem and the head. Evidently some people assumed that as long as their oath did not directly call upon God as witness, it was not binding. So if they said, "I swear by heaven" or "I swear by earth" or "I swear by Jerusalem" or "I swear by my head," then they could break their word because they had not said, "I swear by *God.*" This devious logic says something like this: "Heaven and earth and Jerusalem and my head cannot really take vengeance on me if I break my word—only God can. But I did not call God to witness my words and to hold me accountable, so I am not really in trouble."

Jesus rejects that kind of evasion. He points out that everything

---

[1] Or more literally: "Let your word be yes, yes/no, no; and what is more than these is from evil (or the evil one)."

you swear by has God behind it one way or the other. Heaven is his throne. Earth is his footstool. Jerusalem is his city. And your head is under his control, not yours, because only under his providence does our hair change color. Therefore, your problem is your small view of God and truth. You think truth is insignificant and can be manipulated to your liking. And you think God is off in a corner with little concern for your truthfulness until his name is mentioned. In these two things you are wrong. Truth is precious beyond your ability to imagine, and God is behind every molecule in the universe and is always concerned that his creatures be truthful.

TRUTH EVASION BY BELITTLING GOD

Jesus encountered this evasive strategy in the Pharisees in Matthew 23:16-22. His indignation is unmistakable:

> Woe to you, blind guides, who say, "If anyone swears by the temple, it is nothing, but if anyone swears by the gold of the temple, he is bound by his oath." You blind fools! For which is greater, the gold or the temple that has made the gold sacred? And you say, "If anyone swears by the altar, it is nothing, but if anyone swears by the gift that is on the altar, he is bound by his oath." You blind men! For which is greater, the gift or the altar that makes the gift sacred? So whoever swears by the altar swears by it and by everything on it. And whoever swears by the temple swears by it and by him who dwells in it. And whoever swears by heaven swears by the throne of God and by him who sits upon it.

It is almost incredible that the Pharisees not only use evasions like this, but *teach* them. Jesus says that the blind guides "*say* [that is, they teach others], 'If anyone swears by the temple, it is nothing.'" Perhaps it is not a direct quote but rather the upshot of what they say. In either case, Jesus is furious at the way truth and God are belittled here. Gold is esteemed above God's temple. Sacrifices are esteemed above God's altar. Heaven is esteemed above God who dwells there. All this evasiveness ignores the fact that the holiness of heaven, altar, and temple come from their connection with God. But this means little to those who are bent on finding ways to make peace with falsehood.

What alternative did Jesus demand to these manifold ways of evading the binding claims of truth on our lives? To that we turn in the next chapter.

Do Not Take an Oath— Let What You Say Be Simply "Yes" or "No"

And do not take an oath by your head, for you cannot make one hair white or black. Let what you say be simply "Yes" or "No"; anything more than this comes from evil.—MATT. 5:36-37

But Jesus remained silent. And the high priest said to him, "I adjure you by the living God, tell us if you are the Christ, the Son of God." Jesus said to him, "You have said so."—MATT. 26:63-64

A New Standard of Truthfulness

Over against the creative and corrupt ways people find to evade telling the truth (which we saw in the previous chapter), Jesus says, "But I say to you, Do not take an oath at all. . . . Let what you say be simply 'Yes, yes' or 'No, no'; anything more than this comes from evil" (Matt. 5:34, 37, literal translation). In other words, Jesus now goes beyond the Old Testament standard of keeping our oaths to not using any. His reason seems to be that with the arrival of the kingdom of God in his ministry (Luke 11:20; 17:21) and the presence of the King himself (Matt. 21:15-16) and the sending of the Spirit of truth (John 15:26) and the inauguration of the new covenant (Luke 22:20; see *Demand #23*), the standards of truthfulness should rise and the measure of compromise with evil in this world should decrease.

He argues, "Do not take an oath at all . . . anything more

than [yes, yes, and no, no] comes from evil." Evil in the human heart has created lying and deceit. Jesus said it originated with the "father of lies" (John 8:44) and gains strength from the on-going evil of the human heart. Therefore, truth is in jeopardy all the time. But life in community cannot survive without truth. There must be some measure of trust in marriages and businesses and schools and governments and in the vast realm of contractual agreements, not to mention the precious fabric of personal friendships. Therefore, the evil of lying and falsehood and deceit that pervades the human heart and society has been restrained by devices called oaths.

WE LOOK TO OATHS TO DO WHAT LOVE DOES NOT DO

The evil that ruined trust is essentially selfishness and ill-will. We distort the truth to get what we want, even if it hurts others. Which implies that, for truth to hold sway, love must hold sway. If we were not selfish or unloving to others, we would not break our word or tell lies or act hypocritically. Truth would hold sway.

But love does not hold sway in the world, and so oaths have arisen to compensate for what love should do. Oaths are born out of the necessities created by lovelessness. Since we do not love, and so secure the reliability of our word, we take oaths to assure people we mean what we say. We put ourselves under the threat of deity for breaking our word. Which means we make our own self-regard the measure of our truthfulness. We do not want to be struck down by God. This self-regard we share with all people (even if they don't believe in God). Therefore, this kind of oath carries weight in guaranteeing our truthfulness.

Jesus says in effect, "I am calling you to a different level of truthfulness. I am calling you to witness to the inbreaking of my kingdom and the kind of integrity I have brought into the world. Yes, you still live in a fallen world. There is lying and deceit. Oaths may be necessary among those who do not know my saving power.

They may still help fallen society hang together. They are a kind of dam against the river of human falsehood."[1]

JESUS SIMPLY SAID, "YOU HAVE SAID SO"

Jesus was saying, "But for you—you who know me and follow me and are forgiven and transformed by me—let your yes and no be as good as an oath. Let your integrity be unimpeachable. Look the court clerk in the eye when she asks you, 'Do you swear to tell the truth, the whole truth, and nothing but the truth, so help you God,' and say, 'I will tell the truth.'" When Jesus was adjured by the high priest at his court appearance the night before he died, the priest said, "I adjure you by the living God, tell us if you are the Christ, the Son of God" (Matt. 26:63). In other words, he demanded that Jesus call God to witness with an oath as he made his claim to messiahship.

Jesus would not yield. He answered, in accord with his own command in Matthew 5:37, "You have said so." This is Jesus' simple yes: "You have said it, and you are right" (Matt. 26:64; see Mark 14:62). There was no need for an oath. His yes is as good as an oath. The high priest felt the full force of it and did not need to press for an oath. He tore his robe and said, "He has uttered blasphemy. What further witnesses do we need? You have now heard his blasphemy" (Matt. 26:65).

SHOULD THE FOLLOWERS OF JESUS EVER TAKE AN OATH?

Even though Jesus' main point in his radical demand concerning oaths is that we be people of utter integrity and complete truthfulness, we must still ask the question, should the followers of Jesus, then, ever use an oath? To answer this it may be helpful to note that the question can be asked another way. Not only did Jesus say, "Do not take an oath at all" (Matt. 5:34), he also said the positive coun-

---

[1] I borrowed this image from Adolf Schlatter, *Erläuterungen zum Neuen Testament, Das Evangelium nach Matthäus*, Erster Band (Stuttgart: Calwer Vereinsbuchhandlung, 1928), 76. "Against this flood of sins we seek with the oath to erect a dam; but it does not reach its goal, because it only enlarges the power of the lie" (my translation).

terpart, "Let what you say be simply 'Yes' or 'No'"—or literally, "Let your word be 'yes, yes,' 'no, no'" (Matt. 5:37). So the question of application can also be put this way: Should the followers of Jesus ever make a promise or answer a question or make an assertion with any other words than "yes" and "no"?

The reason it may be helpful to consider this second question is that there are exceptions in Jesus' ministry that would warn us against saying followers of Jesus may not add any words to "yes" and "no" to emphasize the speaker's truthfulness. The most prevalent is Jesus' use of the phrase, "Truly" or "Truly, truly." Over fifty times in the Gospels Jesus says something like, "Truly, I say to you," or "Truly, I tell you." And over twenty-five times he uses the even stronger phrase "Truly, truly I say to you."

D. A. Carson says of the phrase, "Jesus uses it before an utterance to confirm and emphasize its trustworthiness and importance."[2] If anyone in the world ever existed whose integrity did not demand added words to emphasize his truthfulness, it was Jesus. Yet he did so. Evidently the use of reinforcing words do not have to flow from the speaker's lack of integrity, but from an impulse of love that the listeners need to be awakened to the absolute trustworthiness of what is being said because they might not know how reliable the speaker is.

This gives me pause, therefore, that I should be slow to say that a follower of Jesus may have such integrity that there is no situation in which love may not demand some reinforcing expression for the sake of the listeners. Add to this that Jesus knew that God himself, who is the essence of integrity, confirmed his word at times with oaths. This was not to make up for untrustworthiness on his part, but to give multiple encouragements to help us believe him (see Luke 1:73; Gen. 22:16). It seems, then, that Jesus' argument aims at absolute integrity and truthfulness but does not intend to stipulate absolutely the wording that expresses this truthfulness.

---

[2] D. A. Carson, *The Gospel According to John* (Grand Rapids, Mich.: Eerdmans, 1991), 162.

Some Oaths May Be Permitted

Returning then to the seemingly absolute prohibition, "Do not take an oath at all," should we infer from these thoughts that there are exceptions to the prohibition? I am inclined to think we should be open to the possibility that the wording of an oath (like, "I call God to witness that what I say is true") could be one way that we show love to someone who does not know us (and whether we are trustworthy) and whose cultural situation would give credit to our account if we used this form of speech. In other words, Jesus' absolute prohibition relates to the abuses of oaths referred to in Matthew 5:35-36 and 23:16-22, and the principle that is absolute across all time and culture is the demand that we be people of absolute truthfulness and honesty.

But Beware of Taking the Edge Off of Jesus' Radical Demand for Truth

This would imply that we use an oath or some other formula *not* to make up for lack of trustworthiness in us, but only to help others embrace the unvarnished truth that we speak. But even as I write this I feel some of the edge being taken off of what Jesus said. He really was lifting us to a higher level than "You shall not swear falsely, but shall perform to the Lord what you have sworn" (Matt. 5:33). His aim was greater than, keep your promises. There is a call away from oaths.

Our new inclination should be, my oath is not necessary. I should be slow to use an oath. An oath will very likely (if not necessarily) communicate something about the weakness of my trustworthiness that may dishonor Jesus. One of the glories of Jesus is that he frees me from the need to lie and from the need to prove that I don't lie.

The followers of Jesus are not just honest, they are moving toward a condition in which protections against being thought dishonest will not be necessary. Therefore, they will find countercultural ways of declaring the lordship of Christ over their minds and mouths. In the end Jesus aims to be known as the way, the *truth*, and the life. He demands that we live and speak in a way that will make that glory known.

WHAT GOD HAS JOINED TOGETHER LET NO MAN SEPARATE, FOR MARRIAGE MIRRORS GOD'S COVENANT WITH US

Have you not read that he who created them from the beginning made them male and female, and said, "Therefore a man shall leave his father and his mother and hold fast to his wife, and they shall become one flesh"? So they are no longer two but one flesh. What therefore God has joined together, let not man separate. —MATT. 19:4-6

Your Maker is your husband, the LORD of hosts is his name. —ISA. 54:5

Jesus demands that husbands and wives be faithful to their marriages. He does not assume this is easy. But he teaches that it is a great thing because marriage is the work of God himself whereby he creates a new reality of "one flesh" that surpasses human comprehension and portrays to the world in human form the covenant union between God and his people. Marriage is sacred beyond what most people imagine, because it is a unique creation of God, a dramatic portrayal of God's relation to his people, and a display of God's glory. Against all the diminished attitudes about marriage in our day, Jesus' message is that marriage is a great work of God and a sacred covenant breakable only by death.

MARRIAGE: THE MIRROR OF GOD'S COVENANT WITH HIS PEOPLE

Jesus knew his Jewish Scriptures and saw them as coming to fulfill-ment in himself and his work (Matt. 5:17-18). This includes his awareness of what God had said about his relationship with his people when he portrayed it as marriage. For example, God said, "Your Maker is your husband, the LORD of hosts is his name" (Isa. 54:5). And "In that day, declares the LORD, you will call me 'My Husband.' . . . And I will betroth you to me forever. I will betroth you to me in righteousness and in justice, in steadfast love and in mercy. I will betroth you to me in faithfulness. And you shall know the LORD" (Hos. 2:16, 19-20). And "When I passed by you again and saw you, behold, you were at the age for love, and I spread the corner of my garment over you and covered your nakedness; I made my vow to you and entered into a covenant with you, declares the Lord GOD, and you became mine" (Ezek. 16:8). And "Surely, as a treacherous wife leaves her husband, so have you been treacherous to me, O house of Israel, declares the LORD" (Jer. 3:20).

With these Scriptures as the backdrop, it is inevitable that Jesus would see God's creation of marriage in the beginning as a means of portraying his relationship with his people. So Jesus read in Genesis 2:24, "Therefore a man shall leave his father and his mother and hold fast to his wife, and they shall become one flesh." When God said this—and Jesus explicitly says that *God* said this, not just Moses, the writer of Genesis (Matt. 19:4-5)—he had in view (as he has all things in view) that he would call his people his wife and himself her husband. Therefore, the union between a man and a woman is uniquely God's creation with a view to portraying the relationship between himself and his people.

GOD CREATES THE UNION OF EACH MARRIAGE FOR HIS GLORY

Jesus is explicit about marriage as God's creation. He does not leave us to figure this out from the Scriptures, and he does not limit the creation to the first marriage between Adam and Eve. He says, "What therefore *God* has joined together, let not man separate" (Matt. 19:6). God, not man, is the decisive creator of the marriage union. And the point is that *each* marriage is "joined" this way by God, because he tells us not to "separate," and the only marriage we can decisively separate is the one we are in. So this marriage—this particular marriage, not just the concept of marriage or the general ordinance of marriage or the first marriage—is God's work. God has acted in the union of this husband and this wife. These two are one flesh by God's work, not just by their choice.

And as a God-created union of "one flesh" this man and this woman are in a covenant analogous with God's covenant with Israel. Their marriage portrays God's relationship with his people. Through marriage God fills the earth with (mostly unwitting) witnesses to the relationship between him and his covenant people. This is one of the main reasons that divorce and remarriage are so serious. They tell a lie about God's relationship to his people. God never divorced his wife and married another. There were separations and much pain, but he always took her back. The prophet Hosea is a testimony to God's radical love for his wayward spouse. God never abandons his wife. And when he has to put her away for her adulterous idolatry, he goes after her in due time. This is what marriage is meant to portray: God's invincible and gracious commitment to his covenant people—his wife.

In this way marriage is meant to glorify God. In Jeremiah 13:11 God says, "As the loincloth clings to the waist of a man, so I made the whole house of Israel and the whole house of Judah cling to me, declares the LORD, that they might be for me a people, a name, a praise, and a *glory*." God freely chose and married Israel so that they would display his glory. Therefore, marriage is the work of God's creation, the portrayal of his covenant love, and the display of his glory.

BUT WHAT ABOUT MOSES' PERMISSION OF DIVORCE?

This gives some sense of why Jesus' demand for marital faithfulness astonishes the Pharisees. They can hardly believe he would raise the bar so high. They had come to him with a question: "Is it lawful to divorce one's wife for any cause?" (Matt. 19:3). Jesus answers them not by reference to the Mosaic law but by reference to the Mosaic creation account. In other words, he intends to root the meaning of marriage in its original design, not in the way marriage is managed by the law in view of sin.

Jesus says, "Have you not read that he who created them from the beginning made them male and female, and said, 'Therefore a man shall leave his father and his mother and hold fast to his wife, and they shall become one flesh'? So they are no longer two but one flesh. What therefore God has joined together, let not man separate" (Matt. 19:4-6). So the answer to their question is: God made marriage to last, so don't treat it as breakable.

Now the Pharisees think they have Jesus trapped. He seems to have just taken a position contrary to the Law of Moses. So they ask, "Why then did Moses command one to give a certificate of divorce and to send her away?" (Matt. 19:7). In other words, they hear correctly in Jesus' answer the implication that one should never break the marriage covenant. But that is not the way they understand Moses. So they ask, why did Moses make a provision for divorce if, you say, the covenant is not to be broken?

Jesus responds, "Because of your hardness of heart Moses allowed you to divorce your wives, but from the beginning it was not so" (Matt. 19:8). So Jesus takes his stand with Moses in the creation account and says that just as in the beginning the marriage covenant was not meant to be breakable, so now in the kingdom that he was bringing on earth, this original intention is to be rediscovered and reasserted. In other words, Jesus is raising the standard of his disciples above what Moses allowed. He puts it like this: "And I say to you: whoever divorces his wife, except for sexual immorality, and marries another, commits adultery" (Matt. 19:9).

The Devastation of Divorce

We are now at a point where we need to tackle the question, did Jesus make provision for his disciples to divorce and remarry? Are there situations in which he would sanction this? There is no consensus on the answer to this question today among his followers. I want to say clearly from the beginning that I am aware that men more godly than I have taken different views than the one I will give here. I do not claim to have seen or said the last word on this issue, nor am I, I pray, above correction should I prove to be wrong. What follows is an attempt to show why I believe Jesus considered the marriage covenant breakable only by death and therefore forbade remarriage while a spouse is living.

I realize that simply saying this will feel devastating to some, adding more misery to the injury of what they did not want to happen. Divorce is painful. It is often more emotionally wrenching than the death of a spouse. It is often long years in coming and long years in the settlement and in the adjustment. The upheaval of life is immeasurable. The sense of failure and guilt and fear can torture the soul. Like the psalmist, night after night a spouse falls asleep with tears (Ps. 6:6). Work performance is hindered. People draw near or withdraw with uncertain feelings. Loneliness can be overwhelming. A sense of a devastated future can be all-consuming. Courtroom controversy compounds the personal misery.

And then there is often the agonizing place of children. Parents hope against hope that the scars will not cripple them or ruin their own marriages someday. Tensions over custody and financial support deepen the wounds. And then the awkward and artificial visitation rights can lengthen the tragedy over decades.

Because of these and many other factors, people with sensitive hearts weep with those who weep. They try not to increase the pain. And sometimes this care is confused with compromise. People think that loving care is incompatible with confrontation—that the tenderness of Jesus and the toughness of his demands cannot both be love. But surely this is not right.

THE CHALLENGE TO LOVE BIBLICALLY

Jesus was an extraordinarily caring person. His teaching on divorce and remarriage was also firm: "What . . . God has joined together, let not man separate." In fact, firm and loving confrontation with the demands of Christ *is* a form of caring, because a sinful decision is just as harmful to a person as the emotional pain. This is true individually, and it is true for the church and society. Compassionate compromises on the sanctity of marriage that weaken the solidity of the covenant of marriage look loving in the short run but wreak havoc over decades. Preserving the solid framework of the marriage covenant with high standards feels tough in the short run but produces ten thousand blessings the future generations take for granted.

The great challenge to Jesus' followers in the face of divorce and remarriage is to love biblically. The great challenge is to mingle the tears of compassion with the tough love of obedience. This alone will honor Christ and preserve the spiritual health and power of the marriage and the church Jesus founded.

In Matthew 19:3-9 and Mark 10:2-12 Jesus rejected the Pharisees' justification of divorce from Deuteronomy 24 and reasserted the purpose of God in creation that no human being separate what God has joined together. He said that Moses' handling of divorce was owing to the hardness of the human heart and then implied that he had come to do something about that. His aim was that the standard of his followers would be higher than what the Law allowed.

How high? That's the question I try to answer in the next chapter.

What God Has Joined Together Let No Man Separate, for Whoever Divorces and Marries Another Commits Adultery

Whoever divorces his wife and marries another commits adultery against her, and if she divorces her husband and marries another, she commits adultery. —Mark 10:11-12

Everyone who divorces his wife and marries another commits adultery, and he who marries a woman divorced from her husband commits adultery. —Luke 16:18

It was also said, "Whoever divorces his wife, let him give her a certificate of divorce." But I say to you that everyone who divorces his wife, except on the ground of sexual immorality, makes her commit adultery. And whoever marries a divorced woman commits adultery. —Matt. 5:31-32

And I say to you: whoever divorces his wife, except for sexual immorality, and marries another, commits adultery. —Matt. 19:9

J esus set a higher standard for marital faithfulness than Moses or the Jewish teachers of his day. He did not affirm the permission for divorce found in Deuteronomy 24. He said it was owing to the hardness of the human heart (Matt. 19:8) and implied that he was here to change that. In this chapter we will try to discern just how high Jesus' standard of marital faithfulness is.

CLUES IN MOSES THAT DIVORCE DID NOT DESTROY GOD'S UNION

I suspect that Jesus saw a higher standard for marriage implied not only in the creation account of Genesis 2:24 but also in the very wording of Deuteronomy 24:1-4, which shows that the *one-flesh* relationship established by marriage is not completely nullified by divorce or even by remarriage. Consider what Moses wrote:

> When a man takes a wife and marries her, if then she finds no favor in his eyes because he has found some indecency in her, and he writes her a certificate of divorce and puts it in her hand and sends her out of his house, and she departs out of his house, and if she goes and becomes another man's wife, and the latter man hates her and writes her a certificate of divorce and puts it in her hand and sends her out of his house, or if the latter man dies, who took her to be his wife, then her former husband, who sent her away, may not take her again to be his wife, after she has been defiled, for that is an abomination before the LORD. And you shall not bring sin upon the land that the LORD your God is giving you for an inheritance. (Deut. 24:1-4)

The remarkable thing about these four verses is that while divorce is taken for granted, nevertheless the woman who is divorced becomes "defiled" by her remarriage (v. 4). Therefore, it may well be that when the Pharisees asked Jesus if divorce was legitimate, he based his negative answer not only on God's original intention expressed in Genesis 1:27 and 2:24, but also on the implication of Deuteronomy 24:4, that remarriage after divorce, while permitted, nevertheless *defiles* a person. In other words, there were clues in the writings of Moses that the divorce concession was on the basis of the hardness of man's heart and did not make divorce and remarriage the most God-honoring path.

Moses' prohibition of a wife returning to her first husband even after her second husband dies (because it is an "abomination," v. 4) suggests that today no second marriage should be broken in order to restore a first one. I will return to this issue later on. But for now I would say that even a disobedient second or third marriage should not be broken, but confessed as less than ideal and yet sanctified by God's mercy. It is better in God's eyes than more broken covenants.

THE PROHIBITIONS WITHOUT EXCEPTION

Twice in the Gospels Jesus expresses with no exceptions his prohibition of divorce followed by remarriage. In Luke 16:18 he says, "Everyone who divorces his wife and marries another commits adultery, and he who marries a woman divorced from her husband commits adultery." Here Jesus seems to call all remarriage after divorce adultery. These are strong words. Evidently the reason a second marriage is called *adultery* is because the first one is considered to still be valid. So Jesus is taking a stand against the Jewish culture at the time in which all divorce was considered to carry with it the right of remarriage.[1]

Luke 16:18 carries another implication: The second half of the

---

[1] It puzzles me that so many commentators take the opposite approach. They observe that since "any Jewish reader would have taken for granted" that divorce opened the door to remarriage, therefore Jesus agrees with this assumption and does not need to say it in Mark 10:11-12 and Luke 16:18. Hence Andreas Köstenberger, for example, writes, "Rather than concluding that Jesus did not allow for any divorce in sexually consummated marriages, it is much more likely that he did not elaborate on points at which he agreed with the commonly held view in his day." *God, Marriage, and Family: Rebuilding the Biblical Foundation* (Wheaton, Ill.: Crossway Books, 2004), 242. I am inclined to say that Jesus' explicit, unqualified rejection of remarriage in Mark 10 and Luke 16 is a direct repudiation of this cultural assumption as a compromise with the hardness of man's heart. How could he have more clearly addressed and rejected the cultural assumption of the legitimacy of remarriage after divorce? David Instone-Brewer's arguments that (1) the short form of Jesus' saying in Luke 16:18 is a reference to Herod Antipas' marriage of his brother's wife (160-161), and (2) that the omission of any exception clause is explained on the analogy of rabbinic abbreviations (161-167), and (3) that the exception clause, "except for *porneia*," should be "except for indecency," referring to the phrase "some indecency" in Deuteronomy 24:1 and expressing the more conservative Rabbi Shammai's position all seem unlikely to me. David Instone-Brewer, *Divorce and Remarriage in the Bible: The Social and Literary Context* (Grand Rapids, Mich.: Eerdmans, 2002). If one objects that Jesus did not endorse or forbid remarriage after the death of a spouse because he shared the commonly accepted view, my response would be: 1) None of Jesus' discussions of remarriage are aimed at answering the question about what is legitimate in the death of a spouse, but only what is legitimate in the divorce of a spouse. 2) In one place where Jesus comes close to the issue of the death of a spouse (in the question of the Sadducees about the wife who was widowed seven times, Matt. 22:23-32), Jesus finds no fault in her remarriage after a spouse's death.

verse ("he who marries a woman divorced from her husband commits adultery") shows that not only the divorcing man is guilty of adultery when he remarries, but also *any* man who marries a divorced woman commits adultery. This is all the more remarkable because the woman in view here is presumably the innocent party in the divorce, because when her husband divorces her he commits adultery in marrying another. Apparently this is because he had no right to divorce his wife. That is, she has done nothing to make his divorce legitimate. Nevertheless, any man who marries this abandoned woman, Jesus says, "commits adultery."

This is a hard saying. The woman who is forsaken by a man who leaves to marry another is called by Jesus to display the holiness of her marriage vows and the nature of the marriage covenant by not marrying another. Since there are no exceptions mentioned in the verse, and since Jesus is evidently rejecting the common cultural conception of divorce as including the right of remarriage, the first readers of Luke's Gospel would have been hard-put to see any exceptions on the basis that Jesus shared the cultural acceptance of divorce.

The other instance of Jesus' unqualified rejection of remarriage after divorce is found in Mark 10:11-12. He said, "Whoever divorces his wife and marries another commits adultery against her, and if she divorces her husband and marries another, she commits adultery." These two verses repeat the first half of Luke 16:18 but go further and say that not only the man who divorces, but also a woman who divorces and then remarries is committing adultery. And as in Luke 16:18, there are no exceptions mentioned to this rule.

What we have so far is two seemingly absolute prohibitions of remarriage after divorce in Luke 16:18 and Mark 10:11-12 since Jesus sees marrying a second time as adultery, even if you are the innocent party in the divorce. And we have a strong statement in Matthew 19:6 and Mark 10:9 that God has joined married couples together and therefore no man should separate them.

Is There a Permission for Divorce in Matthew 5:32?

But what makes the matter more controversial is that in Matthew 5:32 and 19:9 there seems to be an exception to the rule of no remarriage after divorce. In Matthew 5:32 Jesus says, "Everyone who divorces his wife, *except on the ground of sexual immorality*, makes her commit adultery. And whoever marries a divorced woman commits adultery." Again in Matthew 19:9 he says, "Whoever divorces his wife, *except for sexual immorality*, and marries another, commits adultery." Both these verses are generally interpreted to say that Jesus allowed divorce and remarriage where there has been "sexual immorality" by one of the partners. Is that what the "exception clauses" mean?

According to the wording of Matthew 5:32 (". . . *makes* her commit adultery"), Jesus assumes that in most situations in that culture a wife who has been put away by a husband will be drawn into a second marriage. Nevertheless, in spite of these pressures on the divorced woman to remarry, Jesus still forbids this second marriage. His words imply that the remarriage of an innocent wife who has been put away is nevertheless adultery: "Everyone who divorces his wife, *except on the ground of sexual immorality*, makes her [the innocent wife who has not committed sexual immorality] commit adultery." This would mean that remarriage is wrong not merely when a person is *guilty* in the process of divorce, but also when a person is *innocent*. In other words, Jesus' opposition to remarriage seems to be based on the unbreakableness of the marriage bond, not on the conditions of the divorce.

So Matthew 5:32 does not teach that remarriage is lawful in some cases. Rather, it reaffirms that to remarry after divorce is to commit adultery, even for those who have been divorced innocently, and that a man who divorces his wife is guilty of the adultery of her second marriage, and that a man who marries a woman who is put away by her husband, even innocently, commits adultery. Hence the final clause of the verse: "And whoever marries a divorced woman commits adultery." Before we tackle what the exception clause means, let's put the similar text from Matthew 19:9 before us.

THE EXCEPTION CLAUSE IN MATTHEW 19:9

The other place where Jesus seems to express an "exception clause" to the prohibition of divorce and remarriage is Matthew 19:9, "And I say to you: whoever divorces his wife, *except for sexual immorality*, and marries another, commits adultery." Does this exception mean that there are situations in which a married person may be free to remarry after divorce? That is what most commentators see and what most followers of Jesus think. In my understanding of Jesus' demand this is not what it means. It may help if I describe my pilgrimage to another understanding.

All of my adult life I assumed that adultery and desertion were two legitimate grounds for divorce and remarriage. This was the air I breathed, and I saw a confirmation of this in the exception clause in Matthew 19:9, even though, as I see it now, the rest of the New Testament pointed in the other direction.[2] But there came a point when this assumption began to crumble.

I was initially troubled that the absolute form of Jesus' denunciation of divorce and remarriage in Mark 10:11-12 and Luke 16:18 is not expressed by Matthew, if in fact his exception clause is an opening for divorce and remarriage. I was bothered by the assumption so

---

[2] A fuller statement of my understanding of the rest of the New Testament may be found under the topic "Divorce and Remarriage" at the Desiring God website, specifically, http://www.desiringgod.org/resourcelibrary/articles/bydate/1986/1488/. A survey of three views is offered in *Remarriage After Divorce in Today's Church*, ed. Mark L. Strauss (Grand Rapids, Mich.: Zondervan, 2006), in which Gordon Wenham represents the position of no marriage after divorce, William A. Heth (who no longer holds his view represented in his book coauthored with Wenham, *Jesus and Divorce*, updated ed. [Carlisle, U.K.: Paternoster, 1997; orig. ed. 1984] represents the position of two grounds for divorce and remarriage, and Craig S. Keener represents the position that various other grounds are allowed for divorce and remarriage. In addition, see Craig S. Keener, *And Marries Another: Divorce and Remarriage in the Teaching of the New Testament* (Peabody, Mass.: Hendrickson, 1991); and Carl Laney, *The Divorce Myth: A Biblical Examination of Divorce and Remarriage* (Minneapolis: Bethany, 1981), who argues for no divorce after remarriage. David Instone-Brewer, *Divorce and Remarriage in the Bible: The Social and Literary Context* (Grand Rapids, Mich.: Eerdmans, 2002) and *Divorce and Remarriage in the Church* (Carlisle, U.K.: Paternoster, 2003) argues for a range of grounds for divorce and remarriage including abuse and neglect. Geoffrey W. Bromiley, *God and Marriage* (Grand Rapids, Mich.: Eerdmans, 1980) and Andreas Köstenberger with David W. Jones, *God, Marriage, and Family: Rebuilding the Biblical Foundation* (Wheaton, Ill.: Crossway Books, 2004), offer good overviews of the wider biblical vision of marriage and defend a limited divorce and remarriage position.

many writers make, namely, that Matthew is simply making explicit something that would have been implicitly understood by the hearers of Jesus or the readers of Mark 10 and Luke 16 (see footnote 1).

Would they really have assumed that the absolute statements included exceptions? I began to have serious doubts. Therefore, my inclination was to inquire whether or not, in fact, Matthew's exception clause conforms to the absoluteness of Mark and Luke, not the other way around.

The second thing that began to disturb me was the question, why does Matthew use the Greek word πορνεία (*porneia,* "sexual immorality") instead of the word μοιχεία (*moicheia*) which means adultery? Sexual immorality in marriage would naturally be adultery. But the word Matthew uses to express Jesus' meaning is one that usually means *fornication* or *sexual immorality without reference to marital unfaithfulness.* Almost all commentators seem to make the assumption again that *porneia* refers to adultery in this context. The question nagged at me why Matthew would not use the word for adultery (*moicheia*), if that is in fact what he meant.

Then I noticed something very interesting. The only other place besides Matthew 5:32 and 19:9 where Matthew uses the word *porneia* is in Matthew 15:19 where it is used *alongside moicheia.* Therefore, the primary contextual evidence for Matthew's usage is that he conceives of *porneia* as, in some sense, *different* than adultery. Could this mean, then, that in Matthew's record of Jesus' teaching he is thinking of *porneia* in its more usual sense of fornication or incest or prostitution that does not denote marital unfaithfulness, that is, adultery?[3]

---

[3] Abel Isaksson agrees with this view of πορνεία and sums up his research as follows:

> Thus we cannot get away from the fact that the distinction between what was to be regarded as *porneia* and what was to be regarded as *moicheia* was very strictly maintained in pre-Christian Jewish literature and in the N.T. *porneia* may, of course, denote different forms of forbidden sexual relations, but we can find no unequivocal examples of the use of this word to denote a wife's adultery. [Giving Isaksson the benefit of the doubt here in what may be a technical overstatement, he may mean this (which is what I would say): If a wife sells herself into a life of prostitution, the way Israel did in Jeremiah 3:6 and Hosea 2:2, her acts may be called both *porneia* or *moicheia.* But the fact that the same act may be described in these two ways does not make the words interchangeable. *Moicheia* still denotes the covenant-breaking of marital unfaithfulness, while *porneia* denotes illicit sexual immorality that does *not* denote marital unfaithfulness, but may involve married people.] Under these circumstances we can hardly assume that this word means adultery in the

The next clue in my search for an explanation came when I noticed the use of *porneia* in John 8:41 where Jewish leaders indirectly accuse Jesus of being born of *porneia*. In other words, since they don't accept the virgin birth, they assume that his mother Mary had committed *fornication* and that Jesus was the result of this act. On the basis of that clue I went back to study Matthew's record of Jesus' birth in Matthew 1:18-20.

THE RELEVANCE OF THE EXCEPTION CLAUSES FOR JOSEPH'S BETROTHAL TO MARY

In these verses Joseph and Mary are referred to as husband (ἀνήρ) and wife (γυνή). Yet they are described as only being *betrothed* to each other. This is probably owing to the fact that the words for husband and wife are simply *man* and *woman* in the Greek, and to the fact that betrothal was a more significant commitment at that time than engagement is today. In Matthew 1:19 Joseph resolves to "divorce" Mary though they were only betrothed and not yet married. The word for divorce (ἀπολῦσαι) is the same as the word in Matthew 5:32 and 19:9. But most important of all, Matthew says that Joseph was "just" in making the decision to divorce Mary, presumably on account of her assumed *porneia*, fornication. In other words, this "divorce" was permitted according to Matthew.

Only Matthew has told that story of the crisis Joseph faced in whether to marry his betrothed even though she, as far as he knew at first, had committed fornication (πορνεία). In handling this crisis he called Joseph "just" in the plan to "divorce" her. That means that Matthew, as a follower of Jesus, would not consider this kind of "divorce" wrong. It would not have prevented Joseph (or Mary) from marrying another.

---

clauses in Matthew. The logia on divorce are worded as a paragraph of the law, intended to be obeyed by the members of the Church. Under these circumstances it is inconceivable that in a text of this nature the writer would not have maintained a clear distinction between what was unchastity and what was adultery: *moicheia* and not *porneia* was used to describe the wife's adultery. From the philological point of view there are accordingly very strong arguments against this interpretation of the clauses as permitting divorce in the case in which the wife was guilty of adultery. (Abel Isaksson, *Marriage and Ministry in the New Temple*, trans. Neil Tomkinson and Jean Gray [Lund, Sweden: Gleerup, 1965], 134-135)

Since only Matthew had told this story and raised this question, he was the only Gospel writer who would feel any need to make clear that Jesus' absolute prohibition of divorce followed by remarriage did *not* include a situation like Joseph and Mary's. That is what I think he does with the exception clauses. He records Jesus saying, "Whoever divorces his wife—not including, of course, the case of fornication [πορνεία] between betrothed couples—and marries another, commits adultery."[4]

A common objection to this interpretation is that both in Matthew 19:3-9 and in Matthew 5:31-32 the issue Jesus is responding to is marriage, not betrothal. The point is pressed that "except for fornication" is irrelevant to the context of marriage. My answer is that this irrelevancy is precisely the point of the exception clause. Whether it sounds irrelevant in the context depends on how you hear it. I don't think it sounds pointless if you hear it the way I just suggested or if Matthew 5:32 goes like this: "But I say to you that everyone who divorces his wife—*excluding, of course, the case of fornication* [πορνεία] *during betrothal*—makes her commit adultery." In this way Jesus makes clear that the action his earthly father almost took—to "divorce" Mary because of πορνεία—would not have been unjust. It would have been right. That is the kind of situation the exception clause is meant to exclude.[5]

This interpretation of the exception clause has several advantages:

• It does not force Matthew's Gospel to disagree with the seemingly plain, absolute meaning of Mark and Luke.

• It provides an explanation for why the word *porneia* is used in Matthew's exception clause instead of *moicheia*.

---

[4] I do not know all the words Jesus may have used to express this prohibition over the time of his ministry. Therefore, I am slow to say that Matthew created this exception clause and put it in Jesus' mouth. It is likely that Jesus taught in Aramaic, and so in one sense Matthew and the other Gospel writers, who were writing in Greek, decided what exact wording to use in our Gospels. My own conviction is that these Gospel writers were inspired by the Holy Spirit and that what they wrote in Greek accurately represented what Jesus taught.

[5] Andreas Köstenberger arrays seven arguments against this view in *God, Marriage, and Family: Rebuilding the Biblical Foundation*, pp. 241-243. Though I don't find them compelling, I have tried to take them into account in my thinking and conclusions.

• It squares with Matthew's own use of *porneia* (for fornication) in distinction from *moicheia* (for adultery) in Matthew 15:19.

• It fits Matthew's wider context concerning Joseph's contemplated "divorce" from Mary (Matt. 1:19).

What are the implications of this high standard of marriage? To this we turn in the next chapter.

What God Has Joined Together Let No Man Separate—One Man, One Woman, by Grace, Till Death

The disciples said to him, "If such is the case of a man with his wife, it is better not to marry." But he said to them, "Not everyone can receive this saying, but only those to whom it is given. For there are eunuchs who have been so from birth, and there are eunuchs who have been made eunuchs by men, and there are eunuchs who have made themselves eunuchs for the sake of the kingdom of heaven. Let the one who is able to receive this receive it. —MATT. 19:10-12

IF SUCH IS THE CASE, BETTER NOT TO MARRY?

Not surprisingly, when Jesus had finished teaching on marriage and divorce in Matthew 19:3-9, his disciples were bewildered by how strict Jesus' standards were. So they said, "If such is the case of a man with his wife, it is better not to marry" (Matt. 19:10). This response confirms that we are on the right track when we hear Jesus setting the bar very high. The disciples assume that this standard is so high it is better not to marry. In other words, if there is no back door to marriage, it is better not to walk through the front door. This response would not make as much sense if Jesus had just prescribed a back door as large as infidelity.

Jesus' response is not to lower the bar so that marriage becomes less risky. Instead, he says, in essence, that the ability to remain single if necessary and the ability to stay in a hard marriage if necessary are both a gift of God. In other words, flourishing in singleness and flourishing in marriage are a work of divine grace. "Not everyone can receive this saying [the saying that marriage is permanent], but only those to whom it is given" (Matt. 19:11). The point is not that some disciples are given the grace and some are not. The point is that this grace (or faithfulness in singleness and marriage) is the mark of a disciple. "Those to whom it is given" are followers of Jesus.[1] God gives the grace for what he demands.

Eunuchs for the Kingdom

Then Jesus illustrates that such grace has actually been given to those who for various reasons have not been permitted to marry. "For there are eunuchs who have been so from birth, and there are eunuchs who have been made eunuchs by men, and there are eunuchs who have made themselves eunuchs for the sake of the kingdom of heaven. Let the one who is able to receive this receive it" (Matt. 19:12). The point here is that if you do not marry or if you are divorced and must remain single, you are not alone but are in the company of some who have had singleness forced on them and some who have chosen it for the sake of the kingdom. In all cases God gives grace.

The words "Let the one who is able to receive this receive it" are like the words "He who has ears, let him hear" (Matt. 13:9, 43; 11:15). That is, whether you have ears to hear—or whether you have grace to receive this call to radical respect for marriage—is the mark of being a follower of Jesus. "My sheep hear my voice, and I know them, and they follow me" (John 10:27).

---

[1] Compare the parallel wording between Matthew 19:11 and 13:11, the parallels between Matthew 19:12 and 13:9, 43; 11:15, and the parallel between Matthew 19:11 and 19:26.

The Folly of Homosexuality

Marriage is a great work of God. It is a great gift to the world. It is worthy of books and songs and poetry and life and sacrifice, not just a little chapter like this. Jesus would grieve over the cavalier way that marriage is treated in our day. He would be appalled at any thought of two men or two women calling their homosexual union *marriage*. He would not call it marriage. As much pity as he may feel for the sexual brokenness, he would call the practice of homosexuality sin and the attempt to sanctify it with the word *marriage* folly.

He would respond to this folly the same way he responded to the Pharisees' justification of divorce with Moses' teaching. He would go back to the beginning. Only this time he would underline the words *male* and *female*. "Have you not read that he who created them from the beginning made them *male* and *female*, and said, 'Therefore a *man* shall leave his father and his mother and hold fast to his *wife*, and they shall become one flesh'?" (Matt. 19:4-5). Jesus would root heterosexual marriage in the creation of man as male and female and in the original union of man and woman into one flesh. He would count it a great sadness that the glory of marriage and all that it stands for is so debased as to make it a covering for the sin of homosexuality.

Are Divorce and Remarriage the Unforgivable Sins?

But as great as marriage is, divorce followed by remarriage is not the unforgivable sin. Sometimes I am asked whether my understanding of Jesus implies that divorce is the unforgivable sin. The answer is no. Jesus said that his blood will be the basis of forgiveness for all sins (Matt. 26:28). Therefore he is able to say, "Truly, I say to you, all sins will be forgiven the children of man, and whatever blasphemies they utter, but whoever blasphemes against the Holy Spirit never has forgiveness, but is guilty of an eternal sin" (Mark 3:28-29).

From these wonderful promises we learn that forgiveness for

sins is available on the basis of the shed blood of Jesus. Forgiveness is available for all sins, without exception. Forgiveness is received freely through trusting Jesus to forgive our sins. This implies that we see sin as sin and hate it as a dishonor to Jesus. The only unforgivable sin is the sin that we refuse to confess and forsake. We commit unforgivable sin when we cleave to a sin so long and so tenaciously that we can no longer confess it as sin and turn from it. What Jesus calls "the blasphemy against the Holy Spirit" (in Matthew 12:31-32) and "eternal sin" (in Mark 3:29) is the resistance against the Holy Spirit's convicting work to the point where he withdraws, leaving the sinner in helpless hardness of heart, unable to repent.

Neither divorce nor remarriage is in itself the unforgivable sin any more than is murder, stealing, lying, coveting, adultery, or homosexual behavior. "All sins will be forgiven the children of man" (Mark 3:28). God is faithful and just to forgive—he will honor the worth of his Son's sacrifice for all who confess their sin and bank their hope on the saving work of Jesus.

Marital sin is in the same category as lying and killing and stealing. If someone has lied, killed, stolen, or illegitimately left a marriage, the issue is not, can they be forgiven? The issue is, do they admit that what they did was sin? Do they renounce it? And do they do what they can in order to make it right if possible?

What usually causes the conflict is not whether divorce and remarriage are unforgivable sins, but whether they are sins at all—to be confessed (from the past) and to be avoided (in the future). If a person has stolen things in his past, no one would say that we are treating stealing as the unforgivable sin if we insist that this person confess his sin and begin to make amends to those he defrauded. A sin is not unforgivable because it must be confessed as sin, renounced as an option, and its effects made right (as far as possible).

So it is with divorce or remarriage. It should not keep anyone out of fellowship with the followers of Jesus any more than a past life of robbery. But there should be a heartfelt confession of the sin committed and a renouncing of it and an affirming of what is right, just as with all other sins of the past.

WHAT DOES A FOLLOWER OF JESUS DO WHO HAS DIVORCED AND REMARRIED?

What then would Jesus expect from one of his followers who has sinned and is divorced and remarried? He would expect us to acknowledge that the choice to remarry and the act of entering a second marriage was sin and to confess it as such and seek forgiveness. He would also expect that we not separate from our present spouse. I base this on at least five observations.

First, Jesus seemed to regard multiple marriages as wrong but real. He said to the woman at the well in John 4:18, "You have had five husbands, and the one you now have is not your husband." She is living with a man now, but there has been no marriage—no covenant-making. The others he calls "husbands," but the one she is with now is not her husband.

Second, Jesus knew that Deuteronomy 24:4 spoke against going back to a first husband after marrying a second. He did not go out of his way to qualify this provision.

Third, covenant-keeping is crucial to Jesus as we saw in the previous chapter (also see *Demand #23*). Therefore, even though the current covenant is adulterous in the making, it is real and should be kept. Its beginning in sin does not have to mean that it is continuously sinful and without hope of purification.

Fourth, there are illustrations of God taking acts of disobedience and turning the result into God-ordained plans. One example is the fact that it was sin for the people of Israel to ask for a king to be like the nations (1 Sam. 12:19-22). Nevertheless, God turned the sinfully instituted kingship into the origin of the Messiah and the kingship of Jesus. Another example would be the sinful marriage of David to Bathsheba. The adultery with her, the murder of her husband, and the marriage "displeased the LORD" (2 Sam. 11:27). So the Lord took the life of the first child of this union (2 Sam. 12:15,

18). But the second child, Solomon, "the LORD loved" and chose him as ruler over his people (2 Sam. 12:24).

Fifth, through repentance and forgiveness on the basis of the blood of Jesus and through the sanctifying work of the promised Holy Spirit, a marriage that was entered sinfully can be consecrated to God, purified from sin, and become a means of grace. It remains less than ideal, but it is not a curse. It may become a great blessing.

MARRIAGE: GREAT AND PRECIOUS, BUT NOT ULTIMATE OR PERMANENT

There is no doubt that Jesus' demand for faithfulness in marriage is a radical word to our modern culture. Here is a test for his lordship over our lives. His standards are high. They do not assume that this earth is our final home. He makes it very clear that marriage is an ordinance for this age only. "For in the resurrection they neither marry nor are given in marriage, but are like angels in heaven" (Matt. 22:30). Therefore, marriage is a brief blessing. A great one, but not an ultimate one. A precious one, but not a permanent one.

This eternal perspective explains why Jesus can be so radical. Never to have married is not a tragedy. Otherwise Jesus' life is a tragedy. Tragedy is craving the perfect marriage so much that we make a god out of being married. Jesus' standards are high because marriage does not and should not meet all our needs. It should not be an idol. It should not and cannot take the place of Jesus himself. Marriage is but for a moment. Jesus is for eternity. How we live in our marriages and our singleness will show if Jesus is our supreme treasure.

Demand #43

RENDER TO CAESAR THE THINGS THAT ARE CAESAR'S AND TO GOD THE THINGS THAT ARE GOD'S

*Then the Pharisees went and plotted how to entangle [Jesus] in his talk. And they sent their disciples to him, along with the Herodians, saying . . . "Tell us, then, what you think. Is it lawful to pay taxes to Caesar, or not?" But Jesus, aware of their malice, said, "Why put me to the test, you hypocrites? Show me the coin for the tax." And they brought him a denarius. And Jesus said to them, "Whose likeness and inscription is this?" They said, "Caesar's." Then he said to them, "Therefore render to Caesar the things that are Caesar's, and to God the things that are God's." —*MATT. 22:15-21

Jesus was Jewish. He was part of a people who lived in their homeland under the totalitarian rule of Rome. The Caesar was absolute and claimed even divine status as emperor of Rome. Caesar Augustus was the emperor when Jesus was born (Luke 2:1), and his son, Tiberius Caesar, ruled from A.D. 13-37 during the rest of Jesus' life (Luke 3:1). So when Jesus asked the Pharisees for a coin with Caesar's picture on it, the coin very likely pictured Tiberius.[1]

---

[1] "The silver denarius of Tiberius, including a portrait of his head and minted especially at the Lyon, circulated there in this period; although an earlier coin might be in view, this imperial denarius is most likely. . . . The coin related directly to pagan Roman religion and to the imperial cult in the east: the side bearing his image also included a superscription, namely, 'TI. CAESAR DIVI AVG.F.AVGVSTVS"—"Tiberius Caesar, son of the Divine Augustus"; the other side bore a feminine image (perhaps of the Empress Livia personified as a goddess Roma) and read "PONTIF. MAXIM," referring to the high priest of Roman religion. The Empire actively used such coins to promote the worship of the emperor." Craig S. Keener, *A Commentary on Matthew* (Grand Rapids, Mich.: Eerdmans, 1999), 525.

THE TRAP

When the Pharisees asked Jesus if it was lawful to pay taxes to Caesar, they were trying to hang him on the horns of a politically supercharged dilemma. The Jews were oppressed and were indignant that the promised land where they lived was ruled by pagan Romans. Paying taxes to Rome was a religious offense. But not to pay them would be suicidal. The Pharisees were manifestly making an effort to entangle Jesus in a trap. "Either he will support taxes to Rome, undercutting his popular, messianic support, or he will challenge taxes. . . . [Then] the Herodians could charge him with being a revolutionary—hence that he should be executed, and executed quickly."[2]

So they ask him, "Tell us, then, what you think. Is it lawful to pay taxes to Caesar, or not?" Jesus exposes their hypocrisy and then gives an answer that penetrates deep into the meaning of how his followers should live as dual citizens of his kingdom and the kingdom of this world. He says, "Why put me to the test, you hypocrites? Show me the coin for the tax." So they brought him a denarius. And Jesus said to them, "Whose likeness and inscription is this?" They said, "Caesar's." Then he said to them, "Therefore render to Caesar the things that are Caesar's, and to God the things that are God's" (Matt. 22:17-21).

I don't think Jesus dodged the question. I think he answered it in a way that forces us to think; and in the end the answer demands radical allegiance to God's supreme authority over all things. The first command, "Render to Caesar the things that are Caesar's" gets its meaning from the second one, "Render to God the things that are God's." It's the juxtaposition of these two commands that gives the first one its proper scope.

THE UNEXPECTED, PENETRATING ANSWER

One can picture his hearers holding their breath as he says, "Render to Caesar the things that are Caesar's." Perhaps a smile of devious

---

[2] Ibid., 524.

success began to come over the faces of his adversaries. This sounds very much like a capitulation to the supremacy of Rome. I wonder how long Jesus paused between the two commands. Perhaps long enough to let the words work their way into the mind: "Caesar has a scope of ownership and authority. Comply with that." As that begins to sink in, Jesus adds one short but massive qualification: "Render to God the things that are God's." The smiles that were forming on the adversaries' faces pause. This is not what they were expecting. It is not what anybody was expecting. Jesus has called for a kind of allegiance in two directions: to Caesar according to his ownership and authority, and to God according to his ownership and authority.

Jesus wisely left the scope of these two ownerships and authorities for the listener to answer. Whether this is a compromise with Rome will depend on how a person understands the scope and nature of God's ownership and authority in relation to Caesar's scope of ownership and authority. That is what he forces us to think about.

The starting point for this thinking is the unmistakable assumption of the second command, "Render to God the things that are God's." That assumption is: *Everything* is God's. If a person does not hear that in Jesus' command, he would say, "Hearing they do not hear. They have ears, but they do not hear." In other words, the all-important fact is unspoken and obvious to all who are willing to hear the obvious. By being unspoken, it accomplishes more than getting Jesus out of a trap; it leads to an answer to the question that is far deeper and more far-reaching than what his adversaries were asking.

RENDERING TO CAESAR IS RENDERING TO JESUS, OR IT IS TREASON

The fact that God owns everything and has all authority in the universe puts the first command under the second: "Render to Caesar the things that are Caesar's" becomes a subcategory of "Render to God the things that are God's." All is God's. Therefore what is Caesar's is God's. Therefore rendering to Caesar what is his must be seen as an expression of rendering to God what is God's. This is all-important in understanding how one can be utterly devoted to Jesus as Lord and live in a world with Caesar—or any other authority.

Even though the power of Caesar stood behind the crucifixion of Jesus, Jesus is the supreme Lord over Caesar. Jesus knows this. He is consciously abstaining during his earthly life from exercising the right and power to subdue his enemies. He is choosing to lay down his life. "I lay down my life that I may take it up again. No one takes it from me, but I lay it down of my own accord. I have authority to lay it down, and I have authority to take it up again" (John 10:17-18). Therefore, when he had risen from the dead he said, "All authority in heaven and on earth has been given to me" (Matt. 28:18). That means that he is above all of Caesar's authority. "Render to Caesar the things that are Caesar's" means, therefore: In all your rendering to Caesar, render to Jesus the full honor of the absolute authority that he has over Caesar.

It was fitting during Jesus' earthly ministry that he not draw excessive attention to his universal ownership and authority. He was here to suffer and die. He knew that the day would come when he would rule openly over the nations. That's why he said, "When the Son of Man comes in his glory, and all the angels with him, then he will sit on his glorious throne. Before him will be gathered all the nations" (Matt. 25:31-32). But during his earthly ministry Jesus did not exert this kind of open power. Hence when it came time to express how his followers should relate to Caesar, he called attention to God, not explicitly to himself. He did not say, "Render to Caesar the things that are Caesar's, and to me the things that are mine."

But that is, in fact, what he does call for. He and the Father are one (John 10:30). "The Father judges no one, but has given all judgment to the Son, that all may honor the Son, just as they honor the Father" (John 5:22-23). At his weakest hour the high priest asked him if he was the Messiah, the Son of the Blessed. Jesus answered, "I am, and you will see the Son of Man seated at the right hand of Power, and coming with the clouds of heaven" (Mark 14:62). In other words, "Even though I am weak and despised in your eyes now, very shortly I will sit in the place of absolute authority over you and Pilate and Herod and Caesar." Therefore, "Render to God the things that are God's" means also, render to Jesus the honor of absolute ownership and authority over everything, including all that is Caesar's.

THERE IS NO AUTHORITY EXCEPT WHAT IS GIVEN FROM ABOVE

Therefore, Jesus is demanding absolute allegiance to himself and his ownership and authority. All other allegiances are relativized by this supreme allegiance. All other allegiances are *warranted* and *limited* and *shaped* by this first allegiance.

They are *warranted* because the subordinate authorities in the world, like Caesar, are owing to God's authority. Jesus said to Pilate, who seemed to have authority over Jesus at his trial, "You would have no authority over me at all unless it had been given you from above" (John 19:11). Pilate has authority because God has given it to him. Therefore, such human authority is warranted because it is indirectly God's. When Jesus said, "Render to God the things that are God's," the term "the things that are God's" included Pilate's authority, because it was, indirectly, God's. God had given it to him. He would not have it without God. Therefore, Jesus acknowledges the legitimacy of human authority. It is legitimate, but not absolute. It is *from* God, but it is not God.

It is risky for Jesus to say, "Render to Caesar the things that are Caesar's." That puts a high premium on obedience to the demands of Caesar. One of the realities that warrants this risk is that the heart of rebellion is more dangerous in us than the demands of Caesar outside of us. Jesus wants us to see that the danger to our soul from unjust, secular governments is nowhere near as great as the danger to our soul from the pride that kicks against submission. No mistreatment from Caesar or unjust law from Rome has ever sent anyone to hell. But pride and rebellion is what sends everyone to hell who doesn't have a Savior. Therefore, the subordinate authorities of the world are warranted by God's will in two senses. On the one hand, he wills that we recognize that these authorities are indeed subordinate and that we glorify him as the only supreme sovereign. On the other hand, he wills that we recognize these authorities as God-ordained and that we not proudly kick against what he has put in place.

All our earthly allegiances are not only *warranted* by the supreme authority of God, but also *limited* and *shaped* by that authority. For these functions of God's authority we pass now to the next chapter.

RENDER TO CAESAR THE THINGS THAT ARE CAESAR'S AS AN ACT OF RENDERING TO GOD WHAT IS GOD'S

Then the Pharisees went and plotted how to entangle [Jesus] in his talk. And they sent their disciples to him, along with the Herodians, saying . . . "Tell us, then, what you think. Is it lawful to pay taxes to Caesar, or not?" But Jesus, aware of their malice, said, "Why put me to the test, you hypocrites? Show me the coin for the tax." And they brought him a denarius. And Jesus said to them, "Whose likeness and inscription is this?" They said, "Caesar's." Then he said to them, "Therefore render to Caesar the things that are Caesar's, and to God the things that are God's."—MATT. 22:15-21

I said in the previous chapter that Jesus demands absolute allegiance to himself and his ownership and authority. All other allegiances are *warranted* and *limited* and *shaped* by this supreme allegiance to Jesus as the King of kings. We have seen how they are warranted. Now we turn to see how they are limited and shaped.

WHEN CAESAR DEMANDS WHAT GOD FORBIDS

All our earthly allegiances are *limited* by what God's supreme authority accomplished through Jesus (see John 5:27; Matt. 28:18).

We should do what Caesar says since he has his authority by God's design. But we should not do all that he says. If Caesar says, "Caesar is Lord!" we do not imitate him. If he commands us to bow under his lordship, we do not do it. *Jesus* is Lord. His followers bow to him as supreme and to no one else. Even though human authority is ultimately from God, it does not always act according to God's word. Therefore, it may demand what God forbids.

This is why Jesus warns of impending conflict. He tells his disciples they will have to choose between allegiance to him and allegiance to Caesar's state. This will cost some of them their lives. "They will lay their hands on you and persecute you, delivering you up to the synagogues and prisons, and you will be brought before kings and governors for my name's sake . . . some of you they will put to death" (Luke 21:12, 16). The only way this warning makes sense is if Jesus is telling us not to render to Caesar everything that Caesar thinks is Caesar's. Rendering to Caesar the things that are Caesar's does not include rendering obedience to Caesar's demand that we not render supreme allegiance to God. God's supreme authority limits the authority of Caesar and the allegiance we owe to him.

We Submit to Caesar to Acknowledge the Supreme Lordship of Jesus

All our earthly allegiances are not only warranted and limited by the supreme authority of God but are also *shaped* by that authority. In other words, even the duty we properly render to Caesar is rendered differently because Caesar is not absolute. We render obedience to Caesar where we can, not because he is Lord, but because our Lord Jesus bids us to. In other words, all our obedience to Caesar dethrones Caesar by expressing the lordship of Jesus. We view all our serving of Caesar as serving his owner and Lord, Jesus. There is, therefore, no whiff of worship toward Caesar. He is stripped of his claim to divinity in the very act of submitting to his laws. Even our submission is therefore seditious toward rulers with pretensions of deity.

Jesus illustrates this shaping of submission by the supremacy of God's authority in Matthew 17:24-27.

> When they came to Capernaum, the collectors of the half-shekel tax went up to Peter and said, "Does your teacher not pay the tax?" He said, "Yes." And when he came into the house, Jesus spoke to him first, saying, "What do you think, Simon? From whom do kings of the earth take toll or tax? From their sons or from others?" And when he said, "From others," Jesus said to him, "Then the sons are free. However, not to give offense to them, go to the sea and cast a hook and take the first fish that comes up, and when you open its mouth you will find a shekel. Take that and give it to them for me and for yourself."

This "half-shekel tax" probably refers to a temple tax that the Jewish people paid annually for the upkeep of the temple. The exact identity of the tax is not crucial for the point that is relevant here. The question was, will Jesus and his disciples pay it? The answer is yes. But the way Jesus justifies the payment is what is crucial for us.

He compares the payment to the way a secular king taxes his empire: Does he demand taxes from his children? No. So the children are free. "Now," Jesus says, "that's the way it is with me and my disciples; we are the children of God who has all authority and owns everything, and therefore we do not have to pay this temple tax. But will we? Yes. Why? Not to give an offense."

The principle is this: There are at times reasons to submit to an authority that arise not from the intrinsic right of the authority, but from a principle of freedom and what would be for the greater good. So, applying this to Caesar, the principle would go like this: God owns Caesar. God has absolute authority over Caesar. This all-authoritative God is our Father. We are his children. Therefore, the demands of Caesar to fund his government are not absolutely binding on us. Our Father owns the government. We are free. In fact, the whole earth is ours as heirs of our Father, and we will one day inherit it completely (Matt. 5:5). Nevertheless, in this freedom, should we pay Caesar's taxes? Yes, because that would lead to the greatest good for now and because our Father bids us, "Render to Caesar the things that are Caesar's." In this way we can see how God's supreme ownership over all things not only warrants and limits but also shapes the way we express our earthly allegiances.

How Jesus' Authority Shapes Our Disobedience to Caesar

That shaping effect of Jesus' supreme authority extends even to the way we disobey Caesar. That is, even our disobedience, when it must be, is not indifferent to the proper authority of Caesar. Even our disobedience will be shaped by Jesus' supremacy over, and endorsement of, the perverted authority of Caesar. We saw above that Jesus' authority limits Caesar's authority. We saw this in Jesus' demand that we should die rather than submit to Caesar's demand that we deny Jesus. Jesus himself did not comply with Herod's demands (Luke 23:9) or Pilate's demands (Mark 15:5) or the demands of the high priest (Matt. 26:62-63). Jesus modeled and demanded some civil disobedience. And it is his life and teaching and authority that shape what that disobedience looks like.

We have already devoted whole chapters to Jesus' demands for servanthood (*Demand #17*) and love of our enemies (*Demands #28, 29, 32, 33, 34*) and care of our neighbors (*Demand #21*). These and other demands will profoundly shape the way Jesus' followers engage in civil disobedience. It may be helpful here to apply these demands again to this situation and give some direction.

Shaping Civil Disobedience by the Demands of Jesus

Matthew 5:38-48 contains strong words about non-resistance and active love for your enemy (see *Demand #30*). What we saw, and now see again, is that non-resistance and active love are not always the same. On the non-resistance side, Jesus said,

> You have heard that it was said, "An eye for an eye and a tooth for
> a tooth." But I say to you, Do not resist one who is evil. But if any-
> one slaps you on the right cheek, turn to him the other also. . . .
> And if anyone forces you to go one mile, go with him two miles.
> Give to the one who asks from you, and do not refuse the one who
> would borrow from you. (Matt. 5:38-42)

All of those demands call for compliance to one who mistreats you
or asks you for something. This looks like the opposite of resistance. But then, in the flow of Jesus' sermon, comes something a
little different in verses 43-48, namely, more active love rather than
non-resistance.

> You have heard that it was said, "You shall love your neighbor
> and hate your enemy." But I say to you, Love your enemies and
> pray for those who persecute you, so that you may be sons of your
> Father who is in heaven; for he makes his sun rise on the evil and
> on the good, and sends rain on the just and on the unjust. . . . You
> therefore must be perfect, as your heavenly Father is perfect.

Here a different note is struck. The emphasis falls on seeking the
good of the enemy. Love your enemy. Pray for your enemy—presumably that he would be saved and find hope and life in Jesus. Do
good to your enemy the way God does with rain and sunshine. So
in verses 38-42 the note of compliance is struck (don't resist, turn
the other cheek, go the extra mile). But in verses 43-48 Jesus strikes
the note of positive actions for the good of our enemies with a view
to their blessing.

Now this raises the question of whether the non-resistance and
compliance of verses 38-42 is always the best way to love others
and do them good as prescribed in verses 43-48. One focuses on
passivity—don't retaliate, be willing to suffer unjustly. The other
focuses on activity—seek to do good for your enemy. Is passivity
always the best way to do good?

WHEN LOVE FOR ONE DEMANDS RESISTANCE TO ANOTHER

The answer becomes clearer when we realize that in most situations of injustice or persecution we are not the only person being hurt. For example, how do you love two people if one is the criminal and the other is the victim—if one is hurting and the other is being hurt? Is love passive when it is not only *your* cheek that is being smacked but someone else's—and repeatedly?

Or what about the command to give to the one who asks? Is it love to give your coat to a person who will use it to strangle an infant? And how do you go the extra mile (lovingly!) with a person who is taking you along to support his bloodshed? Do you go the extra mile with a person who is making you an active accomplice to his evil?

The point of these questions is this: In these verses Jesus is giving us a description of love that cuts to the depth of our selfishness and fear. If selfishness and fear keep us from giving and going the extra mile, then we need to be broken by these words. But Jesus is not saying that passive compliance in situations of injustice is the only form of love. It can be a form of cowardice. When love weighs the claims of justice and mercy among all the people involved, there can come a moment, a flash point, when love may go beyond passive, compliant non-resistance and drive the money-changers from the temple (Mark 11:15).

THE GREATEST BATTLE IS TO BE BROKENHEARTED IN OUR RESISTANCE

What guidelines are there, then, for how a follower of Jesus will perform civil disobedience? The words of Jesus rule out all vindictiveness and all action based on the mere expediency of personal safety. The Lord cuts away our love for possessions and our love for convenience. That's the point of Matthew 5:38-42. Don't act merely out of concern for your own private benefit, your clothes, your convenience, your possessions, your safety.

Instead, by trusting Jesus, become the kind of person who is utterly free from these things to live for others (both the oppressed and the oppressors; both the persecuted and the persecutors; both the dying children and the killing abortionists; both the racists and the races). The tone and demeanor of this civil disobedience will be the opposite of strident, belligerent, rock-throwing, screaming, swearing, violent demonstrations.

We are people of the cross. Our Lord submitted to crucifixion willingly to save his enemies. We owe our eternal life to him. We are forgiven sinners. This takes the swagger out of our protest. It takes the arrogance out of our resistance. And if, after every other means has failed, we must disobey for the sake of love and justice, we will first remove the log from our own eye, which will cause enough pain and tears to soften our indignation into a humble, quiet, but unshakable no. The greatest battle we face is not overcoming unjust laws, but becoming this kind of people.

"Render to Caesar the things that are Caesar's, and to God the things that are God's." Let this demand exalt the supremacy of God and his Son Jesus over all earthly powers. Let it bind our hearts in absolute allegiance to the kingship of Jesus. Let it warrant and limit and shape the way we render allegiance to "Caesar." And let it free us to live in this world as citizens of another kingdom—not escaping, not conforming, but living out the radical difference that King Jesus makes in every relationship, including our relationship with the state.

Demand #45

DO THIS IN REMEMBRANCE OF ME, FOR I WILL BUILD MY CHURCH

[Jesus] said to them, "But who do you say that I am?" Simon Peter replied, "You are the Christ, the Son of the living God." And Jesus answered him, "Blessed are you, Simon Bar-Jonah! For flesh and blood has not revealed this to you, but my Father who is in heaven. And I tell you, you are Peter, and on this rock I will build my church, and the gates of hell shall not prevail against it. —MATT. 16:15-18*

Make disciples of all nations, baptizing them in the name of the Father and of the Son and of the Holy Spirit. —MATT. 28:19*

And behold, I am sending the promise of my Father upon you. But stay in the city until you are clothed with power from on high. —LUKE 24:49*

The demand of Jesus, "Do this in remembrance of me" comes from the institution of the Lord's Supper in Luke 22:19. But it assumes something, namely, that there would be a church worshiping Jesus when he was gone. Did Jesus plan for that and provide for the church? That is what this chapter addresses. It is foundational for the next.

"I WILL BUILD MY CHURCH"
Jesus promised to build his church. By "church" he did not mean a building. That is never the meaning of church (ἐκκλησία) in Greek.

He means he will build a people. He will gather a people who trust him as their Lord (John 13:13; 20:28) and Savior (John 3:17; 10:9) and who love each other (John 13:34-35) and their enemies (Matt. 5:44). Jesus describes himself as "the good shepherd" who gathers his sheep into a flock. "I am the good shepherd. I know my own and my own know me, just as the Father knows me and I know the Father; and I lay down my life for the sheep. And I have other sheep that are not of this fold. I must bring them also, and they will listen to my voice. So there will be one flock, one shepherd" (John 10:14-16).

The words "I must bring them also" and "they will listen to my voice" carry the same authority as the words "I will build my church" (Matt. 16:18). "I *must* bring them." "They *will* hear my voice." "I *will* build my church." This is what the power of the kingdom does. Jesus compares the kingdom of God to a net that was cast into the sea of humanity and "gathered fish of every kind" (Matt. 13:47). The kingdom of God, as Jesus presents it, is not a realm or a people, but a rule or a reign. Therefore, it brings a people into being the way a net gathers fish. Some skeptics have tried to find a contradiction between Jesus' message of the kingdom of God and the subsequent rise of the church. But there is no contradiction. The kingdom creates the church. Or, to say it another way, the King, Jesus, builds his church.

Jesus knew and taught that between his first and second coming to earth there would be a lapse of time. For example, Jesus' parable of the wicked tenants is a story of what will happen between his first and second coming. It begins, "A man planted a vineyard and let it out to tenants and went into another country *for a long while*" (Luke 20:9). This is one of the clearest statements indicating that Jesus expected the time before his second coming to be substantial. He knew that he would be away from his "flock," and therefore he made provision for them while he is gone.

Jesus Took Care to Provide for the Church Though the Holy Spirit

This provision includes the sending of the Holy Spirit, the preservation of inspired truth in the writings of his apostles and their close associates, guidelines for how to handle sin in the flock, and the ordinances of baptism and the Lord's Supper.

Jesus was keenly aware of what it would mean to leave his "little flock" (Luke 12:32) in a hostile world and return to the Father. How were they to live without his physical presence? He had been the literal center of their lives for three years, and now he was going to leave. Who would teach them? Who would guide and protect them? How were they to live in his absence? These and many other questions would come when Jesus was gone. Therefore he assured them, "I will not leave you as orphans; I will come to you" (John 14:18).

What he meant by this promise was that he would send the Holy Spirit and that this Spirit of God would be his own presence among them. "I will ask the Father, and he will give you another Helper, to be with you forever, even the Spirit of truth, whom the world cannot receive, because it neither sees him nor knows him. You know him, for he dwells with you and will be in you" (John 14:16-17). "He dwells *with* you, and will be *in* you." Jesus is saying that he himself is now *with* his disciples—physically present—and when the Spirit comes he himself will be *in* them. Jesus comforts his followers with the truth that he himself will be present in the church by the Spirit whom he sends in his place.[1]

"LET NOT YOUR HEARTS BE TROUBLED"

Jesus intends for these promises to give strong encouragement to his followers when he leaves. "Peace I leave with you; my peace I give to you. Not as the world gives do I give to you. Let not your hearts be troubled, neither let them be afraid" (John 14:27). Therefore, even though the church is destined for trouble in a hostile world of unbelief (John 15:20), they should be encouraged because Jesus promises to send the Holy Spirit who will help them and will, in fact, prove to be a manifestation of the presence of Jesus himself.

---

[1] I should make explicit that in describing the coming of the Spirit this way I do not mean to imply that the Person of the Spirit and the Person of the Son are not distinct persons. They are. That the Spirit can manifest the Son and mediate an experience of the presence of the Son is part of the mysterious unity that they have, not a contradiction of their distinct persons.

Jesus promised at the end of his earthly life, "Behold, I am with you always, to the end of the age" (Matt. 28:20). Jesus himself promises to be with his followers even after he is gone from them. This can be true because of the Holy Spirit, who also is the Spirit of Jesus. Therefore, because of Jesus' past work on the cross (Matt. 20:28) and his present work by the Spirit (John 10:16; 12:32) and his future work in coming again in triumph (Matt. 16:27), his church may be confident in a hostile world. "In the world you will have tribulation," Jesus says. "But take heart; I have overcome the world" (John 16:33). "I will build my church, and the gates of hell shall not prevail against it" (Matt. 16:18).

Therefore, in view of this crucial role of the Holy Spirit in Jesus' absence, Jesus demands that his followers wait for the Spirit and not blunder ahead into ministry without this gift. Just before his ascension into heaven, Jesus said, "Behold, I am sending the promise of my Father upon you. But stay in the city until you are clothed with power from on high" (Luke 24:49). All subsequent generations of the followers of Jesus are to receive this Spirit and in this way enjoy the power and presence of the risen King.

Jesus Provides a New Testament for His Church

Not only does Jesus provide for his flock after his departure by sending them the Holy Spirit, but also by preparing for the preservation of inspired truth in the writings of his apostles. Jesus does not refer to the writings of the apostles but puts in place both apostles and the Holy Spirit as the guarantee of their teaching for the foundation of his church.

At a crucial juncture in his earthly ministry Jesus chose twelve apostles from all the disciples who were following him. He did not make these choices lightly. He prayed all night. "In these days he went out to the mountain to pray, and all night he continued in prayer to God. And when day came, he called his disciples and chose from them twelve, whom he named *apostles*" (Luke 6:12). The word "apostle" means "someone who is 'sent' (ἀποστέλλειν)

and who shares the authority of the one who sends, as his representative."[2] Not all whom Jesus sent were appointed as apostles. For
example, he sent out seventy-two ahead of him and said to them, "I
am sending you out as lambs in the midst of wolves. . . . Heal the
sick . . . and say to them, 'The kingdom of God has come near to
you'" (Luke 10:3, 9). But these were not called apostles.

The fact that there were twelve apostles—just as there were
twelve tribes of Israel—and that the word *apostle* carries the implication of special authority to represent him suggests that Jesus
intended for the apostles to be the foundation for the true Israel,
the church. He had said concerning the old Israel that, at least temporarily, they were being replaced. "I tell you, the kingdom of God
will be taken away from you [Israel] and given to a people producing its fruits [Jesus' followers, the church]" (Matt. 21:43; see also
Demand #28). This new "Israel" would have its foundation in the
twelve apostles. They will represent Jesus' authority as they lay the
foundation for this new people.

To secure the future truthfulness of the teaching of the Twelve,
Jesus promised to send the Spirit of truth to preserve his teaching
and lead them into crucial truth that he had not yet given them.
Speaking to the eleven apostles, after Judas had left them on the
night before he was crucified, Jesus said:

> I still have many things to say to you, but you cannot bear them
> now. When the Spirit of truth comes, he will guide you into all the
> truth, for he will not speak on his own authority, but whatever
> he hears he will speak, and he will declare to you the things that
> are to come. He will glorify me, for he will take what is mine and
> declare it to you. (John 16:12-14)

> He will teach you all things and bring to your remembrance all
> that I have said to you. (John 14:26)

---

[2] Donald Hagner, *Matthew 1–13*, Word Biblical Commentary, Vol. 33a (Dallas: Word, 1993),
265. Norval Geldenhuys defines an apostle as "one chosen and sent with a special commission
as the fully authorized representative of the sender." Geldenhuys, *Supreme Authority: The
Authority of the Lord, His Apostles and the New Testament* (Grand Rapids, Mich.: Eerdmans,
1953), 53-54.

This is Jesus' way of caring for his flock after he is gone. He provides an authoritative band of representatives and then gives them the assurance that in their teaching office they will have divine assistance to provide the church with the truth it needs for all of life and godliness. He intends that the teaching of these authoritative spokesmen be preserved for later generations.

We know this because Jesus says to his Father in prayer at the end of his life, "I do not ask for these [twelve] only, but also for those who will believe in me *through their word*, that they may all be one" (John 17:20-21). All subsequent generations of the church will come to faith in Jesus "through their word." This implies that their word should be preserved. This is the origin of what we call the New Testament. The foundation of the church today is the Spirit-guided teaching of the apostles, preserved for us in the writings of the New Testament.[3]

---

[3] There is a controversial passage from Jesus' teaching about the place of Peter in relationship to the foundation of the church. Jesus asked the disciples, "Who do you say that I am?" Simon Peter replied, "You are the Christ, the Son of the living God." Jesus responded, "Blessed are you, Simon Bar-Jonah! For flesh and blood has not revealed this to you, but my Father who is in heaven. And I tell you, you are Peter, and on this rock I will build my church, and the gates of hell shall not prevail against it. I will give you the keys of the kingdom of heaven, and whatever you bind on earth shall be bound in heaven, and whatever you loose on earth shall be loosed in heaven" (Matt. 16:15-19).

Some take this passage to teach that Peter and his successors (such as the bishops of Rome and the popes), have a unique authority and administrative role in the church throughout history. The "keys of the kingdom" would be in their hands and would refer to the unique role of decision-making for what the church believes and does. The direction of my own understanding is given by George Ladd in the following interpretation:

> Another interpretation lies nearer at hand. Jesus condemned the scribes and the Pharisees because they had taken away the key of knowledge, refusing either to enter into the Kingdom of God themselves or to permit others to enter (Luke 11:52). The same thought appears in the first Gospel. "Woe to you, scribes and Pharisees, hypocrites! Because you shut the kingdom of heaven against men; for you neither enter yourselves nor allow those who would enter to go in" (Matt. 23:13). In biblical idiom, knowledge is more than intellectual perception. It is "a spiritual possession due to revelation." The authority entrusted to Peter is grounded upon revelation, that is, spiritual knowledge, which he shared with the twelve. The keys of the Kingdom are therefore "the spiritual insight which will enable Peter to lead others in through the door of revelation through which he has passed himself" [Anthony Flew, *Jesus and His Church*, 1943, p. 95]. The authority to bind and loose involves the admission or exclusion of men from the realm of the Kingdom of God. Christ will build his *ekklesia* [i.e., church] upon Peter and upon those who share the divine revelation of Jesus' messiahship. To them also is committed by virtue of this same revelation the means of permitting men to enter the realm of the blessings of the Kingdom or of excluding men from such participation. (George Ladd, *The Presence of the Future* [Grand Rapids, Mich.: Eerdmans, 1974], 274-275).

This view fits with what I have said about Jesus providing a foundation for the church in the teaching of the apostles. Peter had a prominent role to play in that, but his founding authority was shared by the others and is found today in the New Testament, not in the office of the Pope.

The Spirit and the Word Are Inseparable

In this way Jesus has provided for his church both the Spirit and the word. His Spirit and his teaching are inseparable. He would be critical of any who try to separate the word and the Spirit. The objective teachings of Jesus, brought to memory by the Spirit and recorded for following generations, are the standard for the church. Any attempt to abandon or distort this objective, historical, once-for-all deposit of teaching will go astray from what Jesus demands and teaches and promises.

But it is also true that without the Spirit, no one will receive, or properly grasp, these historical teachings. By nature we are all simply human with no spiritual life. But without spiritual life we do not have eyes to see truly what Jesus taught. The remedy for this blindness and spiritual deadness is to be born again by the Spirit. "Unless one is born again he cannot see the kingdom of God" (John 3:3). This new birth is the work of the Spirit. "That which is born of the flesh is flesh, and that which is *born of the Spirit* is spirit" (John 3:6). If we are going to have the spiritual life and sight that enables us to see what Jesus really teaches, we must be born of the Spirit. (To see more on this important work of the Spirit see *Demand #1*.)

Jesus also made three other noteworthy provisions for his church. In the next chapter we take up Jesus' demand for church discipline and the two ordinances of baptism and the Lord's Supper.

Do This in Remembrance of Me—Baptize Disciples and Eat the Lord's Supper

If your brother sins against you, go and tell him his fault, between you and him alone. If he listens to you, you have gained your brother. But if he does not listen, take one or two others along with you, that every charge may be established by the evidence of two or three witnesses. If he refuses to listen to them, tell it to the church. And if he refuses to listen even to the church, let him be to you as a Gentile and a tax collector. —MATT. 18:15-17

And [Jesus] said to them, "I have earnestly desired to eat this Passover with you before I suffer. For I tell you I will not eat it until it is fulfilled in the kingdom of God." And he took a cup, and when he had given thanks he said, "Take this, and divide it among yourselves. For I tell you that from now on I will not drink of the fruit of the vine until the kingdom of God comes." And he took bread, and when he had given thanks, he broke it and gave it to them, saying, "This is my body, which is given for you. Do this in remembrance of me." And likewise the cup after they had eaten, saying, "This cup that is poured out for you is the new covenant in my blood." —LUKE 22:15-20

How Jesus Demands That We Handle Sin in the Church

In addition to providing his church with the Spirit and the word (which we saw in the previous chapter), Jesus also provided guidelines for how to handle sin in the flock. In one sense, all of his teachings do this. They are the charter for how his followers are to live in the church and in the world. But he gave more specific guidelines for what has come to be called church discipline in Matthew 18:15-17.

> If your brother sins against you, go and tell him his fault, between you and him alone. If he listens to you, you have gained your brother. But if he does not listen, take one or two others along with you, that every charge may be established by the evidence of two or three witnesses. If he refuses to listen to them, tell it to the church. And if he refuses to listen even to the church, let him be to you as a Gentile and a tax collector.

The word "church" signals the fact that Jesus is preparing his followers for the ongoing fellowship of his band of followers in his absence. The implication of the teaching is that persistent, unrepented sin—a refusal to take sin seriously and make war against it in our own lives—will mean we are not really followers of Jesus. In other words, even though Jesus knew that the church would always have false believers in it (Matt. 13:30, 48), nevertheless he made provision for a kind of careful, loving, patient discipline that would not tolerate blatant unwillingness to repent.

Treating an unrepentant "brother" like a "Gentile and tax collector" did not mean treating him with hostility. Jesus had said plainly that such people are to be loved: "And if you greet only your brothers, what more are you doing than others? Do not even the Gentiles do the same?" (Matt. 5:47). What it means to "let him be to you as a Gentile and a tax collector" is to no longer share the unique fellowship of Jesus with him—not to relate with him as if there is no barrier in the fellowship. This would include not sharing, for example, in the Lord's Supper together.

GO, MAKE DISCIPLES, BAPTIZING THEM

Which brings us now to the ordinances that Jesus prepared for his church before he left, namely, baptism and the Lord's Supper. Just before he departed into heaven, Jesus gave the command that we should "make disciples of all nations, baptizing them in the name of the Father and of the Son and of the Holy Spirit" (Matt. 28:19). In other words, part of becoming a disciple or a follower of Jesus is being baptized. This is the outward mark of the inward change that has happened to bring one under the lordship of Jesus as a forgiven sinner.

John the Baptist had baptized people as a call to repentance in preparation for the coming of the Messiah (Mark 1:4). This was in one sense amazing. He was calling on Jewish people to undergo a special sign of repentance as a sign of being part of Messiah's people. But some of the leaders were indignant at this and protested that they were already the people of the Messiah. They were Abraham's offspring. To this John replied, "Do not presume to say to yourselves, 'We have Abraham as our father,' for I tell you, God is able from these stones to raise up children for Abraham" (Matt. 3:9). In other words, "The baptism I demand is a sign that a true people of Israel is being formed. It is not coextensive with the physical offspring of Abraham. It is made up of those who repent and who will very soon meet and believe in the Messiah, Jesus. Do not think," he says to the Jewish leaders, "that if you are rejected for unbelief, God will be unable to fulfill his covenant promises; he can raise up from stones beneficiaries of his promises."

Therefore, already in John's baptism we see how it functioned to distinguish true believers from mere descendants of believers. Now Jesus chooses this sign as the mark of his own followers in his absence. When they are converted from unbelief to belief, they are to be baptized. That is, they are to demonstrate in their obedience to this command that they are truly his.[1] My simple point here is that this act, practiced by almost all Christian churches today, was not invented by the churches. Jesus put this in place before he left

---

[1] I don't intend to go into the controversial issues surrounding infant baptism vs. believer's baptism. I would recommend Paul K. Jewett, *Infant Baptism and the Covenant of Grace: An Appraisal of the Argument That as Infants Were Once Circumcised, So They Should Now Be Baptized* (Grand Rapids, Mich.: Eerdmans, 1978), which defends the truth of believer's baptism. For my own more extended treatment see http://www.desiringgod.org/resourcelibrary/topicindex/23/

and demanded that we do it. Therefore a follower of Jesus should be baptized in the name of the Father, the Son, and the Holy Spirit, as Jesus said. This is part of becoming his disciple and becoming a part of his church.

"Do This in Remembrance of Me"

The other ordinance that Jesus provided for his church is the Lord's Supper. I am calling baptism and the Lord's Supper *ordinances* to signify that Jesus *ordained* them. That is, he established the pattern of their observance. This is clear with regard to baptism because he commanded it as a more or less formal act in the name of the Father, Son, and Holy Spirit. It is also clear in regard to the Lord's Supper because, in the context of a very solemn declaration about the bread and the cup, Jesus commands us to "do this." "'This is my body, which is given for you. *Do this* in remembrance of me.' And likewise the cup after they had eaten, saying, 'This cup that is poured out for you is the new covenant in my blood'" (Luke 22:19-20).

Jesus did not give this ordinance a name. He called the entire meal that he was eating with his disciples that last night the Passover and described it in relationship to his own sacrifice. "I have earnestly desired to eat this *Passover* with you before *I suffer*" (Luke 22:15). The Passover marked the event in Egypt when God spared the Jewish sons from the angel of death because their doorposts and lintel were marked with blood from a sacrificial lamb (Exod. 12:13, 23). Since everything about Jesus' last evening and the following trial and crucifixion was planned by God and followed obediently by Jesus, it would be folly to think his last supper was only coincidentally a Passover meal. "The Son of Man goes as it is written of him" (Matt. 26:24).

Therefore, it is not surprising that the earliest Christian document that refers to this ordinance not only calls it "the Lord's Supper" (κυριακὸν δεῖπνον; 1 Cor. 11:20), but also refers to Jesus as "our Passover lamb" (τὸ πάσχα ἡμῶν; 1 Cor. 5:7). That was surely what Jesus meant to say: "I am instituting a sacred supper for my people when I am gone, and in it they should see a sacred sign of the Passover sacrifice that I will perform tomorrow morning when I die for their sins."

How Is the Cup and Bread the Blood and Body of Jesus?

Of course using the word *sign* in that last sentence is controversial. There have been several different understandings of what Jesus meant by taking the bread and saying, "*This is* my body, which is given for you" (Luke 22:19) and by taking the cup and saying, "*This is* my blood of the covenant, which is poured out for many for the forgiveness of sins" (Matt. 26:28). Was he saying that the cup and the bread were signs of his body and blood, or that they somehow were transformed into the very body and blood of Jesus?

It was natural then, and it is natural today, to point to a representation of something and say that the representation is the thing. For example, I look at a photograph of our house and say, "This is our house." It would not enter anyone's mind to think I mean that the photograph was transformed into my house. If Jesus stooped down and drew a camel in the sand, He would say, "This is a camel." The drawing doesn't become a camel. It represents a camel.

We know he used language this way because in the parable of the four soils, he interprets the images of four kinds of people with these words: "As for what was sown on rocky ground, *this is the one who hears* the word and immediately receives it with joy" (Matt. 13:20). He means the rocky ground *represents* a kind of person. There is nothing modern or strange about this way of thinking, and it is the most natural way to understand Jesus' words. The cup and the bread represent his blood and body.

Moreover, if we insist on saying that "this is my body" and "this is my blood" must refer to the physical body and blood of Jesus, what becomes of the statement, "This cup . . . is the new covenant in my blood" (Luke 22:20)? Are we to say that the cup is the new covenant in the same way that the cup is the blood? Surely, "this cup . . . is the new covenant" means "this cup represents the new covenant that will be purchased and inaugurated by my blood-shedding tomorrow morning." Therefore, it seems wise to understand the words "this is my body" and "this is my blood" to mean: "The cup and bread represent my physical body and blood offered up for you in death as a sacrifice for your sins."

"THE WORDS THAT I HAVE SPOKEN TO YOU ARE SPIRIT AND LIFE"

Sometimes another saying of Jesus is used as a support for seeing the cup and bread as literally transformed into the blood and body of Jesus. In John 6:53-54 Jesus said, "Truly, truly, I say to you, unless you eat the flesh of the Son of Man and drink his blood, you have no life in you. Whoever feeds on my flesh and drinks my blood has eternal life." But Jesus wants us to see this language as a vivid expression of *spiritual* feeding, not physical feeding. He tells us this ten verses later when he makes sure that we understand that the life promised in verses 53-54 is not mediated through flesh but through the Spirit: "It is the Spirit who gives life; the flesh is of no avail. The words that I have spoken to you are spirit and life" (John 6:63). This verse is a warning against taking the words "this is my body" and "this is my blood" in a way that makes eternal life flow through physical eating and drinking.

Therefore, Jesus commands that his followers celebrate the Lord's Supper as a commemoration of his death and an anticipation of his coming again in the glory of his kingdom (Luke 22:18). Knowing that this cup and bread represent the most wonderful act of love in history and that it accomplished the purchase and inauguration of the new covenant—that is, the purchase of forgiveness and a new heart (Jer. 31:31-34)—makes the Lord's Supper a matchless act of communion with the risen Jesus. He draws near by his Spirit and his word and makes himself known to us for our enjoyment in a way that is uniquely shaped by this solemn act.

THE DEMAND OF JESUS: BE THE CHURCH

What we have seen in this chapter is that the church is not an after-thought created by the followers of Jesus because his message of the coming kingdom did not materialize. No, the church did not replace the kingdom. The church is created and sustained by the kingdom. The church was planned by Jesus, and he provided for her in every way.

"I will build my church" is the banner that flies over the gatherings of Jesus' followers today. He is building his people. He is gathering his flock. He is fulfilling his promise to be with her to the end of the age. He is teaching her by his Spirit and through his word. And he is marking her off from the world through the sign of baptism and by making himself remembered and known and enjoyed in the Lord's Supper. "Do this" is a demand of the Lord that calls us today to be not just individual followers but a flock, a gathering, a community, and a church.

LET YOUR LIGHT SHINE BEFORE OTHERS THAT THEY MAY GLORIFY YOUR FATHER WHO IS IN HEAVEN

You are the salt of the earth, but if salt has lost its taste, how shall its saltiness be restored? It is no longer good for anything except to be thrown out and trampled under people's feet. You are the light of the world. A city set on a hill cannot be hidden. Nor do people light a lamp and put it under a basket, but on a stand, and it gives light to all in the house. In the same way, let your light shine before others, so that they may see your good works and give glory to your Father who is in heaven. —MATT. 5:13-16

Salt is good, but if the salt has lost its saltiness, how will you make it salty again? Have salt in yourselves, and be at peace with one another. —MARK 9:50

The demand that we let our light shine before the world has a goal: that people might give glory to our Father who is in heaven. So ultimately, the demand is that we seek to glorify God by letting our light shine. It is fitting then that we devote this chapter to the importance of this goal: the glorifying of God. Then in the following chapter we will turn to what it means to let our light shine.

JESUS' FIRST PASSION AND SUPREME VALUE

The first thing that Jesus demands that we pray is that our Father's name be hallowed. "Pray then like this: 'Our Father in heaven, hallowed be your name'" (Matt. 6:9). In saying this, Jesus signals that his first passion is—and our first passion should be—the manifest holiness of God. I choose the phrase "manifest holiness of God" for three reasons. First, the Greek word behind "hallowed be" (ἁγιασθήτω) is built on the word for "holy" (ἅγιος). Second, when you turn the word "holy" into a verb like this, it means to "show yourself holy"—hence the idea of *manifest* holiness. Third, another way to speak of the manifest holiness of God is to speak of his glory.[1]

The reason it is important to see the connection between the *hallowing* of God's name and the *glory* of God is that numerous sayings of Jesus (as we will see in a moment) show that the glory of his Father and his own glory are supremely important. Nothing in the universe is more valuable than the glory of God. Seeing the connection between the hallowing of God's name as the first passion of Jesus and the glory of God as the supreme value in the universe shows that there is no conflict between these two. Hallowing God's name and glorifying God are largely the same act.

WHAT IS THE GLORY OF GOD?

God's glory is the radiance of his manifold perfections. Those are poor words for the richest reality of all. But though words are inadequate, we must try. God's glory is the outshining of the infinite value of all that God is. It is his moral beauty. It is visible to the physical eye only as the glorious created world points to its invisible but more glorious Maker. "Consider the lilies of the field. . . . Even

---

[1] One way to think of the holiness of God in relation to his glory is that his holiness is the infinite worth of his intrinsic perfection and purity, and his glory is the manifestation or the radiance of that worth. One textual pointer toward this relationship is Leviticus 10:1-3, "Now Nadab and Abihu, the sons of Aaron, each took his censer and put fire in it and laid incense on it and offered unauthorized fire before the LORD, which he had not commanded them. And fire came out from before the LORD and consumed them, and they died before the LORD. Then Moses said to Aaron, 'This is what the LORD has said, "Among those who are near me I will be *sanctified* [ἁγιασθήσομαι], and before all the people I will be *glorified* [δοξασθήσομαι].""" The priests must treat God as holy in their sacrifices, and the result will be that God will be manifested as holy to the people—that is, he will be glorified.

Solomon in all his *glory* was not arrayed like one of these. . . . God so clothes the grass of the field" (Matt. 6:28-30). The glory of the lilies is the work of God. It is meant to get our attention and waken us to a glory of which lily-glory is only a likeness.

We love to look at glory. We were made to enjoy seeing it. This is why Jesus came into the world. He came to reveal the glory of God more fully than nature ever had (John 1:14) and to die in our place so that we could be saved from God's wrath in order to enjoy forever the glory of God's grace (John 3:14-15, 36; 17:24) and to awaken in us a desire for that glory so that we do not perish in our blind love affair with the glory of sin (John 3:19). Jesus consciously aimed to reveal the glory of God. His actions and words were designed to fulfill prophecies like this: "The people dwelling in darkness have seen a great light, and for those dwelling in the region and shadow of death, on them a light has dawned" (Matt. 4:16). He said, "As long as I am in the world, I am the light of the world" (John 9:5; cf. 8:12). That is, he revealed the brightness of God's glory as never before and by this light put everything in truthful perspective.

How Jesus Glorified God

Jesus displayed the glory of God in accomplishing what God had given him to do. So he prayed to his Father at the end of his life, "I glorified you on earth, having accomplished the work that you gave me to do" (John 17:4). That work included many miracles during his life and the great final work of redemption when he died and rose again.

For example, when Jesus did his first public miracle by turning water into wine, John says, he "manifested his glory" (John 2:11). When Jesus healed a paralytic and forgave his sins, "the crowds saw it [and] were afraid, and they *glorified* God" (Matt. 9:8). When the people saw "the mute speaking, the crippled healthy, the lame walking, and the blind seeing . . . they *glorified* the God of Israel" (Matt. 15:31). When ten lepers were cleansed, one grateful man "turned back, *glorifying* God with a loud voice" (Luke 17:15, NASB). When a woman who was bent over for eighteen years was touched and straightened, "she *glorified* God" (Luke 13:13). And when Jesus was about to raise Lazarus from the dead, he said to his sister, "Did I not tell you that if you believed you would see the *glory* of God?" (John 11:40). Everything Jesus did was done with a view to making God look great. His work was to display the greatness and the beauty of the full range of God's perfections.

But the greatest miracle of all was Jesus' death and resurrection so that we might be redeemed from the guilt and power of sin (Mark 10:45) and have forgiveness (Matt. 26:28) and eternal life (John 3:14-15). In this great act of substitution—the guiltless for the guilty—Jesus displayed the glory of the wrath of God and the glory of the love of God. God's wrath is a glorious wrath (Luke 21:23; John 3:36). He could have no other kind. And God's love is a glorious love. When Jesus came to die, as the climax of his earthly work, there was a huge sense that this was the moment of greatest groaning and greatest glory.

In those last hours he said, "The hour has come for the Son of Man to be *glorified*. Truly, truly, I say to you, unless a grain of wheat falls into the earth and dies, it remains alone; but if it dies, it bears much fruit" (John 12:23). The glory of Jesus was manifested both in the suffering and in the triumphal resurrection afterward. Jesus said, "Was it not necessary that the Christ should suffer these things and enter into his *glory*?" (Luke 24:26). The sufferings were the pathway to glory.

THE FATHER AND THE SON GLORIFY EACH OTHER

But they were not just the path. They were an essential part of his glory. "Now [in this very hour of suffering] is the Son of Man *glorified*, and God is *glorified* in him. If God is *glorified* in him, God will also *glorify* him in himself, and *glorify* him at once" (John 13:31). God is shown to be gloriously worthy in Jesus' willingness to die so that God would be just to remove the wrath that rightly falls on sinners. And when the Father is thus glorified in the Son, he then undertakes to glorify the Son with a mighty display of approval in the resurrection.

Back and forth goes the work of the Father and the Son in glorifying each other in the act of salvation. If we have seen that the Son glorifies the Father, and the Father responds by glorifying the Son, the reverse is also true. "Father," Jesus says, "the hour has come; *glorify* your Son that the Son may *glorify* you" (John 17:1; 12:27-28). When Jesus is glorifying the Father in his death, it is the Father at work glorifying the Son as well; and when the Father glorifies the Son in his resurrection and exaltation, it leads to the Son glorifying the Father as well. This mutual display of the glory of God in the work of the Father and of the Son is the supreme passion of their hearts.

No Greater Love Than God's Glorifying Himself in Jesus for Us

And the good news is that this is the very essence of their love for us. They are displaying their glory not only to make it visible for the enjoyment of soul-hungry creatures like us who were made to find ultimate satisfaction in it, but also in a way that pays for our failures to treasure God's glory so that we can escape judgment (John 5:29). In other words, God's passion to glorify himself and his Son is an act of love because of the preciousness of what he gives and the price that he pays to give it. He gives us his glory, and he pays for it with his Son's life. There is no greater gift than God himself in all his glory. There is no greater price than the death of God's Son. Therefore, there is no greater love than God's glorifying himself in the death and resurrection of Jesus.[2]

When that great work of redemption is done in the crucifixion and resurrection, Jesus sets about, over the centuries, to gather a people for himself by sending the Holy Spirit whose central work is to glorify Jesus and draw people to him in faith. So he promised, "When the Spirit of truth comes, he will guide you into all the truth. . . . *He will glorify me*, for he will take what is mine and

---

[2] To see this point unfolded in greater detail and with more texts, see John Piper, *God Is the Gospel: Meditations on God's Love as the Gift of Himself* (Wheaton, Ill.: Crossway Books, 2005).

declare it to you" (John 16:13-14). The central work of the Spirit is to continue the great work of glorifying the Father and the Son. He does that by opening our spiritual eyes to see the truth and beauty of who Jesus is and what he has already done in his life and death and resurrection (John 3:3, 8; Matt. 16:17). When we see him for who he is, we are drawn to receive him and trust him and worship him and obey him.

Now, in view of the passion for God's glory, what does it mean to "let your light shine" for the glory of God? That's the focus of the next chapter.

LET YOUR LIGHT SHINE BEFORE OTHERS—THE JOYFUL SACRIFICE OF LOVE IN SUFFERING

Blessed are you when others revile you and persecute you and utter all kinds of evil against you falsely on my account. Rejoice and be glad, for your reward is great in heaven, for so they persecuted the prophets who were before you. You are the salt of the earth, but if salt has lost its taste, how shall its saltiness be restored? It is no longer good for anything except to be thrown out and trampled under people's feet. You are the light of the world. A city set on a hill cannot be hidden. Nor do people light a lamp and put it under a basket, but on a stand, and it gives light to all in the house. In the same way, let your light shine before others, so that they may see your good works and give glory to your Father who is in heaven. —MATT. 5:11-16*

In the previous chapter we focused on the supreme passion of Jesus, his Father, and the Holy Spirit—namely, that they be glorified in the work of our salvation. Which brings us now to the demand, "Let your light shine before others, so that they may see your good works and give glory to your Father who is in heaven" (Matt. 5:16). After seeing that Jesus' and the Father's and the Spirit's supreme passion is to display the glory of God, it should not be surprising that the followers of Jesus should be drawn into this passion. Live in such a way that people look at your life and make much of your God. That is what Jesus demands.

SHINE WITH THE LIGHT THAT YOU ARE

The light that we let shine is the light that we are. Jesus said, "You *are* the light of the world" (Matt. 5:14). So there is a movement from the inside to the outside. What people see from the outside is our "good works." But that is not who we *are*. The good works have a light source from inside. The key to understanding what the light is that shines out through good works is the aim of the works, namely, that people see and *give glory to God*. Why do they give glory to God and not to us? Because the light that is shining out is the light of God, or the light of Jesus who is the revelation of the glory of God.

WHAT ACTUALLY IS THE LIGHT THAT PEOPLE SEE?

So what does it mean then that we *are* the light of the world? How do good deeds grow from who we are in such a way that they make God look glorious? Here it would be wise to stay close to the context of Jesus' words. He has just spoken the Beatitudes: Blessed are the poor in spirit, those who mourn, the meek, those who hunger and thirst for righteousness, the merciful, the pure in heart, the peacemakers, and those who suffer for righteousness' sake (Matt. 5:3-10). Here is a kind of identity that is very unusual in the world. It is like savory salt when things are tasteless and flat,[1] and it is like hope-filled light when people are stumbling around in the dark.

But the closest beatitude to the demand to let your light shine for the glory of God is that you are blessed when you are reviled. "Blessed are you when others revile you and persecute you and utter all kinds of evil against you falsely on my account. Rejoice and be

---

[1] W. D. Davies and Dale Allison give eleven possible meanings for "you are the salt of the earth" (Matt. 5:13), and then conclude that perhaps that's the point: the many uses of salt. *A Critical and Exegetical Commentary on the Gospel According to Saint Matthew, International Critical Commentary*, Vol. 1 (Edinburgh: T & T Clark, 1988), 472-473. But I follow those who think that the savor of salt is the most natural thing referred to. There is a kind of radical life rooted in the promises of the Beatitudes that has a rare and wonderful taste in a world gone flat with an excess of superficial titillation.

glad, for your reward is great in heaven, for so they persecuted the prophets who were before you" (Matt. 5:11-12). Immediately following this demand to rejoice in persecution comes the statement: "You are the salt of the earth. . . . You are the light of the world" (Matt. 5:13-14). Therefore, I conclude that what is most salty and bright in this insipid and dark world is the almost incomprehensible joy of Jesus' followers in the midst of persecution and the hardships of life.

It is a joy that is meek and merciful and pure and peaceable, but these things alone do not awaken people to the glory of God. In order to waken people to consider God as an explanation for our good works there generally must be an obstacle of suffering that would ordinarily cause them to be angry or despairing, but does not have that effect on us. Rather they see us "rejoice" in hardship. They see that this hardship does not make us self-centered and self-pitying and mean-spirited. Instead they see our joy and wonder what we are hoping in when ordinary props for hope have been knocked away. The answer, Jesus says, is that we have great reward in heaven (Matt. 5:12). That is, Jesus has become a treasure for us that is more precious than what the world offers. Therefore, when persecution or calamity take natural pleasures away, we still have Jesus, and we still have joy.

Now when our good works get their flavor from this salt and glow with this light, the world may well be awakened to taste something they have never tasted before and to see something they have never seen before, namely, the glory of God in Jesus. If we give a word of testimony concerning the truth and beauty of Jesus,[2] and if the Spirit mercifully blows on the hearts of those who see the evidence of that beauty in our lives, then people will "give glory to [our] Father who is in heaven" (Matt. 5:16).

---

[2] Jesus would consider it a great mistake if we took his words to mean that a person could come to a saving sight of the glory of God in our deeds without some verbal testimony as to who Jesus is and what he has done for us and promised to us. This is why Jesus sent his disciples out to *preach* and to *do* good works (Matt. 10:7-8; Luke 9:2; 10:9). Not either-or, but both-and. The great saving task of the followers of Jesus is to speak the gospel along with a life of salt-like, light-like love: "And this gospel of the kingdom will be proclaimed throughout the whole world as a testimony to all nations, and then the end will come" (Matt. 24:14).

Is the Glory of God an "Ulterior Motive" for Love?

The supremacy of the value of the glory of God is seen in the way Jesus makes the demand of Matthew 5:16—"Let your light shine before others, so that they may see your good works and give glory to your Father who is in heaven." He explicitly says that our aim in doing good works for others is that they might glorify God. Sometimes people who talk much of love but are not God-centered the way Jesus is say things like, "If you do good to people to get them to glorify your God, you are not loving them, for you have ulterior motives."

This kind of criticism results from a failure to experience the glory of God as the greatest gift and highest joy imaginable. How could it not be love to lay down your life for someone (in doing good for them) specifically with a view to satisfying them with the glory of God forever? This motive is not ulterior; it is open and front and center. It is the very essence of love: Followers of Jesus are not do-gooders with no eternal aims for those they love. They know exactly what the greatest and highest and most joyful good is: seeing and savoring God in Jesus forever. This is their aim and they are unashamed of it. They think any lesser aim is a failure of love.

Jesus Loved Us by Obtaining for Us at the Cost of His Life God's Glory

We have seen it already, but it is so important we should see it again from different texts: Jesus loved like this. In his darkest hour he let his light shine most brightly in a "good work." As he did the greatest "good work" that has ever been done, he pondered out loud, "And what shall I say? 'Father, save me from this hour'?" His answer is no. Instead he described the ultimate reason why he came to the hour of his death: "But for this purpose I have come to this hour. Father, glorify your name" (John 12:27-28). D. A. Carson rightly calls this "nothing other than an articulation of the principle that has controlled his life and ministry (John 7:18; 8:29,

50)."[3] From beginning (John 2:11) to end (John 12:28) Jesus let his light shine—did his good works—to vindicate and display the glory of God.

The way he thought of this as the supreme act of love was not only that it cost him his life (John 15:13), but that it obtained freely for sinners the greatest gift possible. He prayed for it in John 17:24, "Father, I desire that they also, whom you have given me, may be with me where I am, *to see my glory.*" This was the final, greatest, and most satisfying gift obtained by Jesus in the "good work" that he did on the cross.

This will make no sense at all to a person who does not see and savor the glory of God above all other gifts. But for those who have renounced all that this world offers (Luke 14:33) and set their heart on the "great reward" in heaven, namely, the enjoyment of the glory of Jesus, Jesus' purchase of this reward at the cost of his life will be the greatest act of love imaginable.

LETTING OUR LIGHT SHINE, LIKE JESUS, IN THE WAY WE DIE

When Jesus calls us to let our light shine that others may see our good deeds and glorify God, he is calling us to join him in the work he came to do. And just as he pursued the glory of his Father through his final act of dying, he expects that we will do the same. Therefore, he said to Peter, "'Truly, truly, I say to you, when you were young, you used to dress yourself and walk wherever you wanted, but when you are old, you will stretch out your hands, and another will dress you and carry you where you do not want to go.' (This he said to show *by what kind of death he was to glorify God*)" (John 21:18). Jesus simply takes it for granted that his disciples will make God look good in the way they die.

The only question is, how will we die? That decision lies in the hands of God, as Jesus makes clear with the words, "Are not two sparrows sold for a penny? And not one of them will fall to the

---

[3]D. A. Carson, *The Gospel According to John* (Grand Rapids, Mich: Eerdmans, 1991), 440.

ground apart from your Father. But even the hairs of your head are all numbered. Fear not, therefore; you are of more value than many sparrows" (Matt. 10:29-31). In other words, if God rules over how the birds die, how much more surely will he govern your death.

JESUS' LIGHT AND OURS AT HIS SECOND COMING

The final great historical display of Jesus' shining light—and ours—happens at his second coming. He tells us how it will be both for him and for us. For him, he says, "The Son of Man is going to come with his angels in the *glory* of his Father . . . all the tribes of the earth will mourn, and they will see the Son of Man coming on the clouds of heaven with power and *great glory*. . . . Then shall he sit upon the throne of *his glory*" (Matt. 16:27; 24:30; 25:31, KJV). He came the first time to display the glory of his Father. He will come the second time to complete that revelation and "gather out of his kingdom all causes of sin and all law-breakers" (Matt. 13:41).

What about for us? What will his second coming mean for us? It turns out that letting our light shine will be our *eternal* vocation. We will never cease to have this calling. This is why we were created: to be so satisfied with our great reward, the glory of God in Jesus, that we reflect his infinite worth in acts of love that cause others to see and savor and show more of the glory of God. We can see our eternal shining in Matthew 13:43 where Jesus describes what becomes of his followers at his second coming: "The righteous will *shine* like the sun in the kingdom of their Father."

This is our final destiny. Beholding the glory of Jesus (John 17:24), we will shine with the beauty and the love that he has. The church that he promised to build (Matt. 16:18, see *Demand #45*) will find its final destiny in reflecting to one another the glory of Jesus, so that our enjoyment of him will be all the greater because of the manifold manifestations of it in the shining members.

THE BRIGHT DEMAND

Jesus' demand to the world is that all human beings find in him the all-satisfying glory for which we were made. Then he demands that we turn from trusting in anything else and bank our hope on the great reward of everlasting joy in him. And then, in that hope and joy, he demands that we let that light shine in sacrificial good deeds of love, so that others will see and savor and spread the glory of God.

MAKE DISCIPLES OF ALL NATIONS, FOR ALL AUTHORITY BELONGS TO JESUS

All authority in heaven and on earth has been given to me. Go therefore and make disciples of all nations, baptizing them in the name of the Father and of the Son and of the Holy Spirit, teaching them to observe all that I have commanded you. And behold, I am with you always, to the end of the age. —MATT. 28:18-20

The harvest is plentiful, but the laborers are few; therefore pray earnestly to the Lord of the harvest to send out laborers into his harvest. —MATT. 9:37-38

Go out to the highways and hedges and compel people to come in, that my house may be filled. —LUKE 14:23

I tell you, there will be more joy in heaven over one sinner who repents than over ninety-nine righteous persons who need no repentance. —LUKE 15:7

As the Father has sent me, even so I am sending you. —JOHN 20:21

Before Jesus demanded that his followers go make disciples of all nations, he gave the justification for this seemingly presumptuous mission. He said, "All authority in heaven and on earth has been given to me" (Matt. 28:18). The basis today of any follower of Jesus telling a follower of another lord to repent and turn and follow Jesus is that Jesus has all authority in the universe.

WHAT IS AUTHORITY?

Authority refers to the right and the power to hold sway in a given relationship. So a father has authority over his children, but not necessarily over his neighbor. An army lieutenant has authority over his platoon, but not over the company commander. A teacher has authority over the students in the classroom, but not over their parents. An office manager has authority over the secretaries, but not over the CEO.

We see a picture of the meaning of authority in the story of Jesus' encounter with the Roman centurion. This officer wanted Jesus to heal his servant but did not feel worthy to have Jesus come into his home. So he said to Jesus, "Lord, I am not worthy to have you come under my roof, but only *say the word*, and my servant will be healed. For I too am a man under *authority*, with soldiers under me. And I say to one, 'Go,' and he goes, and to another, 'Come,' and he comes, and to my servant, 'Do this,' and he does it" (Matt. 8:8-9). In other words, authority is the right and power to have your subordinates do what you choose for them to do.

That is the authority Jesus has over everyone and everything. "*All* authority in heaven and on earth has been given to me." The phrase "heaven and earth" is meant to include everything. Therefore, everyone and everything is subordinate to Jesus. Every human. Every angel. Every demon. The devil himself. And all the natural world and what happens in it.

THE TOTAL AUTHORITY OF JESUS

We see this illustrated even during Jesus' earthly ministry. He has authority to forgive sins, which only God can do; and so he was accused of blasphemy (Mark 2:7-12). We see it in the way he taught the people and the way he handled the Jewish Scriptures: "They were astonished at his teaching, for he taught them as one who had authority, and not as the scribes" (Mark 1:22; Matt. 5:17-18). We see it in the way he rebuked the devil (Matt. 4:10) and commanded unclean spirits: "He commands even the unclean spirits, and they obey him" (Mark 1:27). We see it in the way he commanded the forces of nature by healing all kinds of diseases (Matt. 4:23) and turning water into wine (John 2:9; 4:46) and calming the storm: "He awoke and rebuked the wind and said to the sea, 'Peace! Be still!' And the wind ceased, and there was a great calm" (Mark 4:39).

We see Jesus' authority in the matter of life and death, both his own and other's—and ultimately in the matter of eternal life. He raised people from the dead (Mark 5:41-42; Luke 7:14-15; John 11:43-44) and ruled over his own death and resurrection: "No one takes [my life] from me, but I lay it down of my own accord. I have authority to lay it down, and I have authority to take it up again" (John 10:18). And he holds full sway in the final judgment. He said that God the Father "has given him authority to execute judgment, because he is the Son of Man" (John 5:27). And God has "given him authority over all flesh, to give eternal life to all whom [God has] given him" (John 17:2).

How Jesus Lays Claim on the World

There is nothing outside the authority of Jesus. He has the right and the power to demand allegiance from every soul that exists. As the Lord of the universe, Jesus demands that everyone from every nation and every religion become his disciple. The way Jesus pursues this universal claim on every soul is by sending his followers to make disciples from all the nations. After saying that all authority in heaven and earth is his, he says, "therefore . . ." This word shows not only that his universal authority is the *basis* of his universal claim on every person, but also that the *way* he lays claim to those persons follows in the next verse.

What follows is a commission that his followers go and make disciples. "Go therefore and make disciples of all nations" (Matt. 28:19). In other words, Jesus does not lay claim on a person directly from heaven. He lays claim on people through his followers. He laid down the principle while he was still here: "Truly, truly, I say to you, whoever receives the one I send receives me, and whoever receives me receives the one who sent me" (John 13:20; Matt. 10:40). It is true that he said, "*I* will build my church" (Matt. 16:18), and "*I* have other sheep that are not of this fold. *I* must bring them also, and they will listen to my voice" (John 10:16). Yes, he is doing it himself. But he did not mean that he would do it *directly* from heaven without emissaries. We know this because when he prayed for the future church in John 17:20, he described them as "those who will believe in me through their word."

The Mission Lasts as Long as This Age Lasts

In other words, Jesus builds his church and gathers his flock from the nations of the world *through the word* of those he sends. So the universal authority of Jesus issues in a mission that lasts as long as history and extends as far as humanity: "Go therefore and make disciples of all nations. . . . And behold, I am with you always, *to the end of the age*" (Matt. 28:19-20). The words "to the end of the age" show that the mission should last till Jesus comes back. The demand is not given only to the first generation of disciples. The mission lasts as long as the mission-sustaining promise lasts. And that promise is: The all-authoritative Jesus will be with us "*to the end of the age.*" As long as there is time, and as long as there are nations to reach, Jesus' demand to go make disciples is valid.

The Followers of Jesus Speak on His Behalf

This implies several things. First, it implies that Jesus' exclusive claim will be made not just by him, but by his followers. He claimed that he is the one and only Lord of the universe and that every person from every nation and every religion or non-religion should be his disciple. This claim is now given to his emissaries to make disciples among all the nations and all the religions of the world. Jesus sends his followers to go make disciples of all nations, no matter what their religion is—Jews, Hindus, Buddhists, Muslims, animists, atheists, agnostics. He sends his followers, backed by his universal authority, to go and call all people in every nation and every religion to turn to become the disciples of Jesus.

This means that in times of relativism (like our own), when people do not cherish objective, unchanging truth, followers of Jesus will be accused of arrogance. They will proclaim that Jesus has all authority—because it is true—and that everyone should repent and believe in him and become his disciple. They will warn everyone that to reject Jesus as the eternal Son of God who came into the world to redeem sinners by his death and who rose again as Lord of the universe is to forfeit eternal life. Jesus said, "Whoever believes in the Son has eternal life; whoever does not obey the Son shall not see life, but the wrath of God remains on him. . . . Whoever does not honor the Son does not honor the Father who sent him" (John 3:36; 5:23; cf. 15:23).

This is the mandate and promise that sustain Jesus' emissaries: "The one who hears you hears me, and the one who rejects you rejects me, and the one who rejects me rejects him who sent me" (Luke 10:16). The followers of Jesus will be scorned for saying that all authority belongs to Jesus and that everyone must become his disciple or forfeit eternal life. But Jesus knew that would happen: "If the world hates you, know that it has hated me before it hated you" (John 15:18). That is why he enclosed this radical demand to make disciples between the double assurance (1) that all authority really is his and (2) that he will be with his emissaries till the end of the age.

JESUS DEMANDS THAT WE PURSUE ETHNIC DIVERSITY IN HIS KINGDOM

A second implication of Jesus' universal mission is that Jesus cares for all ethnic groups and intends to have disciples from every "nation." When he says, "Go therefore and make disciples of all *nations*," the meaning of the word "nations" is not political states. "Nations"—or its synonym, "peoples" (Luke 2:31; Ps. 117:1)—in the Bible does not refer to political states like America, Spain, Brazil, China, etc., but to ethnic or language or cultural groupings within these political states. For example, within the political state of China there are dozens of "nations"—Dulong, Li, Lisu, Shui, Salar, Yao, etc. And in the Jewish Scriptures that Jesus knew, we read about "the Jebusites, the Amorites, the Girgashites, the Hivites, the Arkites, the Sinites, the Arvadites, the Zemarites, and the Hamathites" (Gen. 10:16-18).

So in our day the demand of Jesus to make disciples of all nations would mean, for example, to make disciples among the Baloch of Pakistan, the Maninka of Guinea, the Bugis of Indonesia, the Wa of China, the Somali and Dakota of Minneapolis. These are the kinds of groups Jesus was referring to when he said, "Go therefore and make disciples of *all nations*." Wherever there is a distinct people group[1] that has no disciples of Jesus, the demand of Jesus is resoundingly clear: "Go as my emissaries with my authority and my word and my love and my power and make disciples there." There is no partiality with Jesus in this mission. He is not western, and he is not eastern. He is utterly committed to ethnic diversity and unity in the truth of his supremacy. In fact, the word from which we get "ethnic" is the word for "nations" in Matthew 28:19, ἔθνος.

It has not always seemed as though God were pursuing all the nations. At times he seemed to be committed to his people Israel, but not the nations. His way has been indirect and at times inscrutable. How shall we understand this roundabout way toward a global church of worshipers from all the nations? That is what we turn to in the final chapter.

---

[1] For a more complete defense and explanation of what "all nations" means in a biblical and missiological perspective, see John Piper, *Let the Nations Be Glad: The Supremacy of God in Missions*, revised and expanded edition (Grand Rapids, Mich.: Baker, 2003), 155-200.

MAKE DISCIPLES OF ALL NATIONS, FOR THE MISSION CANNOT FAIL

I tell you, many will come from east and west and recline at table with Abraham, Isaac, and Jacob in the kingdom of heaven, while the sons of the kingdom will be thrown into the outer darkness. In that place there will be weeping and gnashing of teeth. —MATT. 8:11-12

But before all this they will lay their hands on you and persecute you, delivering you up to the synagogues and prisons, and you will be brought before kings and governors for my name's sake. This will be our opportunity to bear witness. —LUKE 21:12-13

They will fall by the edge of the sword and be led captive among all nations, and Jerusalem will be trampled underfoot by the Gentiles, until the times of the Gentiles are fulfilled. —LUKE 21:24

GOD'S ROUNDABOUT WAY OF PURSUING THE NATIONS: FOCUSING ON ISRAEL

We must not stumble over God's unusual way of pursuing the nations for the glory of his Son. It is true that Jesus taught that God chose to work in a unique way with the people of Israel instead of the nations. Jesus called the Jews of his day "the sons of the kingdom" (Matt. 8:12), that is, those to whom God gave a unique first privilege to be the focus of his saving deeds in history—like the deliverance from Egypt at the Red Sea, and miracles of provision in the wilderness, and the gift of the promised land, and many victories in battle (see Psalm 105 for a narrative of these blessings).

And it is also true that when Jesus came, he came as the *Jewish* Messiah, announcing the coming of the long-expected kingdom of triumph over the enemies of Israel. But he did not intend to bring the kingdom the way they thought. His intention was to suffer and die for their sins before he would reign as their king. This was their only hope of eternal life. Jesus focused his mission on the Jews, giving them every opportunity to know him and believe in him. He even said to the twelve apostles as he sent them out during his lifetime, "Go nowhere among the Gentiles and enter no town of the Samaritans, but go rather to the lost sheep of the house of Israel" (Matt. 10:5-6). And at one point he said, "I was sent only to the lost sheep of the house of Israel" (Matt. 15:24). We may think this a roundabout way to reach the nations. But God has his reasons.

Jesus' Focus Was Rejected, and He Turned to the Nations

There are lessons the nations must learn from the failure of Israel to trust God and welcome a suffering Messiah. During his lifetime on earth most Jews did not believe that Jesus was the Messiah (Matt. 21:39; Mark 15:11-13; John 5:47; 6:36; 8:45; 12:37). They did not expect a suffering servant. Jesus upbraided this failure: "O foolish ones, and slow of heart to believe all that the prophets have spoken! Was it not necessary that the Christ should suffer these things and enter into his glory?" (Luke 24:25-26).

Not only did God intend for his Son, the Messiah, to suffer before he enters his glory, but God also intended all along that this would be the way the door of salvation would be opened to the nations. In the Jewish Scriptures that Jesus knew and loved, the prophecy was clear: The Son of God would one day inherit the nations. God said in Psalm 2 that he would establish his Royal Son in Jerusalem, and then this Son speaks: "I will tell of the decree: The Lord said to me, 'You are my Son; today I have begotten you. Ask of me, and I will make the nations your heritage, and the ends of the earth your possession'" (Ps. 2:7-8).

Again and again in these Scriptures we read the promise that all the nations would one day bow down and worship the true God, and that his Servant-Son would be a light to the nations. "All the ends of the earth shall remember and turn to the LORD, and all the families of the nations shall worship before you. . . . I will make you as a light for the nations, that my salvation may reach to the end of the earth" (Ps. 22:27; Isa. 49:6; cf. Gen. 49:10; Deut. 32:43; Ps. 66:4; 67:3-4; 68:32; 72:8; 86:9; 97:1; 138:4-5; Isa. 11:10; 42:10-12; 45:22; 49:12; Jer. 16:19; Dan. 7:14; Mic. 4:1-4).

When Jesus came as the light of the world, though his focus was on Israel, he began to make it clear that the kingdom he was bringing through suffering would bless the nations and that Israel herself would be, for a season, left to the side. For example, when a Gentile centurion believed in him and the Jewish leaders didn't, Jesus said, "I tell you, many will come from east and west and recline at table with Abraham, Isaac, and Jacob in the kingdom of heaven, while the sons of the kingdom will be thrown into the outer darkness. In that place there will be weeping and gnashing of teeth" (Matt. 8:11-12). The meaning is clear: The natural heirs of the kingdom (Israel) are not going to inherit its blessings because of unbelief, but the Gentile nations, that is, those who come from east and west, will enter the kingdom.

The mystery is opening. Gentiles—the nations—are going to inherit the blessings of Israel. Jesus had signaled this in his very first sermon in his hometown of Nazareth. He said that "there were many widows in Israel in the days of Elijah, when the heavens were shut up three years and six months, and a great famine came over all the land, and Elijah was sent to none of them but only to Zarephath, in the land of Sidon, to a [Gentile!] woman who was a widow. And there were many lepers in Israel in the time of the prophet Elisha, and none of them was cleansed, but only Naaman the [Gentile!] Syrian" (Luke 4:25-27). What was the response among the Jewish hometown people? "When they heard these things, all in the synagogue were filled with wrath" (Luke 4:28).

THE TIMES OF THE GENTILES

More and more it became clear, for those who had ears to hear, that Jesus had come to save all the nations as well as Jews. For example, he told his disciples, "You will be dragged before governors and kings for my sake, to bear witness before them and the *Gentiles* [i.e., the nations]" (Matt. 10:18). When he drove the money-changers out of the temple he said, "Is it not written, 'My house shall be called a house of prayer *for all the nations*'?" (Mark 11:17). He said that in the last judgment "before him will be gathered *all the nations*, and he will separate people one from another as a shepherd separates the sheep from the goats" (Matt. 25:32), and the criterion of judgment will *not* be Jewishness, but how people have related to him in the ministry of his messengers. He said that the judgment of God was going to fall on Jerusalem and that "Jerusalem will be trampled underfoot by the Gentiles, until *the times of the Gentiles are fulfilled*" (Luke 21:24). In other words, there is an appointed time for the mission to the Gentiles when Israel is passed over, until the day comes when Israel will say, "blessed is he who comes in the name of the Lord" (Matt. 23:39).

During this time—the times of the Gentiles—the sovereign promise of Jesus stands firm: "And this gospel of the kingdom *will* be proclaimed throughout the whole world as a testimony to all nations, and then the end will come" (Matt. 24:14). There is no *maybe* here. The mission that he gives to his followers to go and make disciples of all nations *will* come to pass. "I *will* build my church" (Matt. 16:18). "I have other sheep that are not of this fold. I *must* bring them also, and they *will* listen to my voice" (John 10:16). "Thus *it is written* [and cannot be broken!], that the Christ should suffer and on the third day rise from the dead, and that repentance and forgiveness of sins *should be proclaimed in his name to all nations*" (Luke 24:46). The mission to make disciples of all nations *will* succeed.

THE BLESSINGS OF ABRAHAM ARE FOR THE NATIONS

So even though God focused his redeeming work on Israel for many centuries, everything was preparation for the global mission to the nations. This was there from the first promise to Abraham: "Now the LORD said to Abram, 'Go from your country and your kindred and your father's house to the land that I will show you. . . . I will bless those who bless you, and him who dishonors you I will curse, and *in you all the families of the earth shall be blessed*" (Gen. 12:1-3). This is the promise that is coming true in Jesus' command, "Go therefore and make disciples of all nations." When the nations become disciples of Jesus, they receive the Messiah of Israel. And when they receive the Messiah of Israel, they receive the God of Abraham. And when they receive the God of Abraham, they become heirs of all the promises God made to Israel. This is what Jesus meant in Matthew 21:43 when he said, "Therefore I tell you, the kingdom of God will be taken away from you [Israel] and given to a people producing its fruits." That new "people" is the church gathered from all the nations.

HIS FINAL DEMAND: "MAKE A GLOBAL CLAIM ON MY BEHALF"

Jesus' final demand is that we never lose sight of the global scope of his claim on the human race. He is not a tribal deity. He is the Lord of the universe. Every knee will one day bow either willingly or unwillingly (Matt. 25:31-32). All judgment is given to him (John 5:22). The demand is that his followers reach the nations with "all that he has commanded." "Go therefore and make disciples of all nations[1] . . . *teaching them to observe all that I have commanded you*" (Matt. 28:19-20). The mandate is that everything I have tried to set forth in this book (and it is not exhaustive) be taken to the nations. This is what it means to make disciples—not just that they

---

[1] I omit the command to baptize here ("Go therefore and make disciples of all nations, *baptizing* them in the name of the Father and of the Son and of the Holy Spirit") not because it is an unimportant part of becoming a disciple of Jesus, but because I have dealt with this command in *Demand #46*.

make a profession of faith, but that they "observe all that I have commanded you."

By Prayer, Word, and Suffering

The certainty of success is guaranteed (Matt. 24:14). Jesus will see that it gets done. But it is in our hands to do it. We do it by prayer and by the word and by suffering for others. Jesus said, "The harvest is plentiful, but the laborers are few. Therefore pray earnestly to the Lord of the harvest to send out laborers into his harvest" (Luke 10:2). We must earnestly pray that God will do what he promised he would do. Promises do not make prayer superfluous; they make the answer certain.

Then we must open our mouths and speak the truth of Jesus to all nations. "What I tell you in the dark, say in the light, and what you hear whispered, proclaim on the housetops" (Matt. 10:27). "Go out to the highways and hedges and compel people to come in, that my house may be filled" (Luke 14:23). "I tell you, there will be more joy in heaven over one sinner who repents than over ninety-nine righteous persons who need no repentance" (Luke 15:7). And don't be ashamed, Jesus says, because "Everyone who acknowledges me before men, I also will acknowledge before my Father who is in heaven, but whoever denies me before men, I also will deny before my Father who is in heaven" (Matt. 10:32-33).

Finally, in all our praying and speaking we must be ready to suffer. "As the Father has sent me, even so I am sending you" (John 20:21). Jesus was sent to suffer. We will not be able to make disciples of all nations without taking up our cross and following Jesus on the Calvary road of sacrificial love (Mark 8:34). This is the light of Jesus that the world can most clearly see (*Demand #48*).

He Is Worth It

Jesus does not call us to an easy life or an easy mission. "They will lay their hands on you and persecute you, delivering you up to the synagogues and prisons, and you will be brought before kings and governors for my name's sake. This will be your opportunity to *bear witness*" (Luke 21:12-13). There will be no wasted suffering. In the short run, it will always be an occasion to speak and show the reality of Jesus. In the long run, it will lead to eternal life. "For whoever would save his life will lose it, but whoever loses his life for my sake and the gospel's will save it" (Mark 8:35). Therefore, in all your suffering for the advance of Jesus' mission you are increasingly rewarded. "Blessed are you when others revile you and persecute you and utter all kinds of evil against you falsely on my account. Rejoice and be glad, for your reward is great in heaven" (Matt. 5:11-12). That reward is the enjoyment of the inexhaustibly glorious Jesus forever and ever.

❋ desiring God

If you would like to further explore the vision of God and life presented in this book, we at Desiring God would love to serve you. We have hundreds of resources to help you grow in your passion for Jesus Christ and help you spread that passion to others. At our website, desiringGod.org, you'll find almost everything John Piper has written and preached, including more than thirty books. We've made over twenty-five years of his sermons available free online for you to read, listen to, download, and in some cases watch.

In addition, you can access hundreds of articles, find out where John Piper is speaking, learn about our conferences, discover our God-centered children's curricula, and browse our online store. John Piper receives no royalties from the books he writes and no compensation from Desiring God. The funds are all reinvested into our gospel-spreading efforts. Desiring God also has a whatever-you-can-afford policy, designed for individuals with limited discretionary funds. If you'd like more information about this policy, please contact us at the address or phone number below. We exist to help you treasure Jesus Christ and his gospel above all things because he is most glorified in you when you are most satisfied in him. Let us know how we can serve you!

Desiring God
Post Office Box 2901 Minneapolis, Minnesota 55402
888.346.4700   mail@desiringGod.org

SCRIPTURE INDEX

PERSON INDEX

Subject Index